Getting Started SQL Server Integration Services Made Easy

By Indera E. Murphy

Tolana Publishing
Teaneck, New Jersey

Getting Started With SQL Server Integration Services Made Easy

Tolana Publishing
PO Box 719
Teaneck, NJ 07666 USA

Find us online at www.tolanapublishing.com
Inquiries may be sent to the publisher: tolanapub@yahoo.com

Our books are available online at www.barnesandnoble.com. They can also be ordered from Ingram.

ISBN-13: 978-1-935208-38-9
ISBN-10: 1-935208-38-1

Library of Congress Control Number: 2018901194

Printed and bound in the United States Of America

Notice of Liability
The information in this book is distributed on as "as is" basis, without warranty. Every effort has been made to ensure that this book contains accurate and current information. However, the publisher and author shall not be liable to any person or entity with respect to any loss or damage caused or alleged to be caused directly or indirectly, as a result of any information contained herein or by the computer software and hardware products described in it.

Trademarks
All companies and product names are trademarks or registered trademarks of their respective companies. They are used in this book in an editorial fashion only. No use of any trademark is intended to convey endorsement or other affiliation with this book.

About The SQL Server Series

SQL Server Series Volume 3: Getting Started With SQL Server Integration Services Made Easy, is part of a growing series of computer software books that cover a variety of SQL Server tools. This book has been designed to be used as a self-paced learning tool, in a classroom setting or in an online class. All books contain an abundance of step-by-step instructions and screen shots to help reduce the "stress" often associated with learning new software. Some of the titles are shown below.

ISBN: 978-1-935208-37-2

ISBN: 978-1-935208-36-5

ISBN: 978-1-935208-18-1

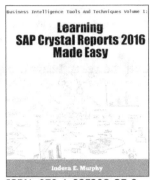

ISBN: 978-1-935208-35-8

ISBN: 978-1-935208-29-7

ISBN: 978-1-935208-34-1

ISBN: 978-1-935208-21-1

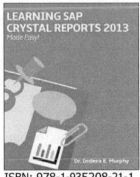

ISBN: 978-1-935208-39-6

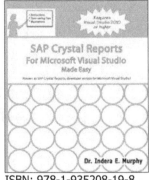

ISBN: 978-1-935208-19-8

ISBN: 978-1-935208-27-3

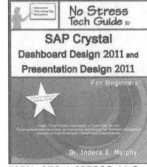

ISBN: 978-1-935208-11-2

ISBN: 978-1-935208-26-6

Visit us online at www.toianapublishing.com for more titles and information

Why A Book On SQL Server Integration Services?

I felt that readers, especially people new to Integration Services, would prefer to have more assistance in learning how to get the most out of the software. I do not feel that flipping between a web site and the software's help file is the most ideal way to learn how to use software.

In general, there are very few books with hands-on exercises for this complex software. I know that many books claim to have "step-by-step instructions". If you have tried to follow books that make this claim and you got lost or could not complete a task as instructed, it may not have been your fault. When I decided to write computer books, I vowed to really have step-by-step instructions that actually included every step. This includes steps like which file to open, which menu option to select and more. In my opinion, it is this level of detail that makes a computer book easy to follow. I hope that you feel the same way.

Over the years, I have come to realize that many people only use a small percent of the features that software has to offer. One of my goals in all of the books that I write, is to point out as many features as possible. My theory is that if more people knew about more than 10% of the features that a software package has, at the very least, they would try a few of them.

About The Author

Dr. Indera E. Murphy is an author, educator and IT professional that has over 25 years of experience in the Information Technology field. She has held a variety of positions including technical writer, programmer, consultant, web designer, course developer and project leader. Indera has designed and developed software applications and web sites, as well as, manage technology driven projects in several industries. In addition to being an Executive Director and consultant, as an online adjunct professor, she has taught courses in a variety of areas including project management, technical writing, information processing, Access, HTML, Windows, Excel, Dreamweaver and critical thinking.

Thank you for purchasing this book!

CONTENTS

SQL SERVER INTEGRATION SERVICES OVERVIEW

After reading this chapter and completing the exercises you will:

- ☑ Have a better understanding of what Integration Services is and what you can use it for
- ☑ Have a better understanding of what the SQL Server components are, that are used in conjunction with Integration Services
- ☑ Have installed the software that is needed to complete the exercises in this book
- ☑ Have downloaded and restored the SQL sample database used in this book
- ☑ Know how to import data from Excel into an SQL database

CHAPTER 1

Welcome To SQL Server Integration Services!

SQL Server Integration Services (SSIS) is a leading data warehouse tool. It is used to extract, transform and load data, (which is commonly known as ETL). As you will see, SQL Server Integration Services (SSIS) does not rely on just one software package. It uses a collection of databases, applications and utilities (aka tools) that make up the SQL Server Integration Services platform. All of the tools work together. Collectively, they support all of the activities associated with managing data.

SSIS is one of the products that make up the SQL Server Business Intelligence platform. Depending on who you ask, SSIS is the most important tool for the platform because without data and the ability to transform and clean the data, there isn't much that the other SSDT tools can do. In my opinion, SSIS is important because the majority of functionality that it has, does not require hours and hours of programming.

As far as I know, SSIS is the original Microsoft extract, transform and load tool, that their newer tool, Power BI Desktop, is based on. The skills that you will acquire from learning SSIS will be very valuable because ETL skills are not going away. For example, when one company buys another company, there is usually a need to combine, integrate or share the data from each companies data warehouse. SSIS is the tool that is used to accomplish these tasks, and it's free! It holds its own against other ETL tools that are not free, like Informatica.

I will be honest and say that even though there is a lot of dropping and dragging in SSIS, there is a little learning curve in the beginning. While history and theory are important to understanding SSIS functionality, I keep it to a minimum, as much as possible, while still explaining the concepts. Don't worry, you can handle it. That is why there are step-by-step instructions. Once you have an understanding of the basics, which is what this book covers, you will understand how to implement the tasks and components that are most frequently used.

I think many people often ask why should I learn SSIS? My first thought is because you are not a programmer and cannot write the code (to create the query) to create the same functionality that SSIS provides, never mind debugging the code when it doesn't work as expected.

The primary goal of this book is to each you how to use SSIS to complete a variety of data related tasks. This book is written from the prospective that you have not used the tools covered in this book before and that your main objective is learning how to create packages that will transform and load data into an SQL database, opposed to learning the intricacies of the SQL Server environment. This book does not cover server related topics, unless they are specific to what is needed to complete the exercises in this book.

A hands-on approach is usually the best way to learn most things in life. As you will see, SSIS is a task driven tool. In this book, I tried to cover tasks that I think are used most often. This book is a visual guide that shows you how to create or modify over 50 SSIS packages. There are over 400 illustrations that practically eliminate the guess work and let you know that you are doing the steps correctly. As you work through the exercises in this book, try to start visualizing how you can take some of the topics covered and apply them to the packages that you need to create on your own.

The good thing is that you have taken a great first step towards learning Integration Services, by purchasing this book. Now, all you have to do, is use this book to learn how to overcome the hurdles. From time to time, I will point out functionality that may not work as expected. When I do this, I am not complaining, merely pointing out things that I think you should be aware of.

It is my sincere hope that whatever your current skill level is with Integration Services, that you will learn more about features that you are already familiar with as you go through this book, and that you learn about features that you did not know existed. Having said that, this book is written for the beginner that has not used SSIS before. I also hope that you find that this book gets you up to speed quickly, as time is money!

Learning new tips and shortcuts will let you work faster and smarter. The more you know about Integration Services, the easier your day to day package design experiences will be.

So sit back and lets get started!

How This Book Is Organized

Topics and exercises in one chapter build on ones covered in previous chapters. To get the most out of this book, it is not advised that you skip around. The first reason is because some of the packages used in later chapters are created in exercises earlier in the book. Another reason is that a topic or option may have been covered in more detail earlier in the book. Additionally, as you will see, many steps are repetitive and instead of listing them in every exercise, they are listed in an exercise tip box. If you decide to skip around and cannot complete an exercise because there is something that you do not understand, you will have to go back and find the section that covers the topic in question. Below is an overview of what is covered in each chapter.

Chapter 1, SQL Server Integration Services Overview discusses the SQL Server environment and which components are often used in conjunction with Integration Services, including SQL Server databases and SQL Server Management Studio (SSMS). Installing SQL Server software, restoring a database and an easy way to import data are also covered.

Chapter 2, Getting Started With SQL Server Integration Services covers the Visual Studio Integration Services interface. Other topics covered include creating solutions and projects, explaining the "Task" and "Package" concepts and creating a basic package.

Chapter 3, Control Flow Tab explains the role of the Control Flow tab, how the connection options work and understanding the Data Flow Task. The following tasks are also covered: Bulk Insert, File System and Execute Process.

Chapter 4, Using The Data Flow Tab To Extract And Load Data introduces the Data Flow tab. The primary focus of this chapter are the source and destination components on the tab.

Chapter 5, Using The Data Flow Tab To Clean And Transform Data picks up where Chapter 4 left off and covers more components on the Data Flow tab, including the following transformations: Character Map, Sort, Aggregate, Conditional Split, Pivot and Unpivot. As you will see, transforming data is where you will spend the most time.

Chapter 6, Joining Data takes packages to the next level. This chapter covers the transformations that can be used to look up data in a different table, merge columns of data from two tables, and write out the data that was looked up, and used in the package.

Chapter 7, Query Builder Crash Course introduces you to Query Builder. This tool is used to create queries for data sources that support SQL queries.

Chapter 8, Using Variables, Parameters And Containers covers creating variables, expressions, parameters and configuring containers. You will also learn how these features work together to make a package dynamic. The SSIS catalog and deployment functionality is also covered.

Objectives Of This Book

This book is written to accommodate self-paced, classroom and online training. While there are no required prerequisites to successfully complete the exercises in this book, having a general knowledge of any of the following would be helpful.

- ☑ Prior version of Integration Services, Power Query in Excel or Power BI Desktop
- ☑ Creating calculated fields
- ☑ Use T-SQL or SQL to create basic queries

Step-by-step instructions are included throughout this book. This book takes a hands-on, performance based approach to teaching you how to use Integration Services and provides the skills required to create packages efficiently. You will get the most from this book if you are sitting in front of your computer and work on the exercises. After completing the exercises in this book, you will be able to perform the following tasks and more:

- ☑ Create and modify packages
- ☑ Import and export data
- ☑ Connect to a variety of data sources
- ☑ Write basic queries
- ☑ Use Containers to group tasks together

☑ Sort and group data
☑ Create parameters
☑ Join tables
☑ Create expressions and use functions

Conventions Used In This Book

I designed the following conventions to make it easier for you to follow the instructions in this book.

☑ The `Courier` font is used to indicate what you should type.

☑ Shortcut key combinations Ctrl+C, means to press and hold down the Ctrl key, then press the C key. This is a shortcut for selecting the Copy command on a menu. Ctrl+V, means to press and hold down the Ctrl key, then press the V key. This is a shortcut for selecting the Paste command on a menu.

☑ SMALL CAPS are used to indicate an option to click on or to bring something to your attention.

☑ 🔆 This symbol indicates a shortcut or another way to complete the task that is being discussed. It can also be a tip or additional information about the topic that is being discussed.

☑ 💣 This symbol indicates a warning, like a feature that has been removed or information that you need to be aware of. This icon can also represent what I call a quirk, meaning a feature that did not work, as I expected it to.

☑ ⋮ This symbol indicates that some of the screen shot/figure is not displayed, because it does not provide any value.

☑ [Text in brackets] references a section, table or figure, that has more information about the topic currently being discussed. If the reference is in a different chapter, the chapter number is included in the reference, like this: [See Chapter 2, Update Options]

☑ When you see "YOU SHOULD HAVE THE OPTIONS SHOWN IN FIGURE X-X", or something similar in the exercises, check to make sure that your screen does look like the figure. If it does, continue with the next set of instructions. If your screen does not look like the figure, redo the steps that you just completed so that your screen does match the figure. Not doing so may cause you problems when trying to complete exercises later in the book.

☑ The section heading EXERCISE X.Y: (X equals the chapter number and Y equals the exercise number) represents exercises that have step-by-step instructions that you should complete. You will also see sections that have step-by-step instructions that are not an exercise. Completing them as you go through the book is optional.

☑ Many of the dialog boxes in Integration Services have OK, Cancel and Help buttons. Viewing these buttons on all of the figures adds no value, so for the most part, they are not shown.

☑ Some of the options and properties in SSIS are multiple words, but are displayed as one word in the software. That may make them hard to read. For example, On Pre Execute is displayed as OnPreExecute. While I understand that it is the way the programmers write code, it can be hard to read. Therefore, as much as possible, I use spaces between the words in this book, to make it easier to read. I didn't want you to think that it is a typo.

☑ "Rename a copy of My package file to" means to make a copy of the package file, then rename the copy with the new file name specified in the instruction. The reason that I have you do this is to keep the packages that you create intact, as some packages are used more than once, as the starting point for other packages.

☑ "E2.1 Package Name" is the naming convention for the packages that you will create. E2.1 stands for Chapter 2, Exercise 1. You may consider some of the file names long. I did this on purpose, so that it is easier to know what topic the package covers. If you do not like to type or do not want to type the full package name, you can just type the first part as the file name. That way, when you have to use a package to complete another exercise, you will be able to find the correct one. For example, if the package name is E5.5 Orders shipped between 4-1-2016 and 6-30-2016, you can type E5.5, as the package file name.

☑ FILE ⇒ NEW ⇒ PROJECT means to open the FILE menu, select the option NEW, then select the option PROJECT, as shown in Figure 1-1.

Options that have an ellipsis (...) after the option name (like Project and File), opens a dialog box.

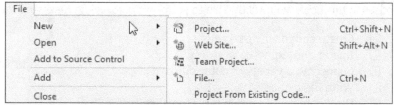

Figure 1-1 Menu navigation technique shown

Assumptions

Yes, I know one should never assume anything, but the following assumptions have been made. It is assumed that . . .

- ☑ You know that the operating system used to write this book is Windows 8.1. If you are using a different version of Windows, any or all of the following can apply:
  - ① Some of the screen shots may have a slightly different look.
  - ② Some of the instructions for Windows tasks may be different.
  - ③ The path to folders and files (for the software) on your computer may be different then the paths listed in this book.
- ☑ You have access to the Internet to download the files needed to complete the exercises in this book and to download updates for any of the software packages used in this book.
- ☑ You know to click OK or the appropriate button to close a dialog box and know to save the changes before going to the next exercise.
- ☑ You know that I am not perfect and sadly, you may find minor mistakes in this book. It is not intentional and I apologize for any inconvenience.
- ☑ You know that when you see <smile>, that it signifies my attempt of adding humor to the learning process.
- ☑ You know that the words "field" and "column" are used interchangeably and are one in the same.
- ☑ You know that "header row" and "column name" are one in the same.
- ☑ You know that "rows" and "records" are used interchangeably, and are one in the same.
- ☑ You understand that there will be options on dialog boxes that will not be referenced in the step-by-step instructions. When that is the case, accept the default value.
- ☑ You know that as a beginner level book, all of the functionality that SSIS offers is not covered in this book. Some topics that are not covered include incremental loads, scalability, data flow engine, scripting, administration, SharePoint, creating your own custom tasks in .NET and third-party components for SSIS.
- ☑ You know that the links in this book can be changed at any time by the web site owner and isn't something that I can control. By searching the web site listed, you should be able to find the information for pages that may have been renamed or relocated.
- ☑ You have Excel installed to be able to view some of the export files that are created. This is optional.

SQL Server Integration Services Software Updates

Many software companies have changed to a faster update release schedule for some of their software titles. Microsoft falls into this category. The core functionality of the software does not change frequently. A large portion of the updates are new features, modifications to existing functionality or name changes of existing options.

One of my favorite features of SSIS is that an updated version (interface changes, new features and bug fixes) is released frequently. For users, that is great. For authors that write books about the software, the frequent updating presents a problem. By the time you read this book, or any book on SSIS for that matter, some parts of the book will be out of date. Sadly, there isn't anything that I can do about this, other then what I am doing right now, and that is to be up front about a situation that I cannot control.

Getting Help With Integration Services (SSIS)

Below are ways to get help if you have a question on how to use a feature or option in Integration Services.

- ① **Read this book** from cover to cover and complete the exercises. Many of the basic questions that you may have are probably covered in this book.
- ② **Forum** You can post questions and learn how other people are using the software. The forum is also a great way to keep current on the latest trends and for getting ideas on how to enhance the packages that you create. It is an invaluable resource. If you do not already have a free account, you will have to create one to be able to post and answer questions. You can use the same account that you will create for the Dev Essentials web site in Exercise 1.1.

SQL Server Integration Services Forum
Use this forum to post questions about Integration Services.
https://social.msdn.microsoft.com/Forums/sqlserver/en-US/home?forum=sqlintegrationservices

SQL Server Forum
Use this forum to post questions about SQL Server.
https://social.msdn.microsoft.com/Forums/sqlserver/en-US/home?forum=sqlgetstarted

SQL Server Integration Services (SSIS)

While I wrote this book for people that want to learn how to create packages using Integration Services, a little knowledge of the other tools behind the scenes, so to speak, is also helpful.

How much you need to know about Integration Services depends on your role and responsibilities. For example, if you are creating packages that will be part of an enterprise solution, you need to know more about the Integration Services environment then someone that needs to create a few packages to get the data that they need for their own use, usually to create reports. The next few sections provide a high level introduction to and overview of the components that make up the SQL Server environment, which SQL Server Integration Services is part of.

SQL Server Data Tools (SSDT)

SSDT (SQL Server Data Tools) is a collection of software tools, that are used to work in a SQL Server environment. SSDT is an add-on for Visual Studio. There are three tools in SSDT: Integration Services (SSIS), **ANALYSIS SERVICES (SSAS)** and **REPORTING SERVICES (SSRS)**. Each tool has its own environment/workspace and own set of project types that can be created in Visual Studio. SSDT uses a custom, for lack of a better word, version of the Visual Studio development environment.

Like Visual Studio, SSDT is a collaborative environment and gives you access to Visual Studio tools, like Visual Basic and Visual C#. You will see options for each of them when you create an SSIS project in Chapter 2.

In the SQL Server environment, especially in a new installation, SSIS is probably the first of the three SSDT tools that is used. There are two ways to use SSIS, as explained below.

① Install SSDT as a stand alone tool. This option runs in a shell of Visual Studio.
② Installing SSDT into Visual Studio provides all of the Integration Services functionality that the stand alone version has. This option also allows you to use all of the Visual Studio features, if needed.

As stated above, Integration Services is an add-on component of SQL Server. What makes this platform unique is that the SSDT tools can be used by people with different job titles or descriptions to get the data that they need, without having to depend on or wait for the IT department to do it for them, as long as they have access to the data. What is needed from the IT department, is access to the database that has the tables or views that you need. Having said that, Integration Services and Analysis Services are primarily used by the IT department and Reporting Services is often used by non IT people to create reports.

SQL Server

SQL Server is Microsoft's relational database management system (RDBMS). It is designed for an enterprise environment. In addition to having database functionality (meaning you can create databases with the software), it also functions as a database server. In this capacity, SQL Server is used to retrieve data requested by other software and store it.

There are several editions of SQL Server. This book uses the Developer edition of SQL Server. This edition has the core database engine and add-on services. This includes several tools for creating and managing an SQL Server platform, just like the Enterprise edition has. The **SQL SERVER DEVELOPER EDITION** offers the full feature set that the Enterprise Edition has. The difference is that the Developer edition should only be used for development and testing purposes. It should not be used in production environments or used with production (live) data.

What Is SQL?

SQL **(STRUCTURED QUERY LANGUAGE)** is the language that is most used to interact with databases. **T-SQL** is the version of SQL that SQL Server supports. It is used to create and populate tables with data, modify data and retrieve data from a data source. The **SQL SELECT COMMAND** is what is used to retrieve data. This is also known as a **QUERY**. Before you start to frown, the answer is no, you do not have to write a lot of T-SQL code to complete the exercises in this book. The graphical interface of the Query Builder creates the SQL code that is used to retrieve the data from the tables, based on the options that you select.

Data Management Tools

The software covered in this section is used to manage and maintain SQL Server databases and use data from other data sources. While you will use the tools covered in this section to complete exercises in this book, depending on your workplace environment, there may be IT staff that specializes in these tools, and may handle these tasks for you.

Knowing what they are, will give you a better understanding of what is involved. It will also help you to communicate your needs better to the IT staff.

SQL Server Management Studio (SSMS)

SSMS stands for SQL Server Management Studio. This tool is used to manage and configure all of the SQL Server instances (local and remote). The Object Explorer is a main section of this software. It is used to browse and select the objects on the server. SSMS has tools to monitor, deploy SQL instances, create scripts and queries. There are graphical tools and script editors that are used to accomplish these tasks. This software can also be used to create a new database, modify an existing database by adding or modifying tables and indexes.

Another use of this software is restoring .bak database files. SSMS is also used to manage scheduled jobs, modify role definitions and more. You will learn how to use the restore database feature, later in this chapter.

Import And Export Wizard

As the name implies, this wizard is used to import data from and export to a variety of file types. This wizard also has the ability to perform a few basic transformations. Most of the time, I suspect that if you use this tool on your own, you will use it to import data from a variety of sources into a SQL Server database, including Azure and Oracle databases, Excel, csv, text files and more.

There are actually two versions of this wizard, one in SSMS, which has an option to create a basic package that can also be used in SSIS, and one in SSIS, which automatically creates a basic package. They both have the same functionality. Later in this chapter, you will learn how to use the wizard in SSMS. Below are the ways to open the wizard.

- ☑ In SSIS ⇒ Solution Explorer window ⇒ Right-click on the **SSIS PACKAGES** folder ⇒ SSIS Import and Export Wizard.
- ☑ In SSIS ⇒ Project Menu ⇒ SSIS Import and Export Wizard.
- ☑ In SSMS, Right-click on the SQL database that you want to import in to or export out of ⇒ Tasks ⇒ **IMPORT DATA** or **EXPORT DATA**, as illustrated in Figure 1-2.

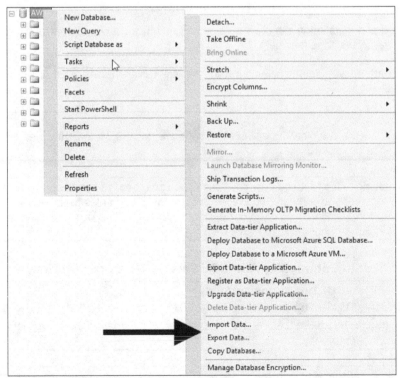

Figure 1-2 Tasks shortcut menu options

Visual Studio Community Edition

Visual Studio includes native support for data programming with Microsoft SQL Server. It can be used to write and debug code. It also includes a data designer that can be used to graphically create, view or edit database schemas. Queries can be created either visually or by using code. The Community edition has almost all of the same functionality that the Professional edition of Visual Studio has. SSDT can be installed in Visual Studio Community Edition.

SSDT vs Visual Studio

As covered earlier, SSDT can be installed with or without installing Visual Studio. If SSDT is installed as a stand alone tool, it is installed with a Visual Studio shell. This shell has the Visual Studio look, but not all of the functionality. As a stand alone tool, it has fewer supported features for SQL Server databases. This is fine because the shell has all of the Integration Services features. If you are trying to figure out which environment is best for you to use on your own, to use Integration Services in, hopefully, this section will help you make a decision. Below are some reasons to consider the Visual Studio option.

① Select the Visual Studio option if the SSIS packages that you are going to create will be part of an application that is being developed in a visual programming language like Visual Basic or C#.
② If you will be working on more than one project at the same time and want a way to be able to easily manage the packages, in several projects at the same time. All of the packages in the same solution, are displayed in the Solution Explorer window, which you can keep visible, at all times.
③ Visual Studio Community is free. <smile>

Download And Install The Required Software To Use Integration Services

If you have installed the following software packages, you can skip the exercises in this chapter. All of these software packages are used in this book. The software is listed in the order that I installed them in.

☑ Visual Studio Community Edition
☑ SQL Server Developer Edition
☑ SQL Server Management Studio (SSMS)
☑ SQL Server Data Tools (SSDT)

Please keep in mind, that the download and installation can change at any time, which I have no control over. If you have trouble installing any of the software, this page may help.

https://docs.microsoft.com/en-us/sql/database-engine/install-windows/install-sql-server-from-the-installation-wizard-setup

Vipre Anti Virus Software
I use this software, but disable it before downloading or installing software because at least for me, it slows down the download and installation process.

To make is easy to find the installation files that you download, you can save them to the desktop, on your computer. Then after you have installed the software, you can move the installation files to a folder on your hard drive or delete them. Saving the installation files to your desktop is optional. You can save them wherever you want on your hard drive. Just remember where you save them.

Exercise 1.1: Download Visual Studio Community And SQL Server Developer Edition

You Can Skip This Exercise If Either Of The Following Apply
① You already have a paid version of Visual Studio and SQL Server 2016 or higher installed.
② You have an MSDN subscription. You can use that service to download SQL Server 2016 (or higher) Developer Edition and Visual Studio Community.

If you already have a paid version of Visual Studio installed on the computer that you will use to complete the exercises in this book, **DO NOT INSTALL THE COMMUNITY VERSION**. You only need to download and install Visual Studio Community if you do not have another version of Visual Studio installed. A trial version is not recommended, because it can expire before you complete the exercises in this book.

The steps and screen shots in this book for Integration Services, are based on SSDT being installed with Visual Studio Community installed.

Create Your Free Visual Studio Dev Essentials Account

1. Go to www.visualstudio.com/dev-essentials/.

2. On the Visual Studio home page, you should see a **JOIN NOW** button for Visual Studio Dev Essentials. Click on this button.

3. Type in the email address that you want to use to create your account ⇒ Click Continue.

4. Click the Create A Microsoft Account link ⇒ On the Create Account page, type in your email address again and type in a password that has at least eight characters ⇒ Click Next ⇒ Leave this web page open.

5. Check your email account for the code and paste it in, on the web page ⇒ Click Next.

6. Fill out the Details page ⇒ Click Continue.
   You should see the Visual Studio Dev Essentials page. In the **SUPPORT** section, you should see a box for **PRIORITY SUPPORT**. As a Visual Studio Essentials member, you have access to free priority support. It is probably a good idea to bookmark this page, to make it easier to find in the future, should you need it.

   In the SQL Server section, you will see a link for SQL Server Integration Services. Unless the question that you have is for SQL Server Developer edition, this is the forum to post your questions in. To post in any of the forums, you have to log in. Use the same email account and password that you just created to set up your free account.

Download Visual Studio Community

1. You should see the **FREE VISUAL STUDIO** button in the upper right corner. Click on this button.

2. You should now see a Download button for Visual Studio Community. Click the Download button.

3. Save the vs_community file to your hard drive ⇒ Leave the Visual Studio web page open because you will use it to download SQL Server Developer Edition, in the next section.

Download The SQL Server Developer Edition Setup File

 If you have the Express edition of SQL Server installed, a large portion of SSIS is not available. The Developer (which is free) and Enterprise (not free) editions have all of the SSIS functionality.

 There are two places to download the Developer Edition from, as explained below.
1. From the Visual Studio Dev Essentials web site. The steps are listed below, in the next section.
2. From this web page https://www.microsoft.com/en-us/sql-server/sql-server-downloads (which does not require you to log in). Click on the Download Now link for the Developer Edition. You will then be prompted to download the file.

Download SQL Server Developer Edition From The Visual Studio Dev Essentials Web Site

1. Go to the same page that you downloaded Visual Studio Community from.

2. In the **TOOLS** section, you should see an option for the Microsoft SQL Server Developer Edition. Click on the **DOWNLOAD LINK** for the software. If you do not see an option for the Developer Edition, scroll down the page.

3. Save the file to your computers hard drive.

Exercise 1.2: Install Visual Studio Community

1. Once the vs_community file has downloaded, right-click on it and select **RUN AS ADMINISTRATOR**.

2. When prompted to choose an installation location and type of installation, accept the default option unless you have a really good reason not to. The installation will take several minutes. If you want, you can start to download any other software that you need, then come back here.

3. When the installation is finished, you will be prompted to restart your computer. If you need to download SQL Server Developer Edition and haven't done so yet, you should download it now before you restart your computer, so that you do not have to go through the log in process again.

4. Restart your computer ⇒ Go to the next exercise.

Exercise 1.3: Install SQL Server Developer Edition

 If you have a previous version of SQL Server installed on the same computer that you are about to install SQL Server Developer Edition (2016 or higher) on, some of the files from the previous version may be updated by this installation.

Download The SQL Server Developer Edition Installation Files

The steps in this section are used to download the SQL Server installation files. Please keep in mind that changes may be made to the download and installation process, when the software is updated.

1. Right-click on the SQL Server Developer Edition file (SQLServer201XSSEI-Dev.exe X is the last digit of the year) that you downloaded in Exercise 1.1, and select **RUN AS ADMINISTRATOR**.

2. On the screen shown in Figure 1-3, select the **CUSTOM** option.

    Figure 1-4 shows where the installation files will be stored. Accept the default location ⇒

    Click the Install button.

    The download will take several minutes. Longer, if your Internet connection is slow.

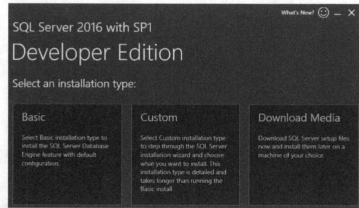

Figure 1-3 Installation type screen

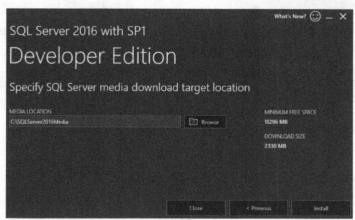

Figure 1-4 Target location options

Install SQL Server Developer Edition

Once the installation package files have downloaded and automatically extracted to the folder (location) shown above in Figure 1-4, the window will automatically close.

The window shown in Figure 1-5 will open. The options on the left provide information, documentation and links to install software.

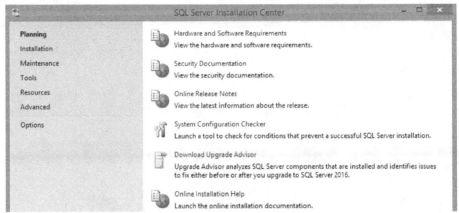

Figure 1-5 SQL Server Installation Center dialog box

1. Click on the **INSTALLATION LINK** on the left. You will see the screen shown in Figure 1-6.

   The first option will install SQL Server.

   The second option will take you to a web page to download SSMS.

   The third option will take you to a web page to download SSDT/Integration Services.

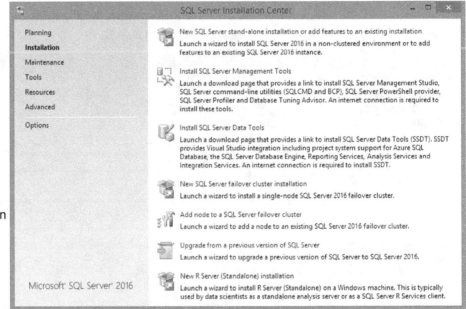

Figure 1-6 Installation screen

I wish that the installation process was much more automated. By that I mean that if the installation page shown above in Figure 1-6, had a check mark for each of the options, you could check all of the software that you want to install and the wizard would download and install the software for the options that you select, instead of having to come back to this screen several times to select and install them, one by one.

How To Reopen The SQL Server Installation Center Dialog Box
If you need to reopen the dialog box shown above in Figure 1-6, after SQL Server has been installed, navigate to the folder, in the Location field, shown earlier in Figure 1-4 ⇒ Double-click on the setup.exe file, illustrated in Figure 1-7.

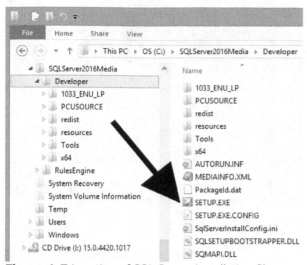

Figure 1-7 Location of SQL Server installation file

2. Click on the first option, New SQL Server stand-alone installation.

3. On the screen shown in Figure 1-8, select the Developer free edition, if it is not already selected ⇒

   Click Next.

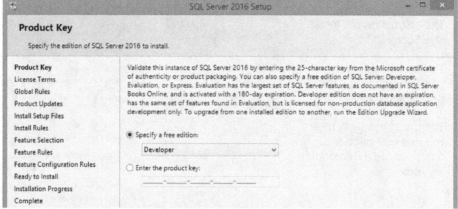

Figure 1-8 Product Key screen

4. On the License Terms screen, check the "I accept the license terms" option ⇒ Click Next.

The next step of the installation wizard will check your computers hard drive, to see if your system meets the Global Setup Rules. These rules are used to determine whether or not your computer has the required prerequisite system configuration.

When the test is complete, you may see the dialog box shown in Figure 1-9.

If your computer did not pass all of the rules, this dialog box will let you know.

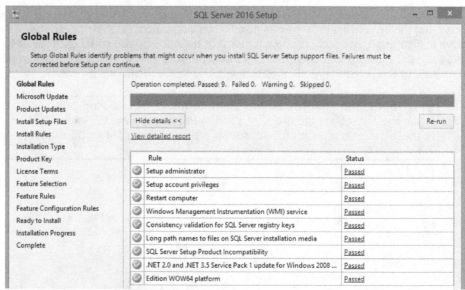

Figure 1-9 Setup Global Rules screen

If your computer passed all of the rules, you can click the **SHOW DETAILS BUTTON**, if you want to see what the rules are.

Clicking the **VIEW DETAILED REPORT** link, displays the page shown in Figure 1-10. This page will be helpful if you need help fixing a rule. When you are finished viewing this page, you can close it.

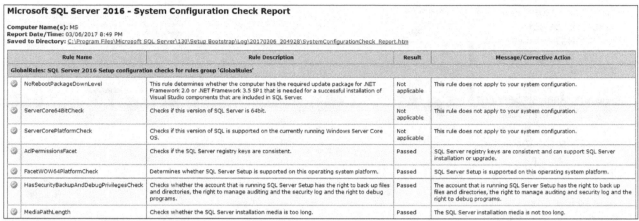

Figure 1-10 System Configuration Check Report

If you computer passed the Global Rules tests, you will see the screen shown in Figure 1-11.

The detailed report from this screen, looks like the one shown above in Figure 1-10.

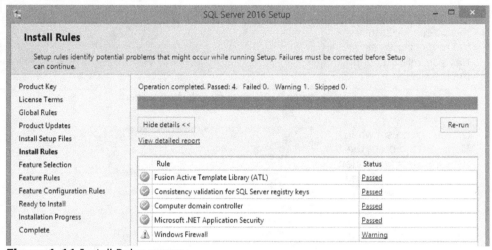

Figure 1-11 Install Rules screen

5. Click Next on the Install Rules screen.

6. On the screen shown in Figure 1-12, check the following options: **DATABASE ENGINE SERVICES, FULL-TEXT AND SEMANTIC EXTRACTIONS FOR SEARCH, ANALYSIS SERVICES, REPORTING SERVICES-NATIVE,** and **INTEGRATION SERVICES.**

    Selecting Analysis Services and/or Reporting Services is optional to complete the exercises in this book.

    If you know at some point that you will use them or want to learn them, it is easier to select and install the software now.

    The options selected on this screen, determine the remaining screens that you will see during the installation.

    Click Next.

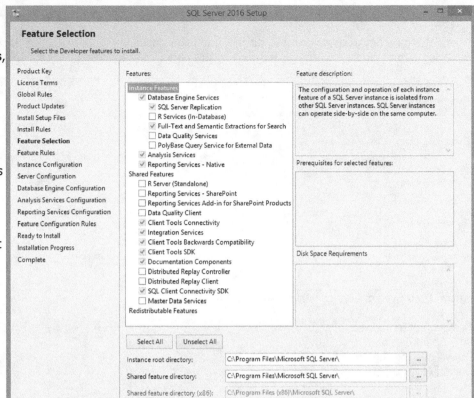

Figure 1-12 Feature Selection screen

7. On the screen shown in Figure 1-13, accept the **DEFAULT INSTANCE** option, unless you have a need to use a specific server name ⇒

    Click Next.

Figure 1-13 Instance Configuration screen

8. On the screen shown in Figure 1-14, accept the default options shown ⇒

Click Next.

The options displayed in the Service column depend on the options selected on the Feature Selection screen, shown earlier in Figure 1-12.

For example, if you did not check the Analysis Services option, you will not see an entry for it on this screen.

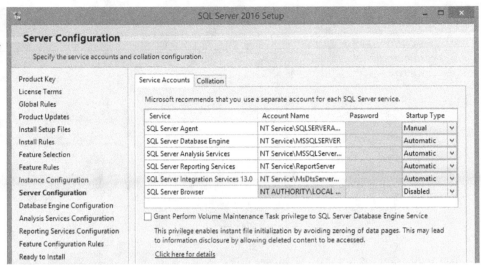

Figure 1-14 Server Configuration screen

9. On the screen shown in Figure 1-15, accept the **WINDOWS AUTHENTICATION MODE** option ⇒

Click the **ADD CURRENT USER BUTTON** to give yourself unrestricted access to the database engine.

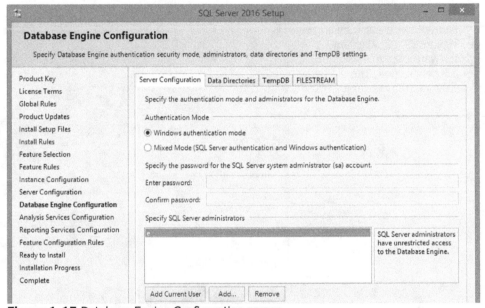

Figure 1-15 Database Engine Configuration screen

10. If you selected to install Analysis Services, you will see the screen shown in Figure 1-16.

Select the **SERVER MODE** that you want to use.

If you want to use **DAX** in Analysis Services, select the Tabular Mode option.

Add at least one user that will have administrator rights to Analysis Services. If that user is you, click the **ADD CURRENT USER BUTTON** ⇒

Click Next.

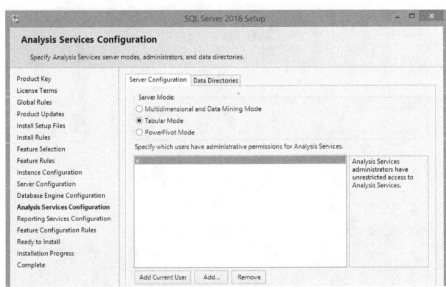

Figure 1-16 Analysis Services Configuration screen

11. On the screen shown in Figure 1-17, the **REPORTING SERVICES NATIVE MODE**, Install and configure option should be selected ⇒

    Click Next.

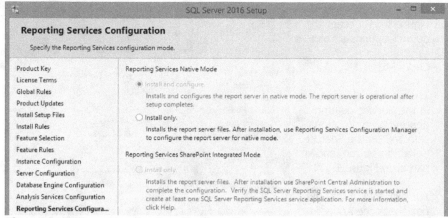

Figure 1-17 Reporting Services Configuration screen

12. You should see the options shown in Figure 1-18 ⇒ Click the Install button.

    You will see the screen shown in Figure 1-19. All of the software that you selected, will be installed. The installation can take a while.

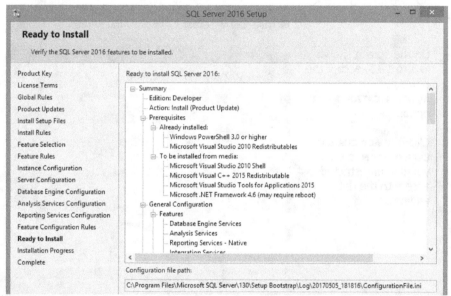

Figure 1-18 Ready to Install screen

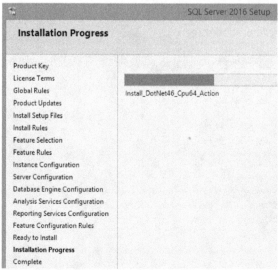

Figure 1-19 Installation Progress screen

13. When the installation is complete, you will see the screen shown in Figure 1-20 ⇒

Click the Close button.

The SQL Server Installation Center window, shown earlier in Figure 1-6, should still be open. Leave it open to complete the next exercise.

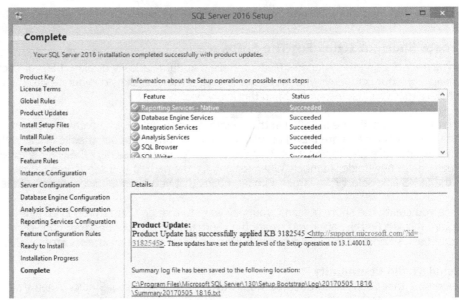

Figure 1-20 Complete screen

Exercise 1.4: Install SQL Server Management Tools (SSMS)

1. On the screen shown earlier in Figure 1-6, click the **INSTALL SQL SERVER MANAGEMENT TOOLS** option.

2. You will see the web page with the download file. Click on the link to download SQL Server Management Studio.

3. Right-click on the file that you downloaded (ssms-setup-enu.exe) and select Run as administrator.

4. On the first screen, click the Install button. You can walk away, as the installation does not require any input from you.

5. When the installation is complete, click the Restart button. After your computer has rebooted, go to the next exercise.

Exercise 1.5: Install SQL Server Data Tools (SSDT)

1. On the screen shown earlier in Figure 1-6, click on the Install SQL Server Data Tools link.

2. On the web page, click on the link to download the SQL Server Data Tools for Visual Studio file ⇒ On the dialog box, click the Save file button to download the file.

3. Right-click on the ssdtsetup.exe file that you downloaded and select Run as administrator.

4. The only option that has to be checked on the screen shown in Figure 1-21, to complete the exercises in this book, is **SQL SERVER INTEGRATION SERVICES**.

   The other options, install software for the other SQL Server tools.

   If you installed Analysis Services and/or Reporting Services in Exercise 1.3, check these options also ⇒

   Click Next.

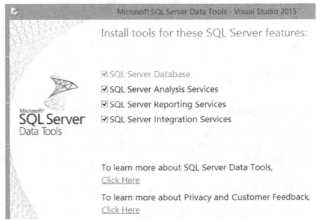

Figure 1-21 SQL Server Data Tools installation options

5. Accept the license terms ⇒ Click the Install button.

6.   When the installation is complete, click the Close button ⇒ Close the SQL Server Installation Center window.

Create Shortcut Icons For The Software

If you are not using the Windows tiled interface that automatically displays tiles for each software package that is installed on your computer, you may want to create shortcut icons on your desktop to be able to access all of the software that you just installed. Doing this is optional.

The path to the software installed in this chapter is listed below. The paths are based on accepting the default installation options and are based on Windows 8.1. If you do not see the file in the path, search your computers hard drive, for the .exe file, to find it on your computer. Some updates of SQL Server software, like SQL Server Management Studio, get a new folder number. When looking for the path, if you see a number greater than "130", as shown below in the SSMS link, select it. A larger number means that you have a newer version of the software.

Once you create the shortcut icons, you may want to change them to run in administrator mode, as some features require this. To do this, after you create the shortcut icon on your desktop, right-click on the shortcut icon ⇒ Properties ⇒ Shortcut tab ⇒ Advanced button ⇒ Select **RUN AS ADMINISTRATOR** ⇒ Click Apply ⇒ Click OK.

Visual Studio Community

Remember that SSDT/Integration Services was installed into Visual Studio. When Visual Studio is opened, so is Integration Services.

C:\Program Files (x86)\Microsoft Visual Studio 14.0\Common7\IDE\devenv.exe

SQL Server Management Studio (SSMS)

C:\Program Files (x86)\Microsoft SQL Server\130\Tools\Binn\Management Studio\ssms.exe

---

Remove The Visual Studio Splash Screen
If you do not like seeing the splash screen (aka waiting for the software to open) every time that you open Visual Studio, you can disable it, by following the steps below. Doing this reduces the time that it takes the software to open.
1. Right-click on the Visual Studio shortcut icon ⇒ Properties.
2. On the Shortcut tab, click in the **TARGET** field ⇒ Press the End key.
3. Press the space bar ⇒ Type /nosplash, as illustrated in Figure 1-22. Typing -nosplash, works the same as the / option above.
4. Click Apply ⇒ Click OK.

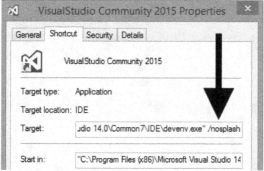

Figure 1-22 Nosplash switch added

Exercise 1.6: Create A Folder For Your Files

You will create and modify several packages in this book. It is a good idea to store all of them in the same folder on your computers hard drive so that you can find them easily. I will refer to this folder as "your folder" throughout the book. The instructions below show you how to create the folder at the root of the C drive.

1.   Open Windows Explorer ⇒ Right-click on the C drive ⇒ New ⇒ Folder.

2.   Type SSIS Book as the folder name, then press Enter ⇒ Right-click on this folder ⇒ New ⇒ Folder ⇒ Type More Files, then press Enter.

3. Additional files needed for some of the exercises in this book are in a zip file. To have the link for the zip file sent to you, send an email to ssisbookfiles@tolanapublishing.com. If you do not receive an email in a few minutes with the subject line Integration Services Book Files, check the spam folder in your email software.

4. When you have the zip file, open Windows Explorer, then click on the SSIS Book folder that you created earlier in step 2 ⇒ Right-click on the zip file and select the option to extract the files. Use the zip software that you currently use or you can use the compression tool in Windows Explorer.

5. Copy (not move) the Ch4 File System Task Exercise.xlsx file to the Move Files folder. Confirm that this file is in both folders that you created in step 2.

 Keep in mind that while all of the software that you will use in this book is installed on your computers hard drive, some components (SQL Server and SSMS for example) are emulating an actual, physical server, which is another piece of hardware. This means that you still have to log in, just like you would have to log in to get connected to these servers, to gain access to the files stored on them, in a corporate environment.

SQL Server Configuration Manager

In addition to the software that you installed earlier in this chapter, on your own, you may also have a need to use the SQL Server Configuration Manager, shown in Figure 1-23.

You may have additional server services then those shown on the right side of the figure. At a minimum, you should have: SQL Server(MSSQLServer).

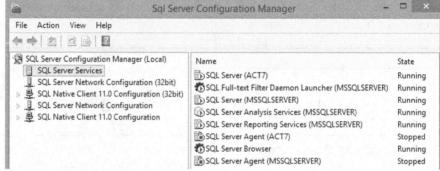

Figure 1-23 SQL Server Configuration Manager

You can create a shortcut to the path below to have easy access to this tool.
C:\Windows\SysWOW64\SQLServerManager13.msc

Understanding The SQL Server Name

I think that it is important to understand the SQL Server naming convention, because you will need to select your SQL Server instance, especially when creating data sources, restoring databases and importing data files. The SQL server name has two parts, as explained below:

① The **COMPUTER NAME**. This is usually the server name. If you install SQL Server on your laptop, the computer name is the name of your computer.

② The **INSTANCE NAME**. An instance name is a separate installation of SQL Server that has its own temporary databases, services and security. Each instance has its own unique name, which is known as a **NAMED INSTANCE**. A **DEFAULT INSTANCE** is one that does not have a unique name. Usually SQL Server (MSSQLSERVER) is installed as the default instance. When that is the case, you can just use the computer name. Otherwise, you have to use the computer name and instance name, in this format: MyComputerName\Instance Name. For example, in addition to the MSSQLSERVER instance, I also have an (ACT7) instance of SQL Server installed, as shown above in Figure 1-23. Having multiple instances means that different versions of SQL Server (like SQL Server 2012 and SQL Server 2016) can be installed on the same hard drive.

Exercise 1.7: Download And Restore The Sample Database

Now that you have read about what SSIS can be used for, a key component of using Integration Services is having access to data. This exercise will show you how to download and restore the sample database. This database will be used in this book.

Download The Sample Database

1. Go to this web page www.microsoft.com/en-us/download/details.aspx?id=49502.

2. Scroll down the page and click on the **DOWNLOAD** button.

3. On the next page, check the first Adventure Works file, shown in Figure 1-24 ⇒ Click Next ⇒ On the Opening dialog box, select the **SAVE FILE** option ⇒ Click OK.

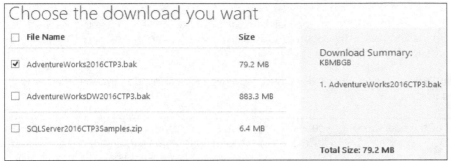

Choose the download you want

☐	File Name	Size
☑	AdventureWorks2016CTP3.bak	79.2 MB
☐	AdventureWorksDW2016CTP3.bak	883.3 MB
☐	SQLServer2016CTP3Samples.zip	6.4 MB

Download Summary:
KBMBGB

1. AdventureWorks2016CTP3.bak

Total Size: 79.2 MB

Figure 1-24 Database backup file to download

4. Double-click on the folder that you created for this book ⇒ Click the Save button. When the download is complete, go to the next section.

Connect To Your SQL Server

1. Open SQL Server Management Studio (SSMS).

2. On the Connect to Server dialog box, open the Server type drop-down list and select **DATABASE ENGINE**, if necessary.

> **Server Name Tip**
> For the exercises in this book, the **SERVER NAME** in SSMS, should be your computers name, if you followed the SQL Server installation instructions earlier in this chapter. In addition to using your computers name, you can also type (localhost) in this field. The Connect to Server dialog box remembers what options you select and displays them, each time that you open the software. If you are using a **NAMED INSTANCE** of SQL Server, the server name needs to be entered in this format: server name\instance name.

3. In the **SERVER NAME FIELD**, do one of the following: Select the server (your computers name) from the drop-down list or type (localhost) in the field.

4. If necessary, change the Authentication option to Windows Authentication ⇒ If you use a password to log onto your computer, enter it in the Password field ⇒ Check the Remember password option, if you do not want to have to type in your log in information, each time you use SSMS.

5. You should have options similar to those shown in Figure 1-25 ⇒

    Click the **CONNECT BUTTON**.

    Once connected, Microsoft SQL Server Management Studio (SSMS) is available. You will see the window shown in Figure 1-26.

Figure 1-25 Connect to Server dialog box options

The **OBJECT EXPLORER WINDOW**, shown on the left of Figure 1-26, displays all of the objects on the database server.

If you do not see this window, View menu ⇒ Object Explorer, or press F8, to display it.

Most of the objects shown, will not be used in this book. You should see the server that you just connected to, at the top of the Object Explorer window, as shown in the figure.

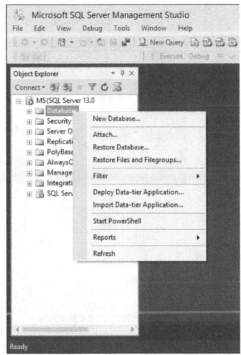

Figure 1-26 Microsoft SQL Server Management Studio

Restore The Adventure Works SQL Server Database

In this part of the exercise, you will restore the database (kind of like unzipping a zip file) that you downloaded earlier in this exercise, so that you can use it.

1. In the Object Explorer window, right-click on the Databases folder and select **RESTORE DATABASE**, as shown above in Figure 1-26.

2. On the Restore Database dialog box, select the **DEVICE** option ⇒ Click the ellipsis button (...) across from the Device option.

3. On the Select backup devices dialog box, click the **ADD BUTTON** ⇒ Navigate to, then click on the folder that you created for this book ⇒ On the right side of the Locate Backup File dialog box, click on the AdventureWorks2016CTP3.bak file ⇒ Click OK. You should see the file, as shown in Figure 1-27 ⇒ Click OK.

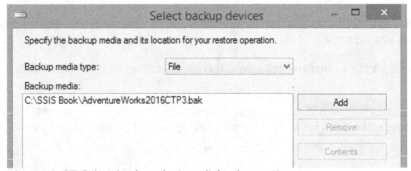

Figure 1-27 Select backup devices dialog box options

 Restore Database Name
You can use the original database name or you can change it. Changing it here, does not rename the actual database. It just lets you use a name that you like or a name that is easier to remember or type, when needed.

4. In the Destination section of the Restore Database dialog box, change the database name to AW, as illustrated in Figure 1-28. AW is short for Adventure Works.

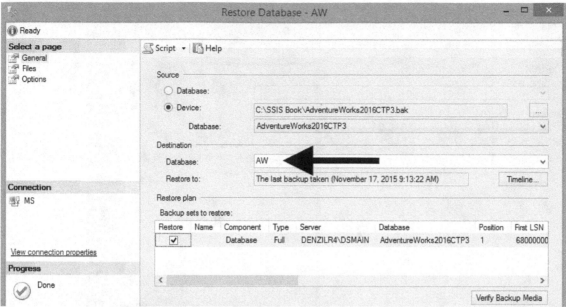

Figure 1-28 Options selected to restore the database

5. Check the Restore box, if it is not already checked ⇒ Click OK. The restore process will start. When complete, you will see a dialog box that says that the database was restored successfully ⇒ Click OK.

6. In the Object Explorer, expand the Databases folder. You will see the database with the new name, as illustrated in Figure 1-29.

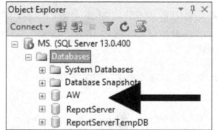

Figure 1-29 Restored database illustrated

Viewing Data In The Database

It helps to view some of the data that you will use to create packages from, especially if you are not already familiar with the data. Doing so will give you a better idea of what data is in the tables.

1. Expand the AW folder ⇒ Expand the Tables folder. As you can see, the database has a lot of tables. Don't worry, you do not have to memorize their names. <smile>

2. Right-click on the Sales.SalesOrderDetail table ⇒ **EDIT TOP 200 ROWS**. This will display up to 200 rows of data in the table, as shown in Figure 1-30.

As shown, there are column names (fields) that end with **ID**. These fields are used to link (create a relationship) to another table in the database. For example, the Sales Order ID field shown in Figure 1-30, is used to link to the Sales.SalesOrderHeader table.

MS.AW - Sales.SalesOrderDetail ⊣ ✕						
SalesOrderID	SalesOrderDetailID	CarrierTrackin...	OrderQty	ProductID	SpecialOfferID	UnitPrice
43659	1	4911-403C-98	1	776	1	2024.9940
43659	2	4911-403C-98	3	777	1	2024.9940
43659	3	4911-403C-98	1	778	1	2024.9940
43659	4	4911-403C-98	1	771	1	2039.9940

Figure 1-30 Order Detail table

3. View the data in a few other tables. When you are finished viewing the data, leave the SQL Server Management Studio (SSMS) software open to complete the next exercise.

. . . .

Import And Export Wizard Overview

This wizard is built on the SSIS framework and can be used without having SSIS installed. This wizard is automatically installed when SQL Server Management Studio (SSMS) is installed. (This wizard is also available in SSIS). In addition to being able to move data from one source to another, this wizard also has the functionality to save the import or export steps as an **SSIS PACKAGE**.

You will probably find this wizard, the easiest way to import data from databases like Access, DB2 and Oracle, as well as data in Excel and text files, into a SQL Server database. This is because it does a large part of the repetitive tasks for you.

How The Wizard Works To Import Data

This section will show you many of the screens that are used to import data. Keep in mind that the screens that you see are dependent on the type of data that is selected to be imported.

Data Source Screen

The screen shown in Figure 1-31 is used to select the data source.

The options shown in the figure are the default data source options.

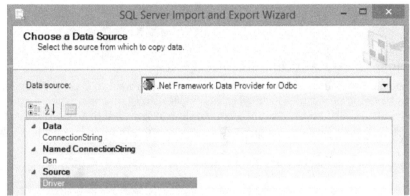

Figure 1-31 Default data source options

Figure 1-32 shows the options to import from an SQL Server database.

When connecting to a SQL Server database, a server name has to be entered. In a production environment, you will also have to enter a user name and password.

If selected, the **USE WINDOWS AUTHENTICATION** option will send your Windows (local or domain) credentials to the data source to log you in.

If you need to connect to a database source (usually a non Microsoft database) that isn't listed, you will have to install the vendors OLE DB provider.

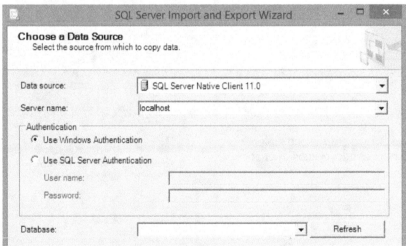

Figure 1-32 SQL Server database connection options

Destination Screen

The screen shown in Figure 1-33 is used to select the file that the data will be copied to.

More than likely, when using SSIS, you will be importing data into an SQL database, which is what will be covered in the rest of this walk thru.

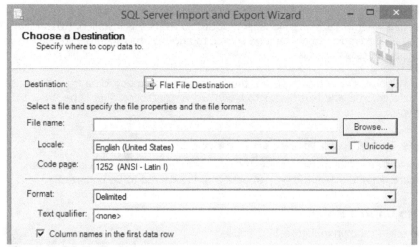

Figure 1-33 Destination screen

Select The Data To Import

The next screen is used to select the tables that you want to import. When importing into a SQL Server database, you have the option of selecting tables and views by name or creating a query to select the data to import, as shown in Figure 1-34. If you know that all of the columns or all of the rows of data in a table are not needed in the SSIS project, you should create a query to only select the data that you need. There is no value in importing data that is not needed.

Selecting the Copy data option shown in Figure 1-34, displays the screen shown in Figure 1-35. It is used to select the table(s) from the data source to import.

Selecting the Write a query option, displays the dialog box shown in Figure 1-36. You can type or paste the query in.

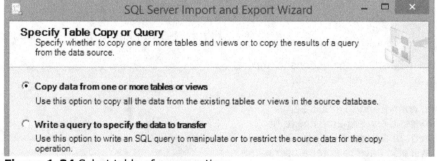

Figure 1-34 Select table of query options

The **EDIT MAPPINGS** and **PREVIEW BUTTONS** are explained in Chapter 3.

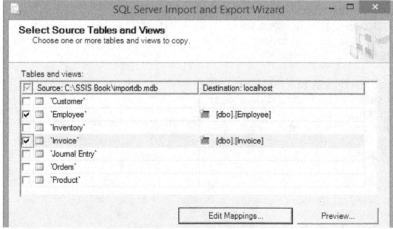

Figure 1-35 Select Source Tables and Views screen

Clicking the **BROWSE BUTTON**, lets you select a query (.sql) file.

This file will have the query (the code) needed to select the data to import.

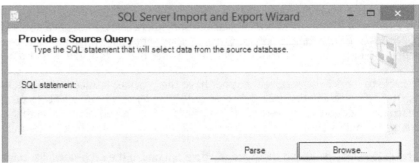

Figure 1-36 Query screen

Save And Run Package Screen

The screen shown in Figure 1-37, is only available when the wizard is run from SSMS. It is not a requirement to run the package now. You can save it now and run it later. This is helpful if you know that you need to add transformations to the package before importing the data to create the new table.

The **SAVE SSIS PACKAGE** option, is used to save the options that are selected on this wizard as a package, so that you can use them again, if you need to import data from the same data source, in the future.

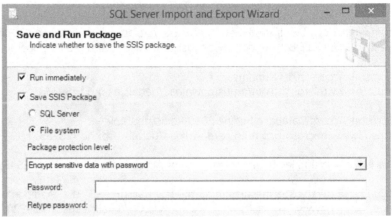

Figure 1-37 Save and Run Package screen

Figure 1-38 shows the screen that is used to create the package name and where the package will be stored.

When enabled, the Save SSIS Package option is used to select whether the package will be saved to the SQL Server or to a file system (a **.DTSX** package file). If you are going to use the package in SSIS, select the File System option.

Figure 1-38 Save SSIS Package screen

This wizard creates the same type of package that you will learn how to create using SSIS. This means that packages created in this wizard in SSMS can be opened and modified in SSIS.

The default location that packages are saved in, when using the wizard in SSMS, is the My Documents folder. If you already have a project set up, save the package to the project folder. Then in SSIS, right-click on the Packages folder and select **ADD EXISTING PACKAGE**, to add the package to the project.

Importing Excel Data Into A SQL Server Database

This section is for readers that do not have a current version of Excel installed that is the same bit (32 or 64-bit) as the bit version of SQL Server that you have installed.

As just covered, SSMS has a wizard to import data. What is not made clear to new users, is that this wizard requires a provider to be installed. Some of the data used in this book is in an Excel workbook and has to be imported into a SQL Server database. You do not need to have Excel installed on your computer to import data from an Excel file, but you do need to have a Microsoft OLEDB provider installed.

If you do not have Excel or Access installed, that is version 2010 or higher, you will have to install a provider, before starting Exercise 1.8. If you are not familiar with providers and do not have access to an IT department to resolve this for you, **before** downloading a provider, search your entire hard drive for "ace.oledb". If the search retrieves the file, ace.oledb.12.0 or higher, your computer has a provider that will let you import data from Excel.

It is possible to have Excel installed, but not have the provider installed. If that is the case, you will get an error in Exercise 1.8, after completing step 3. The error is "The Microsoft.ACE.OLEDB.xx.0 provider is not registered on the local machine". (xx equals the version of the provider for the version of Excel that is selected.) This is why, in the previous paragraph, I suggested searching for the provider on your hard drive, before attempting the exercise.

If you have Excel installed and there are multiple options in the drop-down list on the wizard, that are for Excel 2010 or higher, try them before installing one of the run time files, from the links below.

Read the information in all of the sections on the first two web pages below, before you download a file. Doing this should help you decide which provider to try first, (x86) 32 bit or (x64) 64 bit.

From what I can tell, if prompted to select a version, when installing the provider, selecting Office 2016 may not work, because ACE.OLEDB.16.0, does not consistently work with a 64 bit operating system.

Microsoft Access 2013 Runtime
https://www.microsoft.com/en-us/download/details.aspx?id=39358

Microsoft Access Database Engine 2010 Redistributable
https://www.microsoft.com/en-us/download/details.aspx?id=13255

This issue also applies to importing Excel or Access data into SSIS or SSAS, when using a source component.

If you have **OFFICE 365** installed, read the last paragraph in the "Additional Information" section, on the following web page. https://www.microsoft.com/en-us/download/details.aspx?id=54920

Exercise 1.8: Import Data From An Excel Workbook

Earlier in this chapter, the functionality of the Import and Export Wizard was covered. What I have learned over the years, is that even though there are a lot of databases, a good amount of data is still being stored in Excel workbooks. If you are not familiar with the data in a spreadsheet that you will import data from, you should look at it to make sure that the data is in consecutive rows and preferably in consecutive columns.

In this exercise, you will learn how to import tables in an Excel workbook into the AW database that you restored in the previous exercise. You will use the version of the wizard that is in SSMS.

1. If SQL Server Management Studio is not open, open it now ⇒ In the Object Explorer, right-click on the AW database icon ⇒ Tasks ⇒ Import Data ⇒ On the Welcome screen, click Next.

2. On the Choose a Data Source screen, open the Data source drop-down list and select Microsoft Excel ⇒ Click the Browse button ⇒ Navigate to the folder for this book and double-click on the Import Tables workbook.

3. Open the Excel version drop-down list and select Excel 2013.

    If you do not see that option, select another version of Excel, 2007 or higher.

    If you installed the run time file, discussed in the previous section, select the version of Excel, based on the provider that you installed.

    You should have options similar to those shown in Figure 1-39 ⇒ Click Next.

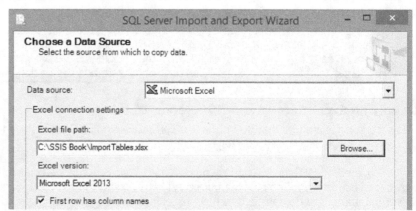

Figure 1-39 Choose a Data Source screen

4. Open the Destination drop-down list and select, **SQL SERVER NATIVE CLIENT 11.0**, or higher. This option indicates the environment that the file, in this case a workbook, will be imported into. This option will select the correct provider to convert the data that is being imported. In this exercise, the Excel data will be imported into a SQL Server database.

5. Select the AW database, as shown at the bottom of Figure 1-40.

    The **NEW** button is used to create a new database to import the data into.

    Click Next.

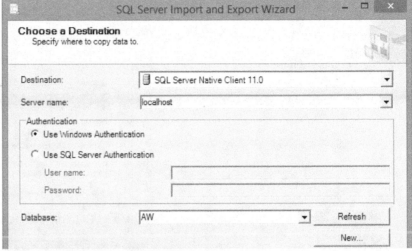

Figure 1-40 Choose a Destination screen

6. Select the Copy data from . . . option, shown in Figure 1-41 ⇒ Click Next.

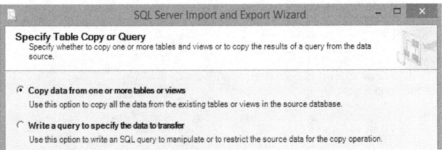

Figure 1-41 Specify Table Copy or Query screen

7. On the Select Source Tables and Views screen, check all of the tables, except for the Duplicate Orders table.

8. Click in the **DESTINATION FIELD** for the Employees table ⇒ Type EmployeeList ⇒
    Click in the Destination field for the Financial Data table ⇒ Type FinancialData ⇒
    Click in the Destination field for the Order Info table ⇒ Type OrderInfo⇒

    Your screen should look like the one shown in Figure 1-42. The names in the Destination column will be the names of the tables in the AW database, that will be created and populated, during the import.

    If the data source has more tables then you want to import, on the screen shown in Figure 1-42, clear the check mark for any tables that you do not want to import.

    In this exercise, the Duplicate Orders table will not be imported.

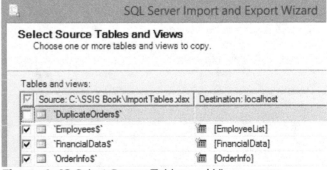

Figure 1-42 Select Source Tables and Views screen

9. Click Next ⇒ On the Save and Run Package screen, check the RUN IMMEDIATELY option ⇒ Click Next.

   Figure 1-43 shows the options that were selected on the wizard.

   Notice in the first three bullets, that new tables will be created, which is what is needed in this exercise.

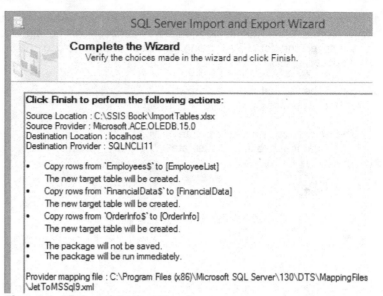

Figure 1-43 Complete the Wizard screen

10. Click Finish.

    The tables will be created in the AW database and the data from the workbook will be copied to the new tables.

    When finished, you will see the screen shown in Figure 1-44 ⇒ Click Close.

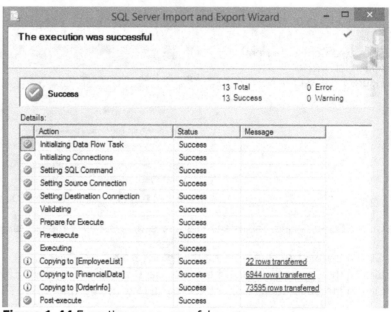

Figure 1-44 Execution was successful screen

11. In the Object Explorer window, click the Refresh (blue arrow) button on the Object Explorer toolbar ⇒ Open the Tables folder, in the AW database.

    You should see the dbo tables, illustrated in Figure 1-45. They are the tables that were created during the import.

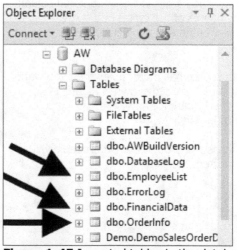

Figure 1-45 Imported tables in the database

12. Click the Save All button on the SSMS toolbar ⇒ Close SSMS.

What Is ETL?

At the beginning of this chapter, ETL was briefly mentioned. This section explains what it is. It is the reason that Integration Services was created.

The process of selecting data, loading data, deleting columns, joining columns from different tables and creating calculated fields are all part of getting the data ready to be analyzed. The IT world refers to this process as **EXTRACT**, **TRANSFORM** and **LOAD** (ETL for short). Yes, Integration Services is an ETL tool. Many Excel users have been completing these same tasks manually for years, without knowing what its called.

It is very possible that you will need to repeat many of the ETL steps several times to get the data the way that you need it. It took me hours and hours to create the practice files for this book. I remember spending six hours creating and loading data into a database, then realized that I had some fields in the wrong table. ETL tools provide the functionality discussed below.

Extract

This is the process of selecting a data source (or as many data sources as needed) and extracting a subset of the data in each data source. Integration Services supports many data sources.

Transform

Transformation shapes and cleans the data. This is the process of changing the data by using one, some or all of the following data enhancement techniques:

① **DATA INTEGRATION** Appending, joining and grouping data are examples of integration.
② **DATA CLEANSING** Deleting rows or columns of data that are not needed. Other examples of data cleansing include formatting, which includes changing the data type, or filtering data.
③ **DATA ENRICHMENT** Usually refers to adding new data. Adding a new column by combining data from existing columns or creating a calculated field, are examples of data enrichment.

Load

Load takes the data set from the source and transformation process and adds it to the destination.

Learning To Create SSIS Packages

For some, learning to create packages in SSIS can be intimidating. **LEARNING TO CREATE PACKAGES REQUIRES TIME, PATIENCE, DEDICATION AND ATTENTION TO DETAIL.** The SSIS tasks covered in this book are very robust and have a lot of features and options. SSIS is task driven, so as you go through the exercises in this book, take your time and try to understand how the concepts that you are learning can be applied to packages that you will create on your own. It is possible to go through this entire book in a few days, if you already have some experience with SSIS or a software package like Power Query in Excel, that provides similar functionality.

The reality is that you will make some mistakes along the way. If you think that I created all of the exercises in this book correctly on the first try, you are sadly mistaken. <smile> If you have a fear of making mistakes, this is the time to let go of the fear, because the fear will prevent you from learning. It is also normal to initially get confused on what to do next. Even though you may not understand why you are being instructed to do something, the steps in each exercise will allow you to achieve the expected result. This is how you will begin to build a foundation for creating packages and learning Integration Services.

The first time that a concept or technique is presented, a lot of information is provided. Each subsequent time that you have to perform the same task, less and less information (aka hand holding) will occur. As you will see, there are a lot of repetitious tasks involved in creating packages. These are the tasks that less and less information will be provided for, as you go through this book. The purpose behind this learning technique is to allow you to rely more on your knowledge, instead of flipping through this book months from now, to find the answer.

Overview

After reading this chapter and completing the exercises you will:

☑ Understand the Visual Studio interface options that are relevant to creating packages in Integration Services
☑ Know how to create a solution and project
☑ Know how to create a basic package

CHAPTER 2

SSIS Overview

The previous chapter covered the tools that are used in conjunction with SSIS. SSIS is used to design, develop and deploy packages. As you saw in the previous chapter, the Import and Export Wizard can also create an SSIS package. The difference is that in SSIS, you can add a lot more functionality, in addition to importing data, to a package. You can however, create the basic package using the wizard, then add more functionality to it in SSIS.

SSIS, like any Visual Studio development environment, is designed for collaborative development, including multi user project management. While SSIS is now free, even when used with data on a production server, it has not been scaled back or reduced in any way. The same is true for all of the SSDT tools.

Integration Services provides the framework for you to create and control the workflow of packages, down to a granular level. Features and functionality that you may think that the only solution to, is to write code or create scripts for, can be done by the tasks and other components that SSIS has. All data is not perfect. To accommodate this, SSIS has pretty extensive error handling capabilities.

This chapter introduces you to SSIS. It is used to build workflow processes. This includes extracting, transforming and loading data, also known as **EXTRACT, TRANSFORM AND LOAD (ETL)**. The ETL framework that you create can fully or partially load data in time intervals that you select. SSIS has the tools that you need to move data to and from a variety of data sources, including databases like SQL, MySQL and Oracle. Data in Excel workbooks and flat files, like text files, are also supported. The packages that can be created in SSIS can include any or all of the following to create an ETL solution:

- ☑ Clean data
- ☑ Transform data
- ☑ Merge, aggregate and look up data
- ☑ Extract data from several data sources
- ☑ Execute SQL tasks
- ☑ Load data

The reason that SSIS can process data so quickly is because the data is loaded into the servers memory, then transform it in memory before writing the data to the destination. Think of SSIS as a super upgrade to staging data and executing stored procedures.

Using Integration Services (SSIS) In Visual Studio

The first time that you open Visual Studio, you may see the tab shown in Figure 2-1. View ⇒ Start Page, will display this tab. Parts of the tab that you may use, are explained below. The options on the left side of the tab are also available on a menu.

Figure 2-1 Start Page tab

The **START SECTION** has options to create a new project, open existing projects and reports.

The **RECENT SECTION** displays projects that have already been created. If there are projects that you use all the time, you can pin them to this section, by clicking the push pin icon next to a project, as shown above in Figure 2-1.

The rest of the Start Page tab contains links for features that you can read about or watch videos for.

SSIS Workspace

Figure 2-2 shows the workspace that is used to create and modify SSIS packages. It consists of the following components: SSIS Toolbox, SSIS Designer, Solution Explorer and the Properties window. The middle section is the **SSIS DESIGNER**, and is covered in this chapter. This white space is also known as the **CANVAS**. It is where you create the package, by dragging tasks and components to this section.

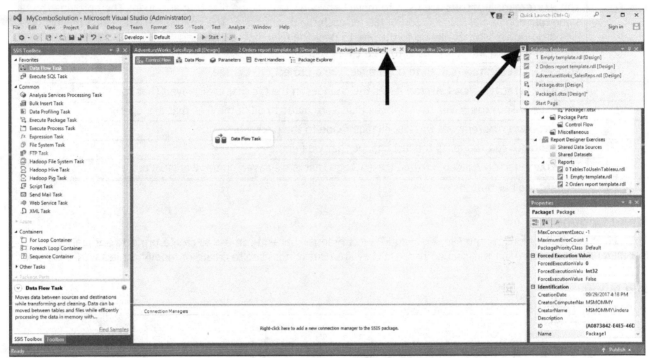

Figure 2-2 SSIS Workspace

Tabs

A tab is displayed above the canvas for each file that is open. If you have a lot of files open or the file names are long, you will not see all of the tabs. When that is the case, clicking the button to the left of the Solution Explorer window, illustrated above on the right side of Figure 2-2, will display all of the files that are open, even if you cannot see the tab for the file. You can select a file to view from this drop-down list.

 What Does The * After A File Name Mean?
Files that have changes that have not been saved, have an * (asterisk) after the file name on the tab, as illustrated above in Figure 2-2, next to the third tab.

 If you have created SSAS or SSRS projects or files, those files can be opened also and the workspace will change to reflect the file type that is open.

Toolbars

Visual Studio has a lot of toolbars. This section covers the one that you may find helpful when creating and modifying packages.

 Tools ⇒ Customize ⇒ Toolbars tab, displays the toolbars that can be added to the workspace.

Standard Toolbar

Figure 2-3 shows the options on the toolbar. The numbered buttons are explained in Table 2-1.

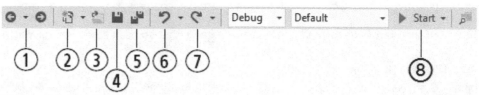

Figure 2-3 Standard toolbar

Button	Description
①	The **NAVIGATION BUTTONS** are used to move between the package files that are open. They provide the same functionality as clicking on the tab for each file that is open. The first button also has a recent files drop-down list that has up to the last 15 package files that you opened.
②	The **NEW PROJECT BUTTON** is used to create a new project.
③	The **OPEN FILE BUTTON** is used to open a file, like a project or package.
④	The **SAVE SELECTED ITEMS BUTTON** saves the changes in the file that is displayed (has focus).
⑤	The **SAVE ALL BUTTON** saves the changes that were made to all of the files that are open.
⑥	The **UNDO BUTTON** removes the last change made to the package.
⑦	The **REDO BUTTON** reapplies the last change that was undone.
⑧	The **START BUTTON** executes (runs) the package that is displayed on the workspace.

Table 2-1 Standard toolbar buttons explained

Menu Options

This section covers options on the File, View and Project menus, that you can use to create projects and packages. Not all menus are covered in this section because they are usually not used to create or modify projects, in this book.

File Menu

Figure 2-4 shows the options on the File menu, when a package file is open.

The **NEW** option is used to create a new project or file.

The **OPEN** option is used to open an existing project or file.

The **RECENT FILES** option displays up to the last 10 files that you opened. (1)

The **RECENT PROJECTS AND SOLUTIONS** option displays up to the last 10 projects or solutions that you opened. (1)

Figure 2-4 File menu

(1) This option is helpful when you want to open a file or project that is not in the solution that is currently open. This could be an SSIS, SSAS or SSRS file or project.

View Menu

The majority of options shown in Figure 2-5 add a window to the workspace. The windows that you will use the most in this book, are explained below.

The **SOLUTION EXPLORER** option displays the Solution Explorer window, shown later in Figure 2-8, in the upper right corner of the workspace.

The **TOOLBOX** option on this menu is not the SSIS Toolbox shown later in Figure 2-20. The toolbox that this option displays is not used in SSIS. It is for other software that uses the Visual Studio interface, like SSRS. The SSIS Toolbox is covered later in this chapter.

The **TOOLBARS** option displays toolbars that you can add to the workspace. The toolbars displayed, depend on the SSDT tools that are installed on your computer.

The **PROPERTIES WINDOW** option displays the Properties Window, shown later in Figure 2-18. It is displayed in the lower right corner of the workspace. The options on this window change, based on the item that is selected in the package.

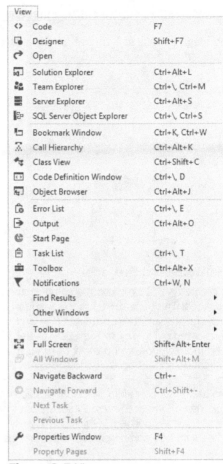

Figure 2-5 View menu

Project Menu

Figure 2-6 shows the options on the Project menu. The options are used to add functionality to the project. Many of the options on this menu are also on the shortcut menus in the Solution Explorer, which is covered later in this chapter.

Figure 2-6 Project menu

SSIS Menu

Figure 2-7 shows the options on the SSIS menu.

The menu options shown, are only available when a package is displayed on the workspace.

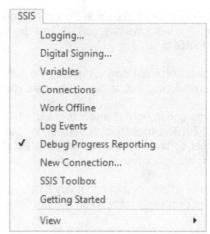

Figure 2-7 SSIS menu

Solutions And Projects

To create an SSIS package, a solution and project are required. Solutions and projects are containers (folders) for packages. They are stored in the Solution Explorer and are used to keep the components together and organized. All of the Visual Studio products (C# and Visual Basic, for example) use solutions and projects to store files. Files that are created using any of the SSDT tools (SSIS, SSAS and SSRS) also use solutions and projects. A package also has to be in a solution and project to run it in debug mode to troubleshoot any problems. Packages for the same application should be saved in the same project folder, because projects are what gets deployed.

A solution is a container in Visual Studio that has one or more projects. An SSIS project can have one or more packages and related files. What may not be obvious is that projects can be created with other software tools like Visual Basic, Reporting Services and Analysis Services and be stored in the same solution. This is done so that the projects can be combined and rolled out as a single large scale application, into a solution that meets the business requirements.

For example, the business requirements include an application to maintain inventory, 29 inventory reports and a database that has inventory and product tables that is stored in an Oracle database that needs to be moved into a new SQL Server database. To accomplish this, the following tools are used and each will have its own project folder in the same solution in Visual Studio.

- ☑ Visual Basic will be used to create the inventory front end application.
- ☑ SSIS will be used to transform and move the data from the Oracle database to a SQL Server database.
- ☑ Reporting Services will be used to create the 29 inventory reports.

SSIS File Extensions

In SSIS, you can create a variety of files. Each file type that you create has a unique extension. The file extensions are explained below.

.DESIGNER is a package part file saved in a package.
.DTPROJ is a SSIS project file.
.DTSX is a SSIS package file.
.SLN is a solution file. This file type is also created by other tools like SSRS and Visual Basic.
.CONMGR is a shared connection manager file.
.DS is a shared data source file.
.PARAMS is a shared parameter file.
.DTSXP is a Control Flow package part.

What Is A Solution?

A solution is the top container if you will, for storing projects and resources. It is used to keep the files in one or more projects organized. Figure 2-8 shows the Solution Explorer window. If no solution is open when you create a new project, a solution is also created automatically.

A solution can store different types of projects. The projects in a solution should be related. For example, Figure 2-8 shows a solution that I created.

It has two projects: My SSIS Project, which contains one package and the Report Designer Exercises project. It is a SQL Server Reporting Services (SSRS) project. This project has shared data sources and shared data sets, that were created for the reports shown in the project.

Having this type of functionality is helpful if the package uses files from a different type of project.

For SSIS projects, the Solution Explorer stores project connection managers, SSIS packages, package parts and project parameters. Other files needed for packages are stored in the Miscellaneous folder shown in the figure. Files that do not have their own folder or that do not have one of the following extensions, are also placed in the Miscellaneous folder: **.CONMGR**, **.DTSX** or **.PARAMS**.

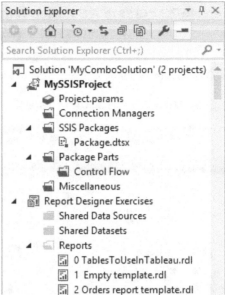

Figure 2-8 Solution with two projects

What Is A Project?

A project is like a file cabinet. It has folders that are automatically created, when the project is created. Because the project name is used to create a folder for all of the package files, the project name must use Windows naming conventions. The folders contain the resources for the packages in each project. The folders that are automatically created, like the Connection Managers and Miscellaneous folders, are used to store files that the packages need. On your own, you will probably create a project folder for each project (no pun intended) that you work on.

Each SSIS project has a **SSIS PACKAGES FOLDER**, as shown above in Figure 2-8. This folder can store an unlimited number of packages. Projects can be deployed (put into production). This means that more than one package can be deployed at the same time. Packages can also be deployed individually.

Often, SSIS projects are part of a bigger business project, as discussed earlier. This means that other types of files will be created and stored in the same solution. As you will see, the three SSDT tools each have their own project folder templates and all can be in the same solution folder (container), as shown above in Figure 2-8, hence the term "Enterprise System".

Copy Packages Between Projects
If needed, a package can be copied and pasted from one project to another project in the solution, by right-clicking on the package that you want to copy ⇒ Select Copy ⇒ Right-click on the project folder that you want to paste the copy of the package into ⇒ Select Paste.

Understanding Project Templates

SQL Server Data Tools supports a variety of project types, as shown below in Figure 2-9. Each project type has a few project templates that you can select from. Projects created using Integration Services functionality, use one of the following Integration Services templates. Both will create a package project.

①	**INTEGRATION SERVICES PROJECT** This template is used to create an Integration Services project that has an empty package.
②	**INTEGRATION SERVICES IMPORT PROJECT WIZARD** As its name suggests, a wizard is used to walk you through creating a new project that is based on an existing Integration Services Catalog or to import packages from an existing deployed project.

Exercise 2.1: Create A Solution And Project

In this exercise, you will learn how to create a solution and project that will be used as the starting point for the next exercise in this chapter.

1. Open Visual Studio if it is not already open ⇒ If any solutions or projects are open, close them.

2. File ⇒ New ⇒ Project. You will see the dialog box shown in Figure 2-9.

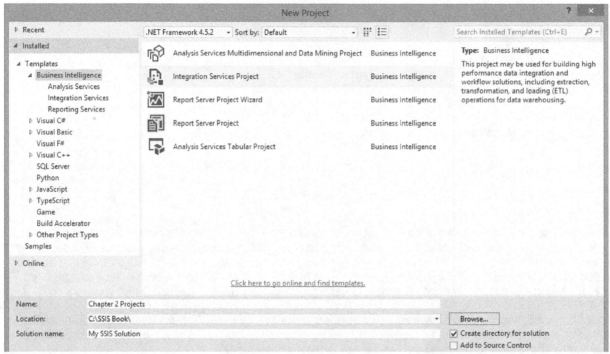

Figure 2-9 New Project dialog box

3. On the left side of the dialog box, display the Templates section ⇒ Click on the Business Intelligence or Integration Services option. I don't know why the Integration Services Import Project Wizard option does not appear on the Business Intelligence screen.

4. Select the Integration Services Project option, to the right.

5. In the Name field, type Chapter 2 Projects. This will be the project name.

By default, the Solution name will be the Project name. You can also change the Solution name on the Solution Explorer, if you are not creating a directory for the solution.

6. Click the Browse button ⇒ Navigate to and select the folder that you created for this book ⇒ Click the **SELECT FOLDER** button.

7. Check the **CREATE DIRECTORY FOR SOLUTION** option ⇒ In the Solution name field, type My SSIS Solution, as shown above in Figure 2-9 ⇒ Click OK. The solution and project folders will be created.

In the lower right corner of the workspace, you will see the Getting Started (SSIS) and Properties tabs. You can close or hide the Getting Started tab, as it is not needed to complete the exercises in this book.

8. On the Visual Studio Standard toolbar, click the Save All button.

Options Dialog Box

This section covers some of the options that you may have the need to change for SQL Server Integration Services.

What To Do If The Solution That You Created Is Not Displayed In The Solution Explorer
If by chance you do not see the solution that you just created in Exercise 2.1, it is probably because an option needs to be enabled. In Visual Studio, if a solution only has one project, the solution is hidden by default. I know in older versions of SSIS, the option was not checked by default. This also happens when a solution only has one project. The steps below show you how to enable the option.
1. Tools ⇒ Options.
2. Click on the Projects and Solutions category ⇒ Check the **ALWAYS SHOW SOLUTION** option, illustrated in Figure 2-10.

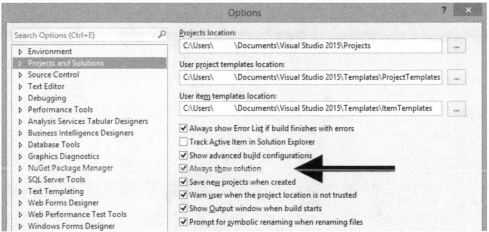
Figure 2-10 Projects and Solutions options

Changing The Default New Project File Location

The **PROJECTS LOCATION** field in Figure 2-11, shows where projects will be saved by default. If that is not where you want to save projects, click the button at the end of the field and select the folder that you want to use as the default location. This figure shows the default project location set to the folder used in this book. Doing this is optional to complete the exercises in this book, but you may find it helpful.

Figure 2-11 Project location changed

Displaying Precedence Constraint Labels

The **SHOW PRECEDENCE CONSTRAINT LABELS** option, illustrated in Figure 2-12, is used to display the labels on precedence constraints (the arrows), when viewing packages.

If checked, labels (success, completion and failure) will appear next to each precedence constraint arrow on the tab, when the package is run. [See Chapter 3, Figure 3-8] This is helpful to make it easier to tell what the expected outcome is, for each arrow. Displaying the labels is not a requirement to complete the exercises in this book, but displaying them will be helpful.

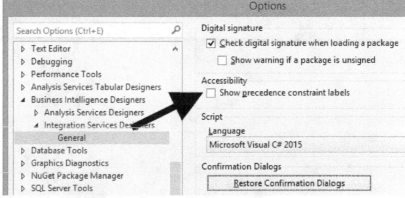
Figure 2-12 Integration Services Designers options

Selecting What Is Displayed After Visual Studio Opens
You can customize what is displayed when you first open Visual Studio, by doing the following:
On the Options dialog box shown above in Figure 2-12, select Environment ⇒ Start Up ⇒ Select an option in the **AT STARTUP** drop-down list, shown in Figure 2-13. You may find it helpful to change the At startup option to **LOAD LAST LOADED SOLUTION**. This will automatically open the solution used in this book. Once you complete the exercises in this book, you can change this option to your own project.

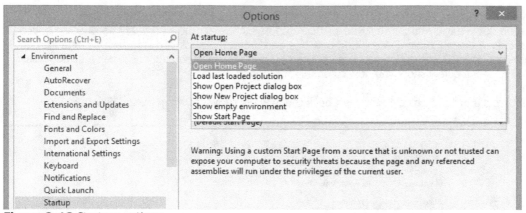

Figure 2-13 Start up options

SSIS Workspace Tools

The tools discussed in this section are displayed on the workspace. You will use them to create and modify packages.

Solution Explorer

Figure 2-14 shows the Solution Explorer right after the new solution and project were created in Exercise 2.1. It contains one package and empty folders. You can use the package file shown in the figure to create your own package because it is empty. You can also rename the package.

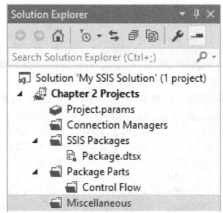

This window also stores all of the shared parameters and shared connection managers for all of the packages that are created in the solution. Parameters, connection managers and packages are stored in the project that they are created in. The shared resources are only available in the **PROJECT DEPLOYMENT MODEL**.

Almost all of the items in the Solution Explorer, including the Solution name, has a shortcut menu. The exceptions are the Package Parts and Miscellaneous folders.

Figure 2-14 Solution Explorer

Project Folder Shortcut Menu

Figure 2-15 shows the Project folder shortcut menu.

The **ADD** option is used to add new and existing items and packages to the corresponding project.

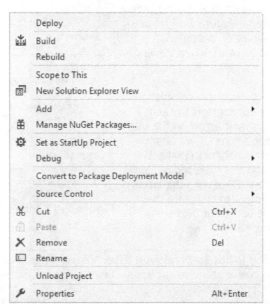

Figure 2-15 Project folder shortcut menu

SSIS Packages Folder Shortcut Menu

Figure 2-16 shows the shortcut menu for the SSIS Packages folder.

The **NEW SSIS PACKAGE** option is used to create a new package in the project.

SSIS IMPORT AND EXPORT WIZARD opens a wizard that is similar to the wizard that you learned how to use in Chapter 1.

ADD EXISTING PACKAGE is used to add a copy of an existing package, from another project, to the current project.

Figure 2-16 SSIS Packages folder shortcut menu

Package File Shortcut Menu

Figure 2-17 shows the shortcut menu for a package file.

EXECUTE PACKAGE runs the package.

DEPLOY PACKAGE [See Chapter 8, Integration Services Deployment Wizard]

VIEW CODE displays the code (on a tab on the SSIS Designer) that was created, based on the options and tasks selected to create the package.

EXCLUDE FROM PROJECT removes the package from the SSIS packages folder, for the project, but does not delete the package from your computers hard drive.

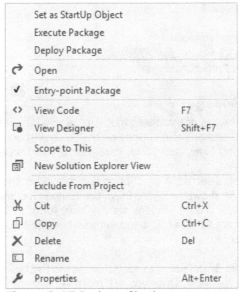

Figure 2-17 Package file shortcut menu

Miscellaneous Folder

The Miscellaneous folder stores any file that is not for any of the other folders in the project. This includes spreadsheets and word processing documents. Often, packages have installation or deployment instructions, which could be in a word processing document. Placing those files in this folder would be helpful. Selecting the Add option, on the Project folder ⇒ Existing Item, will let you add a Word document, text file, spreadsheet or another file type to the Miscellaneous folder.

Properties Window

The options on the Properties window shown in Figure 2-18, are used to customize the selected item. While each item on the Control Flow and Data Flow tabs, has its own set of properties (on each items editor), there are other options on the Properties window that are not on the editor. (Pressing the F4 key or View menu ⇒ Properties Window, displays this window)

Right below the window name, you will see the name of the selected object in bold and the control type. If the object has not been renamed, it uses the control type and a number as the objects name, as shown at the top of Figure 2-18. If the object has been renamed, that name is displayed, as shown at the top of Figure 2-19.

The column on the left of the Properties window is the list of properties that are available for the selected object. The column on the right, contains the current setting for the property. This is the column that you use to change the settings. What may not be obvious is that some properties display a description of the property, at the bottom of the Properties window, when you click on the property. In Figure 2-18, the Offline Mode property is selected and you see a description for the property, at the bottom of the window. If you do not see the description section, drag the light gray line above the description section up, until the description section is visible.

Properties that have (**COLLECTION**) in the column on the right, as shown in Figure 2-18, indicates that there are more properties that can be used to customize the object.

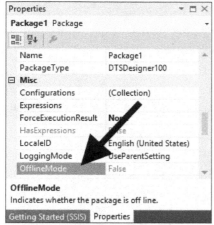

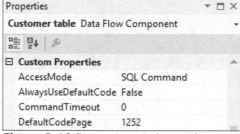

Figure 2-19 Properties window with a named object

Figure 2-18 Properties window

SSIS Toolbox

This toolbox has all of that tasks that can be used to create a package. The sections and options on the toolbox change, based on the tab (Control Flow, Data Flow, Parameters, etc) that is selected.

When a task is selected, a description is displayed at the bottom of the toolbox. As shown in Figure 2-20, the toolbox has the sections explained below. These sections are available for most tabs. The sections that are tab specific are covered when the tab is covered, later in this book.

① **FAVORITES** By default, this section contains the tasks that you may use the most. Once you are more familiar with the options in the toolbox, you may want to add tasks to this section, that you use the most. Doing so will keep you from having to scroll down the list. To add a task, right-click on it and select **MOVE TO FAVORITES**.

② **COMMON** Contains tasks that are frequently used.

③ **OTHER** The name of this section changes, based on the tab that is selected. It contains additional tasks that can be used to create a package.

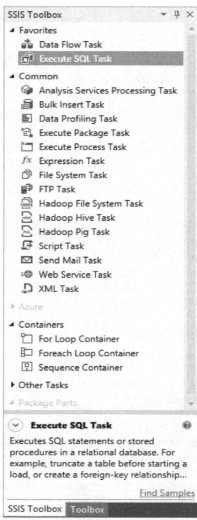

Figure 2-20 SSIS Toolbox (Control Flow tab)

Each of the sections on the toolbox can be collapsed, as needed. If you only use five tasks, you could move them to the Favorites section, then collapse the other sections, as shown in Figure 2-21.

If you change your mind later and want to remove a task from the Favorites folder, right-click on it and select the first **MOVE TO** option on the shortcut menu, shown in Figure 2-21. The first Move to option is the location that the task was originally in, except for containers.

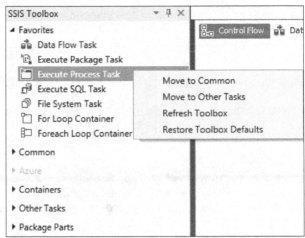

Figure 2-21 Customized toolbox

Saving The Workspace Layout

This option is helpful when you have the workspace set up the way that you want it. If something happens to your layout, and trust me, it is possible <smile>, having it saved will be a welcomed relief. Yes, you can manually set up your workspace again and hopefully you remember every tweak that you made. For the rest of us, the steps below show you how to save a layout.

1. Place all of the objects where you want them on the workspace.

2. Window ⇒ Save Window layout.

3. On the Save Window layout dialog box, type in a name for the layout. I used MY SSIS Layout, because I also have a saved layout for SSRS.

Restore A Layout

To restore a layout, open the Window menu ⇒ Apply Window layout ⇒ Select the layout that you want to restore.

SSIS Designer

By default, the designer displays five tabs at the top of the canvas, as shown in Figure 2-22. The Control Flow and Data Flow tabs are used to create packages.

Once a task is added to the workspace, double-clicking on it, displays the options that are used to configure the task. Each task has its own editor.

The exception is the Data Flow Task. It uses the Data Flow tab to add and configure tasks. These tabs and the Event Handler tab, covered later, have options on the toolbox.

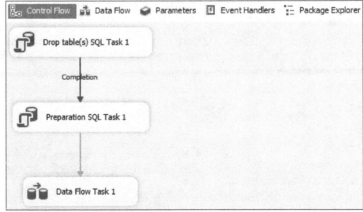

Figure 2-22 SSIS Designer

The Control Flow and Data Flow tabs are used the most to create a package. After you have added a few tasks, you can run the package to test it, by doing one of the following.

- ☑ Press the F5 key on your keyboard.
- ☑ On the Solution Explorer, right-click on the package that you want to run ⇒ Execute Package.
- ☑ Click the Start button on the toolbar. [See Figure 2-3, button 8]

Running a package takes you out of design mode and into debug mode. Figure 2-42 shown later, shows the Debug Mode window.

Control Flow Tab

This tab manages the entire workflow of the package. It controls the order that tasks are executed in. Each package can only have one control flow. The toolbox has two types of tasks for the Control Flow tab: Workflow (the Common section) and Containers. Tasks add the functionality to the package. Containers add order and structure to the workflow. The precedence constraints connect and control the flow of tasks.

Data Flow Tab

This tab handles the movement of data. The following are also created on this tab: Data cleansing, transforming data, sorting data, combining data from different data flows, aggregating data and more. The toolbox options for this tab, has data source, data destination, maintenance and transformation tasks.

☑ The data source tasks are used to extract data from a variety of sources.

☑ The data transformations are used to clean, create new columns of data and prepare the data to meet the needs of the business request.

☑ The data destination tasks are used to load (write) data to a variety of data sources.

While each package can only have one Control Flow, it can have many data flows. Each Data Flow Task that the Control Flow has, generates a new Data Flow tab. A package can have an unlimited number of data flows. Most of the time, the primary reason to have multiple data flows is to keep from having to recreate the same transformation for the same field, several times in the same package. For example, one package can have all of the data flows listed below. Each would be on its own tab.

① Loads data from several tables into memory that will be used by multiple data flows.

② Perform data conversion on date and numeric fields, that will be used by the same source files on different data flow tabs.

③ Create derived columns of data that multiple destination files need.

> **Control Flow vs Data Flow Tabs**
> I think that it is important to understand the differences between these tabs, especially since they both have tasks. The **CONTROL FLOW TAB** is used to handle the workflow of the package. The **DATA FLOW TAB** is used to load (import and export) and transform the data to configure the Data Flow Task on the Control Flow tab.

Parameters Tab

The options shown in Figure 2-23 are used to create a parameter. Parameters are created to pass values to a specific part of the package. A parameter is a placeholder that must have a name, data type and value. Parameters are covered in Chapter 8.

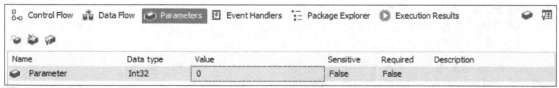

Figure 2-23 Parameters tab

Event Handlers Tab

Behind the scenes, each task and container has events that run. These events can be trapped when necessary. This is done by setting up workflows that will run when an event is triggered. This process is called **EVENT HANDLERS**. In addition to handling errors, event handlers can be created for warnings or when a task, package or container has completed.

The options on the Event Handlers tab are used to create tasks that are for a specific task or created for the entire package. The options on this tab are the same as the ones on the Control Flow tab. Workflows can be created on this tab, just like they can on the Control Flow and Data Flow tabs. Figure 2-24 shows the Event Handlers tab. The options are explained below.

The **EXECUTABLE** drop-down list has all of the components that an event handler can be applied to. An executable is a task, container or package. The package is the highest level executable. Selecting the package means that the event handler will be applied to all components on the package. Selecting a component (task or container, for example) sets the **SCOPE** for the event handler. This means that the option selected in the Event handler drop-down list will only be applied to a specific component.

The **EVENT HANDLER** drop-down list, shown in the figure, has the handlers that can be used with the selected executable task. In addition to being able to create an On Error handler, a handler can be created for a task that fails, or for something that you want to have happen after the package is run, like clean up temporary data storage after the package finishes running or refresh the data in a table when a lookup fails. A popular use of event handlers is to use the **ONERROR** event scoped to the package, to send an email if any part of the package generates an error.

The options in the Event handler drop-down list contain options to handle warnings and errors. There are also options to use when a task or container has completed. Table 2-2 explains the events that can be applied to a package.

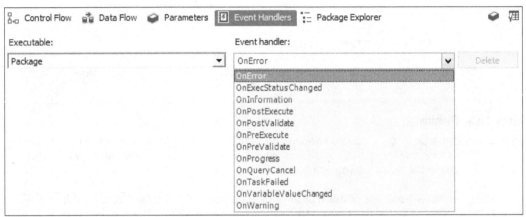

Figure 2-24 Event Handlers tab

Event	The Event Is Triggered . . .
OnError	When an error occurs. This event can be used to replace the failure precedence constraint, to redirect the workflow.
OnExecStatusChanged	When the execution status changes on a task or container.
OnInformation	When an informational event occurs, while an executable task is being validated or run.
OnPostExecute	When a task or container is finished processing.
OnPostValidate	When the validation of a task has completed.
OnPreExecute	Before a task or container runs. It is often used to check the value of a variable that will be used in the next task.
OnPreValidate	Just before the validation of a task starts.
OnProgress	When measurable progress is made.
OnQueryCancel	When a task checks to see if it should continue or stop running.
OnTaskFailed	When a task or container fails without generating an actual error.
OnVariableValueChanged	Anytime the value in a variable changes.
OnWarning	When a warning occurs.

Table 2-2 Event Handlers explained

When several event handlers are added to a package, the workflow of the package can look overwhelming, if the event handlers were on the Control Flow tab. That is why they are on their own tab.

Package Explorer Tab

This tab displays all of the components, tasks, event handlers, connections and variables, that were used to create the package, in a tree view layout (like Windows File Manager), as shown in Figure 2-25. This tab makes it easy to find an item and to see how a task effects other tasks, in the package. Connection managers, executables, precedence constraints, parameters and transformations are also displayed in this summarized view.

Double-clicking on an item, except for system variables and the Data Flow Task, opens the corresponding editor, so that changes can be made or review the current options. By default, this tab does not have any options on the toolbox.

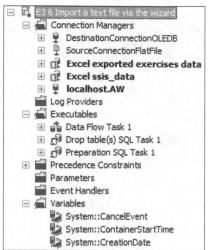

Figure 2-25 Package Explorer tree view of the components in a package

Once the package is run (executed), you will see the Debug window, shown later in Figure 2-42 and a new tab named **PROGRESS**, shown later in Figure 2-44.

Adding An Annotation To A Package

This feature can be used to document a package. The **ADD ANNOTATION** option is on the shortcut menu on the following tabs: Control Flow (Figure 2-26), Data Flow (Figure 2-27) and Event Handler. Selecting this option displays a text box, shown at the top of Figure 2-28. Type in the text that you want.

The text box stays visible on the canvas. A good use of this feature is to keep a log of changes that are made to the package. The shortcut menu options (in Figure 2-28) are used to customize the annotation. The text box can be resized. It is a good idea to include a date on the annotation. When you are finished, save the changes to the package.

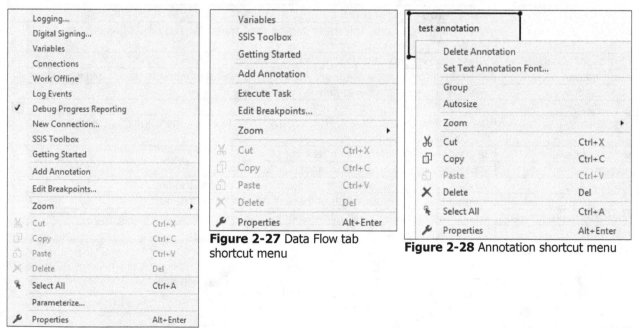

Figure 2-27 Data Flow tab shortcut menu

Figure 2-28 Annotation shortcut menu

Figure 2-26 Control Flow tab shortcut menu

Connection Managers Tab

Connections to a data source are called **CONNECTION MANAGERS** in SSIS. Each connection to a different data source that you create, will have its own Connection Manager, so it is a good idea to give Connection Managers a name that makes sense. The connections on this tab can be used by tasks on the Data Flow tab. The **CONNECTION MANAGERS TAB** is below the SSIS Designer. It is used to create connections to data sources. By default, connections created here can only be used in the package that it is created in.

The connections can be used as a source or destination connection. As you will see with an Excel workbook that has multiple sheets or a database, as long as the connection does not select a specific sheet or table, it can be used for any sheet or table in the file.

What Is A Task?

A task is a set of self-contained instructions (like a macro) that complete a specific action. A task adds functionality to the package, like sorting data, merging rows of data, sending an email, copying files from one location to another or creating a new column of data. These are tasks (also called **COMPONENTS**) that can be used in the ETL process. They are on the toolbox. The tasks usually have to be put in a specific order because one task creates or manipulates data that another task needs. Tasks can be sequenced on the Control Flow, Data Flow and Event Handlers tabs.

To add a task, drag it from the toolbox to the canvas, then right-click on the task (on the canvas) and select **EDIT** on the shortcut menu, to open its editor.

Another Way To Open The Task Editor
In addition to right-clicking on a task, you can double-click on the task to open the editor. Double-click on the icon to the left of the task name to open the editor. Double-clicking on the task name is used to **RENAME THE TASK**.

Task Editor

Each task, except the Data Flow Task, has its own editor. Once the task is added to the canvas, open the editor. The Task Editor is used to configure and customize the task. Figure 2-29 shows the Task Editor for the File System Task.

What you will see is that there are some generic properties that most task editors have. Two properties that come to mind are Name and Description. The default for these properties are the task name.

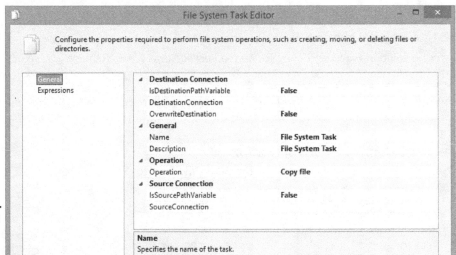

Figure 2-29 File System Task Editor

It is not a requirement to give each task a name, but you may find it helpful because you will be better able to know what the task has been configured to do. Another reason to give each task a descriptive name is because the name is used in the error log. If the package uses the same task more than once, it will be difficult to know which task is causing the problem, because they will have the same name.

What Is A Package?

A package is a collection of tasks, that when combined, create an automated workflow to accomplish a business objective. For example, a package can be created that imports data from several workbooks, once a day, checks the data to make sure that it is in the format needed to append it to tables in a database.

Technically, a package is an XML file. Packages use the **.DTSX** file type, which is really an XML file. Don't frown. You do not have to learn XML to create a package. <smile> The SSIS designer creates the XML file for you. Unless you specifically look for the XML file, you will never see it. If you have used Reporting Services and are familiar with **.RDL** files, the XML file created in SSIS, is the same concept.

Right-clicking on a package file in the Solution Explorer and selecting View Code, will display the XML code for the package. Before you faint over the fact that XML files are not secure by default, packages are automatically encrypted with your Windows user key. This key protects your Windows user credentials on your computer.

A package is what SSIS was designed to create. In a way, a package is like an executable (.exe) file, because it is self contained. A package is designed to solve all or part of a business need, from a data perspective. In many companies, the data is stored in a variety of systems, often different platforms, like an Oracle™ financial system, a warehouse management system in Microsoft Dynamics™ and a customer relationship management (CRM) system in Sales Force™.

Having data on so many different platforms can be a challenge to get them to all work "nice" together. Often, there is a need to feed or extract data between these systems. This is where SSIS steps in. It can feed warehouse data to the financial system. It can also extract specific data from the CRM system, place it in an Excel workbook to be used by a specific department. A package can also be used to create what are known as views and extract data for people that need to create reports.

> **Default Package**
> Each project that is created, has a default package named **PACKAGE.DTSX** that is automatically created. You can rename the package and use it to create a package.

Exercise 2.2: Create A Package

In this exercise, you will learn how to create a basic package that connects to a table in the AW database, then create a query that retrieves the Customer ID, Customer Name and Email address fields. The data retrieved from the query will be written to a text file. While the package that will be created is considered "basic", it uses enough functionality, for you to get a good idea of the overall steps required to create a package. Some of the task configuration topics may not make sense now, but they are explained later in this book.

Create A New Package File

1. In the Solution Explorer, right-click on the Package.dtsx file ⇒ Rename ⇒ Type E2.2 Basic package, as the file name ⇒ Press Enter.

2. If the package file is not open (meaning there is no tab for it displayed for it at the top of the canvas), double-click on the package file in the Solution Explorer.

Select The Control Flow Tab Options

In this part of the exercise, you will use the Data Flow Task to create a connection to the Adventure Works database.

1. From the toolbox, drag the Data Flow Task to the canvas.

2. Click on the words on the task ⇒
    Type Connect to AW database, as shown in Figure 2-30.

    The location of the task on the canvas, is not all that important right now. I placed it near the top, to take the screen shot.

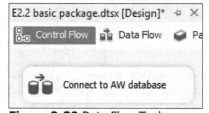

Figure 2-30 Data Flow Task renamed

Create A Connection To An SQL Server Database

In this part of the exercise, you will use the OLE DB connection options to connect to the SQL database that you restored in Chapter 1.

1. Right-click in the **CONNECTION MANAGERS** section at the bottom of the workspace ⇒ New OLE DB Connection, as shown in Figure 2-31.

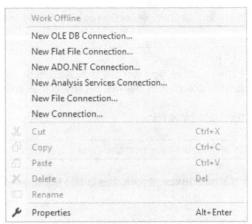

Figure 2-31 Connection Managers shortcut menu

2. On the Configure OLE DB Connection Manager dialog box, click New.

3. On the Connection Manager dialog box, type `localhost` in the Server name field. Localhost points to a server on your computers hard drive, opposed to a physical server.

4. In the Select or enter a database name field, type `AW`, as illustrated in Figure 2-32. This is the name that the Adventure Works database was given, when it was restored.

   The **SERVER NAME** field is used to type in or select the Server name, in this case, the name of the SQL Server.

   When using a local (on your computers hard drive) instance of SQL Server, you should be able to type **LOCALHOST**, as the server name and use the Windows Authentication option.

   Select the **AUTHENTICATION** option that is needed to give your logon account the permission to read and write to the database.

   On your own, you may have to enter a user name and password to connect to a data source.

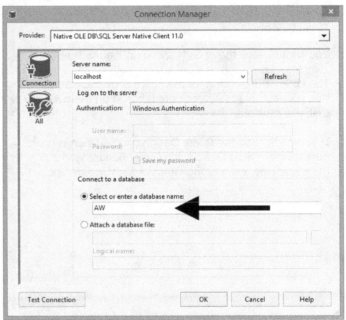

Figure 2-32 Options to connect to a SQL Server database

5. You can click the **TEST CONNECTION** button to make sure that you can connect to the database in SSIS ⇒ Click OK. You should have the data connection options, shown in Figure 2-33 ⇒ Click OK ⇒ Click the **SAVE ALL** button to save the changes to the package.

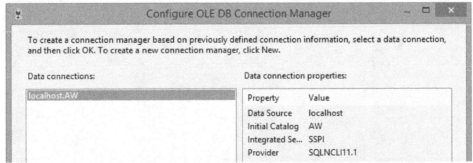

Figure 2-33 Data connection options for the Adventure Works database

Keep in mind that this connection can be used for a source or destination connection to the AW database.

Select The Table

In this part of the exercise, you will use the OLE DB Source task to create a query using the Query Builder, that will select the table and columns in the AW database that will be used to retrieve the data.

1. Click on the Data Flow tab.

 You can also double-click on the Data Flow Task on the Control Flow tab, to display the Data Flow tab.

2. Drag the **OLE DB SOURCE** task (in the Other Sources section) to the canvas ⇒ Rename the task to `Customer table`.

3. Double-click on the task. This will open the editor for the task ⇒ Open the Data access mode drop-down list and select the **SQL COMMAND** option ⇒ Click the Build Query button. The Data access mode options are covered in detail in Chapter 4. [See Chapter 4, OLE DB Source Editor And Data Access Mode]

4. Right-click in the white space at the top of the dialog box ⇒ Add Table ⇒ Scroll down the list of tables and double-click on the Customer PII (Sales) table ⇒ Close the dialog box.

5. Check the Customer ID, First Name, Last Name and Email Address fields.

   You should have the options shown in Figure 2-34.

   The code at the bottom of the figure is the SQL query that was automatically generated, based on the options that you selected.

   If you have used the Query Designer in SQL Server Reporting Services (SSRS), the Query Builder works the same way, even though it looks slightly different.

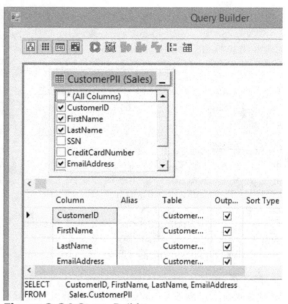

Figure 2-34 Query Builder

6. Click OK. You will see the options shown in Figure 2-35. Notice that the SQL query that was automatically generated in the Query Builder, shown above in Figure 2-34, is displayed in the SQL command text field, on the source editor.

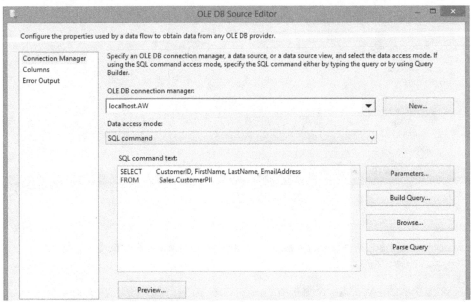

Figure 2-35 Options to retrieve data from the Customer table

Clicking the **PREVIEW BUTTON**, shown above in Figure 2-35, displays up to the first 200 rows of data that will be retrieved, as shown in Figure 2-36.

This dialog box is helpful when you type in the SQL code on the editor shown above in Figure 2-35 or click the Browse button to select a query file to retrieve data. This dialog box will let you confirm that the query works and is retrieving the data that you are expecting. If you use the Query Builder, you can view the data that will be retrieved, on that dialog box.

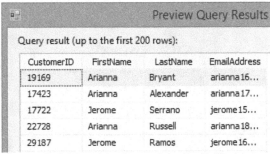

Figure 2-36 Preview Query Results dialog box

7. Click OK.

Create A Derived Column

As you saw in Figure 2-34, the Customer Name is stored in two fields. Most of the time, the first and last names will be displayed together. The solution is to combine the data in the two fields into a new field. This new field is known as a derived column. Doing this is optional, as it can be done by the person that will use the file that will be created by the package. Other times, it is not optional. Combining the fields can also be done using the Query Builder.

1. Add the **DERIVED COLUMN TASK** to the canvas ⇒ Rename it to `Customer Name`.

2. Click on the Customer table task. You should see blue and red arrows ⇒ Drag the blue arrow to the Customer Name task. This is how you connect the tasks.

3. Double-click on the Customer Name task ⇒ Display the fields in the Columns folder.

4. Click in the Derived Column Name cell ⇒ Type `CustomerName`. This will be the name of the new (derived) field that will be added to the table of data that will be exported.

5. The Derived Column should have **<ADD AS NEW COLUMN>**. If not, select it now.

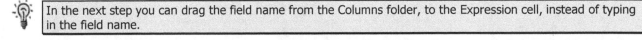

In the next step you can drag the field name from the Columns folder, to the Expression cell, instead of typing in the field name.

6. Click in the Expression cell and type `[FirstName]` + `" "` + `[LastName]`. There is a space between the quotes. You should have the options shown in Figure 2-37 ⇒ Click OK.

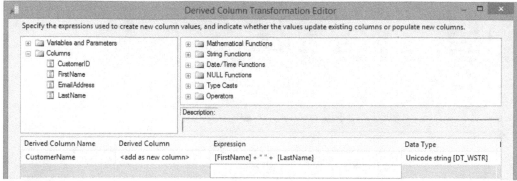

Figure 2-37 Derived column options

Select The Destination Options

In this part of the exercise, you will configure the **FLAT FILE DESTINATION** component, which is the file type that the customer data, that the query retrieved, will be written to.

1. Add the Flat File Destination Task to the canvas ⇒ Rename it to Send customer data to a text file.

2. Drag the blue arrow from the Customer Name task to the Send customer data task.

3. Double-click on the Send customer data task.

4. Click the New button. On the dialog box shown in Figure 2-38, select the Delimited option ⇒ Click OK.

   You will see the Flat File Connection Manager Editor.

   The options on this dialog box are used to select what character or width type will be used to separate the columns in the destination file.

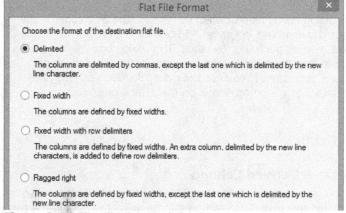

Figure 2-38 Flat File Format dialog box

5. In the File name field, type C:\SSIS Book\Ch2 Customer data.txt. This file will be created when the package is run. The records selected from the query will be written to this file.

6. Check the **COLUMN NAMES IN THE FIRST DATA ROW** option. You should have the options shown in Figure 2-39. On your own, you may want to give the connection manager a name and enter a description, so that if you have to edit it, you will know which file connection manager to edit ⇒ Click OK.

7. On the Flat File Destination Editor, click on the **MAPPINGS** option. You should have the options shown in Figure 2-40 ⇒ Click OK. If you do not see this, click on the Connection Manager option ⇒ Click the Update button ⇒ View the Mappings page again.

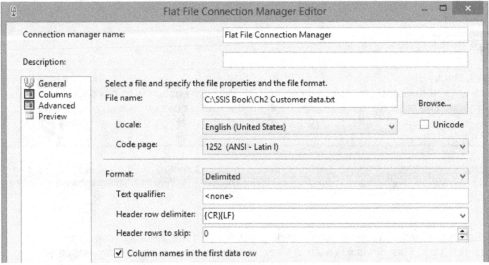

Figure 2-39 Flat File Connection Manager options

These are the columns of data that will be written to the text file. Because the Customer Name field has the first and last name, it may not be necessary to write the individual name fields to the destination file. At best, the last name field could be written to the destination file, as it could be used to sort the customers by the last name, which is a common thing to do.

It is not a requirement to write out all of the fields shown in the figure. If there are fields that you do not want to send to the destination file, open the drop-down list for the field, in the Input Column, and select <ignore>, as shown on the second row in the figure.

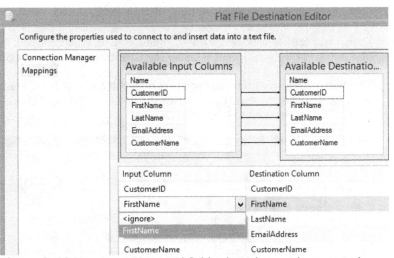

Figure 2-40 Mapping options and field selected to not be exported

The other way to not write a column to the destination file is to remove the link between the fields at the top of the dialog box.

8. Save the changes. Your Data Flow tab should look like the one shown in Figure 2-41.

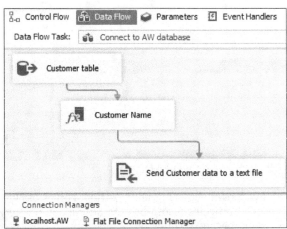

Figure 2-41 Data Flow tab options

Run The Package

In this part of the exercise, you will run/execute the package that you just created. The end result will be that the Ch2 Customer data file has data by the query and a new field of data.

 Running (Executing) A Package
As covered earlier, there is more than one way to run a package. My preferred option is to run packages from the Solution Explorer window. The reason is because other options that can be used to run a package, like the Start button on the toolbar, can cause other items to run, in addition to the package. This may or may not be what you want to have happen.

When a package is run, the design mode changes to the execution/debug mode, as shown in Figure 2-42. As you can see, several windows are displayed. When the package is finished running, the execute mode is still displayed.

Debug Mode Window

This window is automatically displayed when you run/execute a package. It displays the tasks and components and the number of rows sent to the next task. This window is used to view how the package is processing, hopefully, without any errors. <smile>

1. In the Solution Explorer window, right-click on the E2.2 package ⇒ Execute Package.

2. You should see the window shown in Figure 2-42 ⇒ When finished, click the Package execution completed link (illustrated in the figure), that is below the Connection Managers section to return to the workspace.

    The green check mark next to each task means that the task was executed without a problem. Notice the number of rows. Because the steps have the same number, it means that no filter was applied, so all of the rows in the source file were written to the destination file.

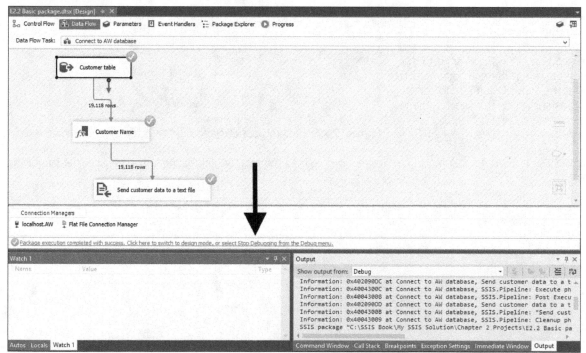

Figure 2-42 Debug Mode window

The **OUTPUT WINDOW** shown above in the lower right corner of Figure 2-42, is a place that you can look to find out what this problem is. It provides a step-by-step description of everything that is going on, in the package. This window will be your best friend because by default, it lets you see what is going on, while the package is running. While this figure shows the Output window on the right, on my own, I have it displayed across the entire bottom of the workspace, because I am very concerned about the status of the package. <smile>

While changes can be made in debug mode, they are not available until the package is run again. New tasks cannot be created in debug mode.

3. In your folder for this book, you should see the Ch2 Customer data.txt file.

    If you view it, you should see the records shown in Figure 2-43.

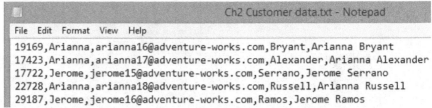

Figure 2-43 Text file created and populated from the package

Notice that the First and Last Names are combined in the new field, at the end of the row. That is the derived column that you created. As shown above in Figure 2-42, this file has 19,118 rows of data.

Progress Tab

As soon as the package is run, the **PROGRESS TAB**, shown in Figure 2-44 is available. The Progress tab is another place to look when the package has a problem that you need to debug.

When you click the Stop button on the toolbar, to stop the debug mode, the Progress tab goes away and the Execution Results tab appears. This tab can also be used when there is a problem with the package. It provides another step-by-step view of what happened, while the package was running.

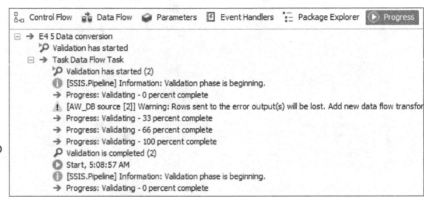

Figure 2-44 Progress tab

The Progress tab contains a detailed list of every step taken while the package was running, including any validation that was done and the execution of every task in the package. When the package has finished running, the execution results are displayed on the Execution Results tab, shown in Figure 2-45.

View The Execution Results

As you can see, there is a new tab on the workspace. The **EXECUTION RESULTS TAB** is shown in Figure 2-45.

This tab displays all of the steps that were executed and the progress of each step, when the package was run. The Execution Results tab displays the information about the last time the package was run.

Keep in mind that I did say that this exercise creates a "basic package". <smile> The rest of this book will show you how to use many of the tasks on the toolbox on the Control Flow and Data Flow tabs.

Figure 2-45 Execution Results tab

CONTROL FLOW TAB

 Overview

After reading this chapter and completing the exercises you will:

☑ Have a better understanding of the role that the Control Flow tab plays in creating a package.
☑ Have a better understanding of how the connection options work.
☑ Understand the Data Flow Task.
☑ Be able to use the following control flow tasks: Bulk Insert, File System and Execute Process.

CHAPTER 3

Control Flow

The control flow manages the order that the components and tasks are executed in, in the package. Precedence constraints are used to control the order. Not surprising, the control flow is created on the Control Flow tab.

The primary focus of this chapter is to learn more about the Control Flow tab and the tasks that can be created on it. Additionally, connection options and precedence constraints are covered, because they are an integral part of creating packages. Without creating the connections properly, there isn't much that you can do in Integration Services, without data. Some of the exercises in this chapter will be the starting point for the exercises in the Data Flow chapters.

Control Flow Tab

This tab is also known as the **CONTROL FLOW DESIGNER**. This tab has the following types of workflow options to manage and organize the package.

☑ There are two control flow types: Execution and Container tasks. These are on the toolbox.

☑ Containers are used to add order and structure to the workflow, by using loop or sequence functionality.

☑ Precedence constraints are used to connect and control the flow.

The Control Flow tab is often the starting point of creating a package. Packages can also be started from the Data Flow tab because data connections can be created from that tab also. The toolbox components for the Control Flow tab have two types of categories (tasks), as explained below.

☑ **CONTROL FLOW TASKS** Items in this category include execution tasks like Execute SQL, File System, Execute Package and containers. Containers are covered in Chapter 8.

☑ **MAINTENANCE TASKS** Items in this category include Back Up Database, Check Database Integrity and Rebuilding Indexes. These tasks are used to maintain the SQL Server database.

Connection Options

While creating connections is usually associated with the Data Flow tab, they need to be discussed early in the learning process, as just about every task, at some point in the process needs data. For the rest of this book, the connections that will be used in more than one package, will be created in or added to the Connection Managers folder in the Solution Explorer, so that they will be available to all packages in the same project. This means that the rest of the packages created in this book need to be saved in the same project.

What may not be obvious is that once you create a connection to a database for example, any time that you need to use any table or view in that database, you can use the same connection. The same applies to sheets (tabs) of data in an Excel workbook.

An advantage to creating project level connections, is that if any of the connection information needs to be changed, like the name or location of the data file, it only has to be changed in the connection file, opposed to having to change it in multiple package files. The project connections that are created, are displayed in the Connection Managers folder, in the Solution Explorer. The default name for a connection is the server and database names, but they can and should be renamed.

In the real world, packages, databases and other data files can be moved from one server to another. Therefore, it is a good idea to rename the connection to something appropriate. If you need to know the type of connection (to a spreadsheet or database for example), you can include that as part of the connection name.

As you will see, the options on the Connection Manager dialog box change, based on the type of data file that you are creating the connection for. This means that the options for creating a connection to a spreadsheet are different form those for a connection to a database, as shown in Figures 3-1 and 3-2. Figure 3-4 shows some of the file types that you can connect to.

While the instructions in this book will have you create a connection in the first exercise that the data file is needed, on your own, you can create all of the connections at one time, in the Solution Explorer.

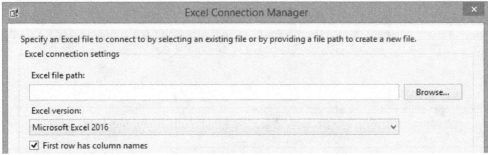

Figure 3-1 Connection options for an Excel workbook

The options in the drop-down list in this figure vary, depending on the software that is installed on your computer and the DSN connections that you may have already created.

In addition to selecting an option from the drop-down list, you can create a connection string (DSN), to select a driver for the data source that you want to connect to, by selecting the driver on the dialog box shown in Figure 3-3.

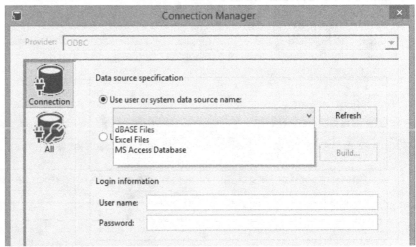

Figure 3-2 ODBC connection options for a database

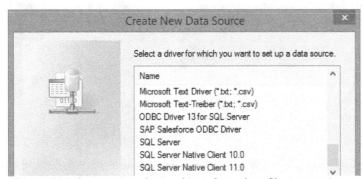

Figure 3-3 Options to select a driver for a data file connection

Many of the connection types on this dialog box are also on the toolbox, on the Data Flow tab.

This dialog box can be opened in one of the following ways:

☑ On the Control Flow tab, right-click in the Connection Managers tab section ⇒ New Connection.
☑ In the Solution Explorer, right-click on the Connection Managers folder shortcut menu and select New Connection Manager.

Add SSIS Connection Manager

Select the type of connection manager to add to the package.

Connection manager type:

Type	Description	File Na...	File Ver...
ADO	Connection manager for ADO connections	C:\Pro...	2017.14...
ADO.NET	Connection manager for ADO.NET connections	C:\Pro...	2017.14...
CACHE	Connection manager for cache	C:\Pro...	2017.14...
DQS	Connection manager for DQS server	Micros...	14.0.0.0
EXCEL	Connection manager for Excel files	C:\Pro...	2017.14...
FILE	Connection manager for files	C:\Pro...	2017.14...
FLATFILE	Connection manager for flat files	C:\Pro...	2017.14...
FTP	Connection manager for FTP connections	C:\Pro...	2017.14...
Hadoop	Connection manager for Hadoop	Micros...	14.100...

Figure 3-4 Add SSIS Connection Manager dialog box

Project Level Connections

Creating a connection using the Connection Managers folder in the Solution Explorer, allows the connection to be used by all of the packages in the project. This is helpful because you only have to create the connection to a data source once.

Connections
Once a connection is created, it can be used as a **SOURCE** or **DESTINATION** connection. Separate source and destination connections for the same data file are not needed. Also keep in mind that a "connection" only configures access to the data file. It does not specify how the data file can be used.

Package vs Project Connection
Connections created on the Connection Managers tab start off as a **PACKAGE LEVEL** connection. This tab is the only place that package level connections are displayed. Connections created from the Connection Managers folder in the Solution Explorer, are **PROJECT LEVEL** connections and are displayed on the **CONNECTION MANAGERS TAB**, in every package. This is in addition to being displayed in the Connection Managers folder. They have the word (project) in front of the connection name, as shown in Figure 3-5.

Figure 3-5 Connection Managers tab with project and package level connections

The **ASSISTANT** components on the Data Flow tab are also used to create a connection to a data file. However, by default, they create package level connections.

Converting A Connection
Connections that are created for a specific package can be converted to a project connection if needed, by right-clicking on the connection on the Connection Managers tab, at the bottom of the workspace and selecting **CONVERT TO PROJECT CONNECTION**, as shown in Figure 3-6. You will then see (project) at the beginning of the connection name.

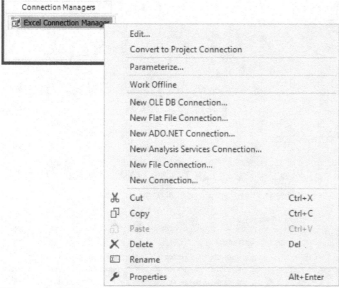

Figure 3-6 Package connection managers shortcut menu

If you have used other software that could create connections to data files, some of the terminology in SSIS could be confusing. For example, outside of SSIS, the term **DATA SOURCE** refers to a file that has data that will be used. A data source can be read from or written to. There isn't different terminology for a file that is written to, outside of SSIS. In SSIS, the term **SOURCE** only refers to the data file that will be used to get data from.

Understanding Precedence Constraints

Precedence constraints are used on the Control Flow tab, when two or more tasks are added to the tab. These constraints are used to connect the components that control the order that tasks are run in. They control when tasks and containers should run. Precedence constraint labels were covered in Chapter 2. [See Figure 2-12]

Precedence constraints are like traffic cops, as they direct the flow of tasks, containers and components. To control the flow, you have to set the constraint value or create an expression to set the constraint value.

If the concept of precedence constraints has you frowning or scratching your head, think of it this way. In this formula, (4 + 3) * 5, the 4 + 3 would be processed first, then that value would be multiplied by 5. The order of precedence is to process the part of the formula in parenthesis first. This means that the formula 5 * (4 + 3) will produce the same result, as the first formula. This is how precedence constraints work also.

Basic Precedence Constraints

Precedence constraints are represented by the **ARROWS** (green, black and red) between the tasks and containers on the Control Flow tab. They help manage the package workflow and handle error conditions. They also determine if the next task (the one connected by the arrow) will be executed, based on the state (value) of the constraint. The values are explained below.

- ☑ The **SUCCESS** state (green arrow) means that the attached task will only be executed if the preceding task completed successfully.
- ☑ The **COMPLETION** state (black arrow) means that the attached task can be executed, as long as the preceding task has run. It does not matter if the preceding task succeeded or failed.
- ☑ The **FAILURE** state (red arrow) means that the attached task will only be executed if the preceding task failed.

Constraint values determine how or if the current tasks proceeds. This is based on the previous task that it is linked to. Constraints default to "success".

In Figure 3-7, this means that the items in the Foreach Loop Container will not execute until the Connect to AW database task successfully completes, because the arrow is green.

When the need arises that the Control Flow will need several sets of tasks, or tasks that need to be repeated, they are often placed in a container. Doing this is not a requirement.

Figure 3-7 Items with a constraint

Figure 3-8 shows a control flow and shortcut menu. The flow is explained below.

The **PREPARATION SQL TASK** will run regardless of whether the Drop table task completes successfully or if it fails.

If the **DROP TABLE TASK** completes successfully, the Success Get Data task will run.

If the **DROP TABLE TASK** fails, the Script Task will run.

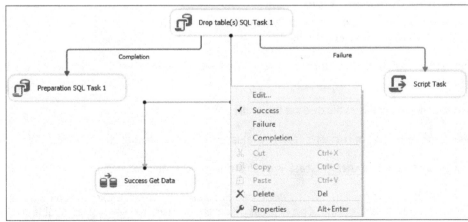

Figure 3-8 Control flow

You can change the workflow (the precedence constraint) between tasks by double-clicking on the arrow to open the editor or by right-clicking on the arrow between the tasks, to display the shortcut menu shown in the figure. The **EDIT OPTION** opens the Precedence Constraint Editor, shown below in Figure 3-9.

Advanced Precedence Constraints

As you saw, the basic constraints provide a lot of functionality in terms of workflow control. There are two types of advanced precedence constraint options, as explained below.

① Using a logical **AND** or logical **OR** evaluation, as shown at the bottom of Figure 3-9. These logical options are used when a task has multiple constraints. This option allows the current precedence constraint to be combined with other precedence constraints. Logical options are used when the workflow needs to have two or more precedence constraints pointing to the same task. When this is the case, both conditions must evaluate to True, for the task that the other two tasks are connected to. Select the **LOGICAL AND** option when you only want the task to run if the previous tasks have completed. When this option is selected, the precedence constraint line is a solid color. Select the **LOGICAL OR** option if any of the previous tasks have completed. When this option is selected, the precedence line is dotted.

② Creating expressions (to select how the task is evaluated), by selecting one of the expression options in the **EVALUATION OPERATION** field drop-down list, shown in Figure 3-9. This will let you create **BOOLEAN EXPRESSIONS** (true/false) in addition to or instead of, the basic constraint options.

It is not a requirement for all items to have a precedence constraint. Tasks can have more than one restraint, meaning one task can be linked to two other tasks. This is what the logical options are used for, at the bottom of Figure 3-9.

The options that you change are only for the constraint line that you opened the editor from. If you wanted the tasks in the container to run, as long as the Data Flow Task has run, regardless of whether it was successful or failed, you would change the Value field to Completion.

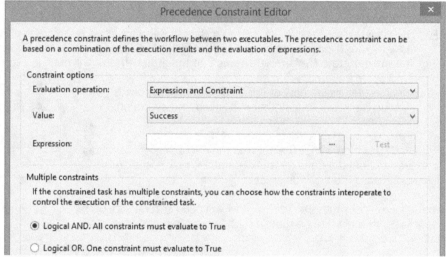

Figure 3-9 Precedence Constraint Editor

Evaluation Operation Field

As covered in the previous section, this field is used to select how the task will be evaluated. The evaluation options in the drop-own list are explained below.

CONSTRAINT does not create an expression. The task is evaluated on the success, failure or completion of the previous task.

EXPRESSION The task is evaluated on the expression.

EXPRESSION AND CONSTRAINT The task is evaluated on the constraint that is selected and the expression that is created.

EXPRESSION OR CONSTRAINT The task is evaluated on either the constraint or the expression that is created.

When one of the expression options discussed above is selected, the Expression field shown above in Figure 3-9 is used to type in the expression. The expression created is used to evaluate a variable to determine if the next task should be executed. Clicking the ellipsis button at the end of the field, opens the Expression Builder, which can also be used to create the expression.

Exercise 3.1: Create A Shared Connection To A Database

SSIS is somewhat project driven, meaning items like connections and package parts can be used by any package in the project. Many of the steps to create a package are repetitive. To help reduce the repetition, this exercise will lay the ground work for a project that will be used in the rest of this book. Learning how to create a shared connection to the AW database is also covered in this exercise.

Create A New Project

As explained in the previous chapter, data source connections can be shared by all of the packages in the same project. To do that, this part of the exercise will create a new project that will be used for the rest of the exercises in this book.

1. In the Solution Explorer, right-click on the Solution name (Solution My SSIS Solution) ⇒ Add ⇒ New Project. The Integration Services Project should be selected and the solution name that was created for this book, should be in the Location field, on the Add New Project dialog box.

2. In the Name field, type SSIS Book.

   You should have the options shown in Figure 3-10.

   This is the project folder that you will save all of the remaining exercises in, that you create in this book.

   This will make is easier months from now, if you want to look at a specific package that was created in this book. You will know where to find it.

   Click OK.

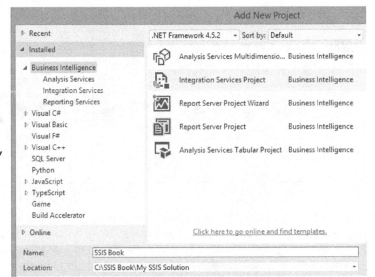

Figure 3-10 Options to create a new project

In the Solution Explorer window, you may find it helpful to close the Chapter 2 Projects folder, so that you do not accidentally use it to create any more packages in.

Create A Connection That Can Be Shared

As many of the exercises will use the Adventure Works database, as a source or destination file, creating a **SHARED CONNECTION** to it will be very helpful and save time. This connection will be available to all of the packages created in the SSIS Book project.

1. Right-click on the Connection Managers folder in the SSIS Book project ⇒ New Connection Manager.

2. Select the OLEDB connection manager option ⇒ Click Add.

3. Because a connection to the Adventure Works database was already created in this solution, you should see the connection on the Configure OLE DB Connection Manager dialog box. You can use it here ⇒ Click OK. In this exercise, this is the same as selecting the **CONVERT TO PROJECT CONNECTION** option on the Connect Managers tab.

Notice on the Connection Managers tab that the connection is referenced as a project connection, as shown earlier in Figure 3-5.

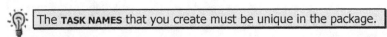
The **TASK NAMES** that you create must be unique in the package.

Data Flow Task

The Data Flow Task is an executable task, just like the Execute SQL Task. It moves data from the data source to a destination. By "move", I mean the task makes a copy of the data to place in another file. This task does not actually delete data in the data source. This task is probably the most important task because the data source and destination are defined in this task. The Data Flow Task requires using the Data Flow tab to create a connection to a data source. In addition to mapping input and output columns, this has it's own transformation components that are used to manipulate the data that comes from the source, before being sent to the destination. These transformation components are on the Data Flow tab. Hence, the similarity in the task and tab names. <smile> The Data Flow Task is different from the other tasks, because it has its own tab. It is used to load and transform data. This is the only task that can use the Data Flow tab.

When other tasks on the Control Flow tab are added to the canvas and you right-click on it and select Edit, the Task Editor opens. When you right-click on the Data Flow Task, the Data Flow tab is enabled and displayed. The majority of the options shown in the toolbox on the Data Flow tab are the transformation components.

More than one Data Flow Task can be added to the Control Flow tab. Each Data Flow Task that is added, has its own Data Flow tab, as shown in the drop-down list in Figure 3-11. In addition to selecting the Data Flow Task from the drop-down list, on the Data Flow tab, you can double-click on the Data Flow Task on the Control Flow tab, to open the corresponding Data Flow tab.

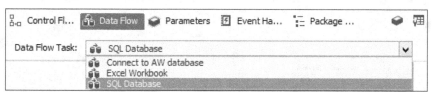

Figure 3-11 Data Flow tab with multiple Data Flow Tasks on the Control Flow tab

The Data Flow Task has the following functionality:

- ☑ It can handle large amounts of data.
- ☑ As you learned in Chapter 2, Exercise 2.2, the source and destination file types do not have to be the same.
- ☑ The same data can be saved to more than one location (destination) on the same Data Flow Task.
- ☑ It can be used to move data from one database to another database.
- ☑ Data flows that do not have any transformations (meaning that the data flow only has a source task and a destination task), will copy the data from one location to another location, without changing the data.

 The **DATA FLOW TASK** is what links or binds the control flow and data flow together. Packages can be created only using tasks on the Control Flow tab.

 Exercise Tips
The following tips should help make completing the exercises in this book easier.

① When I reference the Toolbox, I am referring to the SSIS Toolbox, shown in Chapter 2 Figure 2-20.

② It is probably best to use the **SAVE ALL BUTTON**, opposed to the Save button, to ensure that the project and all of the changes made to all of the packages that are open, are saved. The **SAVE BUTTON** only saves changes to the package that is displayed (has focus) on the canvas.

③ When instructed to "Rename a new package file" or "Add a package file", right-click on the SSIS Packages folder ⇒ **NEW SSIS PACKAGE**. This creates a new, empty package.

④ When instructed to rename the package, right-click on the file and select Rename.

⑤ When instructed to rename a task, click on the words on the task and type in the new name or right-click on the task and select Rename.

⑥ You should run Visual Studio/SSIS in Administrator mode. [See Chapter 1, Create Shortcut Icons For The Software]

⑦ When instructed to add a task (from the SSIS toolbox), drag or double-click on it (in the toolbox) to add it to the canvas.

⑧ When a task is first added to the control flow, it will display an X in a red circle. This symbol indicates that the task needs to be configured or that something is missing. Ignore the symbol until you have selected all of the options that you need for the task and have linked it to another task.

⑨ In SSIS, a source task has the same functionality as **IMPORTING DATA**. A destination task has the same functionality as **EXPORTING DATA**.

Exercise 3.2: Connect To A CSV File

1. Rename a new package file to `E3.2 CSV data connection`.

2. Add the Data Flow Task ⇒ Rename it to `Connect to CSV file`.

3. On the Data Flow tab, add the **FLAT FILE SOURCE** task ⇒ Rename the connection to `Connect to ssis_products csv`.

4. On the Flat File Source Editor, click the New button.

5. On the Flat File Connection Manager Editor, in the Connection manager name field, type `Connect to csv file`.

6. Click the Browse button ⇒ Select the ssis_products.csv file.

   You may have to change the File type drop-down list to csv files or All files, to see the file ⇒ Click Open.

   You should have the options shown in Figure 3-12.

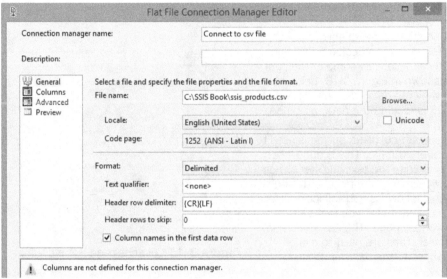

Figure 3-12 CSV connection options (general page)

The **TEXT QUALIFIER** option is used to specify that you want string data to be enclosed in quotes or enclosed with another qualifier. **<NONE>** is the default value for this option. Using this option is helpful. For example, when the file is delimited by commas (meaning that at the end of the data in each field, a comma is added), and some (or all) text fields also have a comma in the data that you do not want to separate by. Setting a text qualifier will ignore commas in the text data.

For example, if one column contains the city and state, with a comma between them and this option was used, quotes would be placed at the beginning and end of the column. This would keep the comma between the city and state from being used as a delimiter. Keep in mind that the options selected here can be changed on a per field basis, on the Advanced page.

The **HEADER ROWS TO SKIP** option is used when the source has empty rows or rows that you do not want to use, that are at the top of the data source. This happens more with data in an Excel spreadsheet or with a text file. If you are not sure if the source has either of these potential problems, look on the Preview page on this dialog box to see the first few rows of data.

 Changes made on a connection editor are processed when the data is imported into the package. It is a good idea to take a good look at all of the options on the editor. Doing so will save you time. If you plan to save the connection as a **PACKAGE PART**, you will not have to make the same changes in every package that needs to use the same data source.

 At the bottom of the dialog box, you will see warning messages, from time to time. I tend to ignore them until I have finished selecting all of the options for the connection. The reason is because most of the time, the warning messages will go away, once you have selected the options that are needed. Having said that, the next tip box discusses a message that you cannot ignore.

Enabling The OK Button On The Editor
As you can see, at the bottom of the Flat File Connection Manager Editor, shown above in Figure 3-12, is a warning that says that the columns have not been defined. This warning message is displayed for a flat file source connection. I could not find a way to make this go away, or enable the OK button, without displaying one the other pages on the dialog box. When you see this warning, you can click on any of the other pages, to enable the OK button if you do not need to make any changes. If you need to change column information, display the Columns page. It is, what it is, I guess. <smile>

Columns Page

1. Display the **COLUMNS** page.

The **COLUMN DELIMITER** option is used to select the character that signifies or marks the end of data in a column.

In addition to being able to select different row and column delimiters, you can also view some of the data, as shown in Figure 3-13. Being able to view the data, lets you know that SSIS is reading the data, as expected.

The **RESET COLUMNS** button is used to re-query the file. This is done when you change the text qualifier or header row delimiter options. Use this button with caution, as you will loose all of the changes that you make on the Advanced page. The Advanced and Preview tabs are used to make changes to the data as needed.

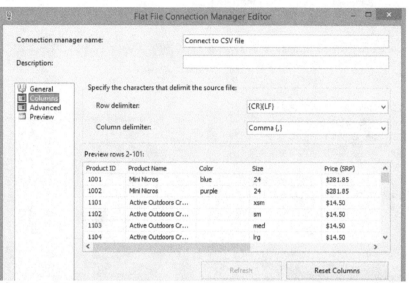

Figure 3-13 Columns page (for a csv file)

Advanced Page

The options shown in Figure 3-14 are used to configure the fields. This is probably the most important page on the Connection Manager because these properties are sent to the next task or component in the data flow. That is why it is important to get the data type correct.

By default, the data type is set to string, for all fields in text files. Being able to select the correct data type here means that you do not have to convert it in the package, by adding a transformation task to the package.

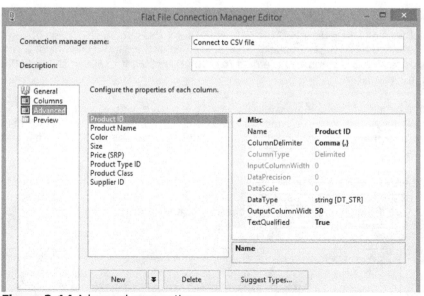

Figure 3-14 Advanced page options

While the exercises in this book do not change the data type of most columns, on your own, you should view and change the data types, especially for data that will be written to an SQL database. Doing this will keep the destination table as small as possible in terms of the space that it takes up and your data will have a data type that SQL Server databases support. It is also more efficient to make changes to the data while it is being loaded into memory and definitely before it is written to the destination file.

If you need to set the same setting for two or more columns, you can select the columns by holding down the Shift or Ctrl key and selecting the columns.

Making column or data type changes after the package is run means that the connection manager needs to be refreshed. Refreshing the data, updates the metadata throughout the data flow. Some of the properties and options on the Advanced page shown above in Figure 3-14, are explained below.

The **NAME** property is used to rename the field.

As needed, the value in the **OUTPUT COLUMN WIDTH** property may need to be made longer, so that the data is not truncated.

The **TEXT QUALIFIED** property is used to select whether string data is surrounded by text qualifier characters like quotes. True means that text data in the flat file is qualified. False means that text data in the flat file is not qualified.

The **NEW BUTTON** is used to create a new column, using the options shown in Figure 3-15.

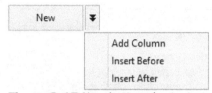

Select **ADD COLUMN** to add a column to the end of the table.
INSERT BEFORE adds a column before the column that is currently selected.
INSERT AFTER adds a column after the column that is currently selected.

Figure 3-15 New button shortcut menu

The **SUGGEST TYPES BUTTON** opens the dialog box shown in Figure 3-16. The options are used to suggest and change the data type and field length for the fields that will be imported. This is helpful if you are not sure what data type to select. If you use this option, it is a good idea to check the results on the Advanced page.

Data Type For Zip Codes
Whether you use the Suggest Types button or not, if the table has a zip code field, check the data type. It should be set to **STRING [DT_STR]**. This is to accommodate zip codes in the north east part of the country that start with a zero. Additionally, change the **OUTPUT COLUMN WIDTH** property to 5, if the zip codes do not have the plus 4. If the zip code has the plus 4, change this option to 10. Also change the **TEXT QUALIFIED** property to False.

If a field (including fields with numeric data) will not be used in a calculation, it is probably okay not to change the data type, as long as the field that it will be mapped to, will accept the data with a string data type.

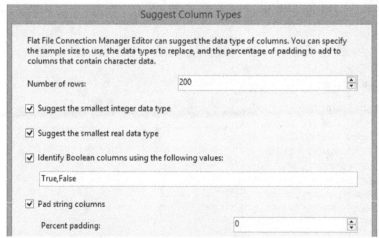

Figure 3-16 Suggest Column Types dialog box

Change Some Field Properties

In this part of the exercise, you will change a few properties.

1. On the Advanced page, select the Product ID field ⇒ Change the Name property to `Product Nbr`.

2. Select the Price (SRP) field ⇒
Open the Data Type drop-down list and select
CURRENCY [DT_CY] ⇒
Change the Text Qualified property to False,
as shown in Figure 3-17.

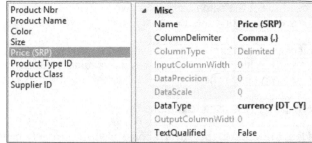

Figure 3-17 Price (SRP) field property changes

 Changing The Data Type Of A Date Field
When changing the Data Type property to **DATE [DT_DATE]**, or to any date data type for that matter, change the Text Qualified property to False.

Preview Page

The options shown in Figure 3-18 are used to preview the data after you have made changes to it, on the other pages on the dialog box.

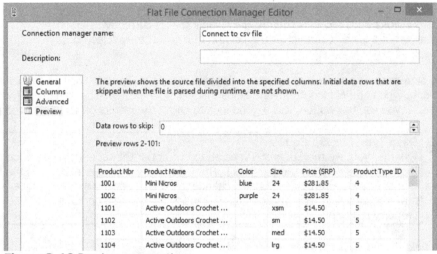

Figure 3-18 Preview page options

1. Click OK. Notice that the OK button is now enabled on the editor.

Flat File Source Editor

If you know or think that the data has null values or fields with no data (also known as a **ZERO LENGTH STRING**), you may want to check the **RETAIN NULL VALUES** option, shown in Figure 3-19.

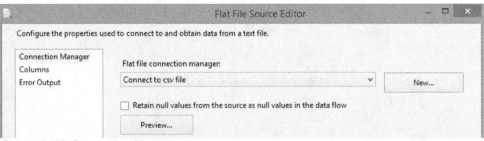

Figure 3-19 Connection Manager page

Columns Page

The options shown in Figure 3-20 are used to confirm the fields that will be imported.

If there is a field that you do not want to import, clear the check mark for the field. This is the same as deleting a field on the Advanced page, shown earlier in Figure 3-14.

Neither option deletes the field from the actual source file. The options prevent the field from coming into the SSIS package.

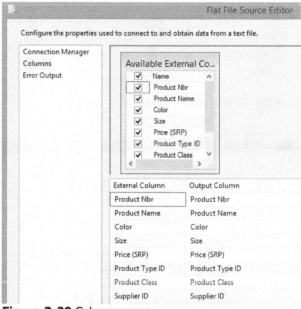

Figure 3-20 Columns page

Error Output Page

The options shown in Figure 3-21 are used to select error handling options.

The default options shown, will cause the source import connection to fail it any of the fields have data that would be truncated or have another error.

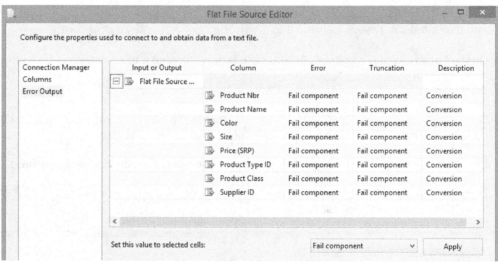

Figure 3-21 Error Output options

The other options that can be applied are in the drop-down list in the Error and Truncation columns and in the drop-down list at the bottom of the figure. This page is covered in more detail in Chapter 4.

1. Click OK. You should see the connection for the csv file at the bottom of the workspace. At this point, you would use other tasks on the toolbox to complete the package.

Multi Flat File Connection

The previous exercise showed you how to create a connection to one flat file. If you have the need to process more than one flat file in a data flow, you can use the **MULTI FLAT FILE** connection manager type on the Add SSIS Connection Manager dialog box. [See Figure 3-4] This connection can be used to copy or move several files. The metadata for all of the files must match.

The dialog box shown in Figure 3-22 is used to select the files that you want to use.

It looks like the Flat File connection manager.

The difference is that you type all of the files on the File names field. The files must be separated by a | (vertical bar).

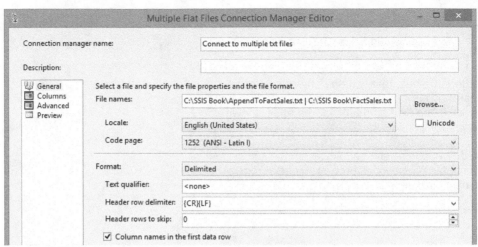

Figure 3-22 Multiple Flat Files Connection Manager Editor

In the data flow, this connection manager combines/merges the records from all of the files listed, into a single file. This is different from using a Foreach Loop Container, because the process (on the Data Flow tab) only happens once.

Exercise 3.3: Connect To An Access Database

In this exercise, you will create a package that will use the Data Flow Task to connect to an Access database.

1. Rename a new package file to E3.3 MS Access data connection.

2. Add the Data Flow Task ⇒ Rename it to Connect to Access database.

3. On the Data Flow tab, add the OLE DB Source task ⇒ Rename it to Connect to Access importdb.

4. On the editor, click the New button ⇒ Click the New button again.

5. Open the Provider drop-down list and select **MICROSOFT JET 4.0 OLD DB PROVIDER** ⇒ Click OK. If you do not have this option, see Chapter 1, Importing Excel Data Into A SQL Server Database.

6. Click the Browse button ⇒ Navigate to your folder and select the importdb.mdb database.

7. Delete Admin from the User name field. You should have the options shown in Figure 3-23 ⇒ Click OK.

   You should see the connection to the database, as shown in Figure 3-24 ⇒ Click OK.

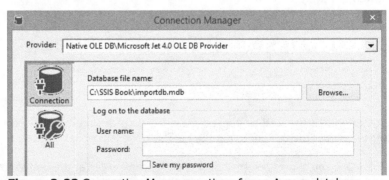

Figure 3-23 Connection Manager options for an Access database

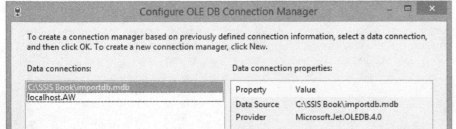

Figure 3-24 Configure OLE DB Connection Manager options for an Access database

8. Open the Name of the table or the view drop-down list and select the Customer table, as shown in Figure 3-25.

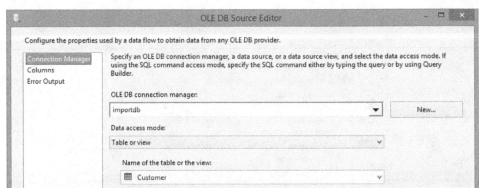

Figure 3-25 Table in Access database selected

9. On the Columns page, clear the check mark for the Customer Credit ID field, as illustrated in Figure 3-26 ⇒ Click OK.

The options on the Error Output page are the same as the ones shown earlier in Figure 3-21.

At this point, you would add data cleansing or transformation tasks to the Data Flow tab, as needed, and then load the data to the destination file.

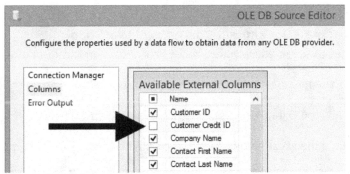

Figure 3-26 Columns page options

Connecting To Spreadsheets Created In Excel 2007 Or Later
If you have trouble connecting to the Excel workbook in the next exercise, hopefully this tip will resolve the issue. There are two options that you can check, as explained below.

① If you cannot connect to a spreadsheet that was created in Excel 2007 or later, make sure that you select the correct version on the Excel Connection Manager, shown later in Figure 3-29. The default Excel driver is 32-bit only and packages have to run in 32-bit mode, when using an Excel connection. You will get the following error message if you do not have the correct driver installed: The 'Microsoft.ACE.OLEDB.12.0' provider is not registered on the local machine. You can check, by following steps 1 and 2 below, then add the OLE DB Source task to the workspace and open the editor ⇒ Click the New button twice ⇒ On the Connection Manager dialog box, open the provider drop-down list ⇒ If you see one of the Access Database OLE DB providers illustrated in Figure 3-27, select a higher version of Excel, on the dialog box shown later in Figure 3-29.
② If the version of Windows that is installed on your computer is 64-bit, the projects properties have to be set to 32-bit, because of the same Excel driver issue discussed above in the first option. To check the properties of the project, follow the steps below.
1. In the Solution Explorer, right-click on the SSIS Book folder ⇒ Properties.
2. Configuration Properties ⇒ Debugging ⇒ Change the **RUN 64 BIT RUN TIME** property to False, as illustrated in Figure 3-28 ⇒ Click Apply ⇒ Click OK.

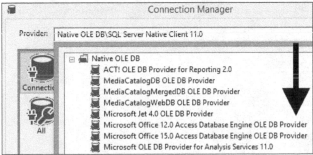

Figure 3-27 Access OLE DB providers illustrated

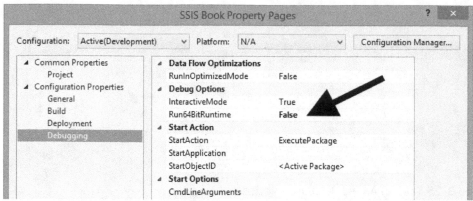

Figure 3-28 Property Pages dialog box

Exercise 3.4: Connect To An Excel Workbook

In this exercise, you will learn how to connect to an Excel workbook and get data from one sheet, in the workbook.

1. Rename a new package to `E3.4 Excel data connection`.

2. Add the Data Flow Task ⇒ Rename it to `Connect to Excel`.

3. Add the **EXCEL SOURCE** task to the Data Flow tab ⇒ Rename the task to `Connect to ssis_data`.

 Excel Connections
For Excel connections, I do not use the extension as part of the name, because the Excel logo is on the button. Doing this is optional. I just try to make it as easy as possible to be able to know what each task is doing.

4. On the editor, click the New button ⇒ On the Excel Connection Manager, click the Browse button ⇒ Navigate to your folder and select the ssis_data.xlsx file. You should have the options shown in Figure 3-29 ⇒ Click OK.

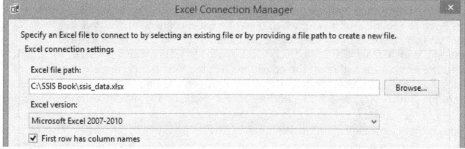

Figure 3-29 Excel Connection Manager options

5. Open the Excel sheet drop-down list and select the Orders$ file.

   You should have the options shown in Figure 3-30 ⇒ Click OK.

   Like the previous exercises, more tasks would be added to this package.

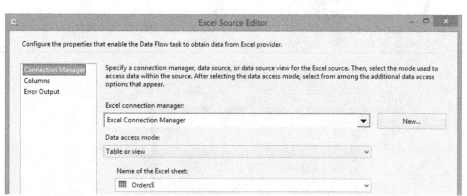

Figure 3-30 Excel Source Editor options

6. On the Connect Managers tab, rename the Excel connection to `Excel ssis_data` ⇒ Right-click on the connection manager option ⇒ Convert to Project Connection.

When using the Excel connection manager to import data, you may discover that some data is replaced by NULLS. I have seen this happen when numeric and text data is in the same column. If the column will not be used in an expression, setting the data type to string should resolve the conflict.

Multiple File Connection

Earlier in this chapter, you learned about connecting to multiple flat files at one time. The same concept is available for connecting to multiple files or folders, by selecting the **MULTI FILE** connection manager on the Add SSIS Connection Manager dialog box. [See Figure 3-4]

The dialog box shown in Figure 3-31 is used to select the existing files or folders that you want to connect to.

Also notice that new files and folders can be created and connected to.

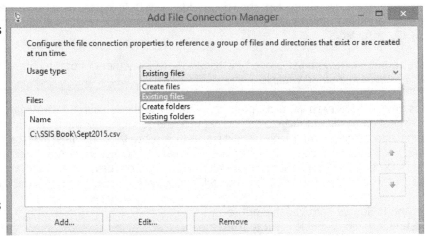

Figure 3-31 Add File Connection Manager

Data Preparation

There will be times when you need to verify or validate the data before it is written to a destination file. The following tasks on the Control Flow tab provide this functionality.

- ☑ Execute SQL Task (1)
- ☑ Bulk Insert Task (1)
- ☑ Data Profiling Task
- ☑ File System Task
- ☑ FTP Task
- ☑ Web Service Task
- ☑ XML Task

(1)   This task is known for using data in a relational database management system (RDBMS).

File System Task

This task is used to handle directory and file operations. This includes creating file or folder (which SSIS calls a directory) tasks, like copy, delete and rename. This task is helpful if you need to have files in a specific location to create the package. For example, there are data source files in three folders, but you need all of them in the same folder. The File System Task only performs the action once. If you need to repeat the task to copy several files in the same folder, place this task in a **FOREACH LOOP CONTAINER**.

What I like about this task is that it does not require creating a custom script. The actions that this task can perform are in the **OPERATION** drop-down list, shown later in Figure 3-32. The options are explained in Table 3-1. Most of the operations require you to select the source and destination folders.

Operation	Description
Copy directory	Copes all of the files in one folder to another folder.
Copy file	Copies one file from one folder to another folder.
Create directory	Creates a folder. (2)
Delete directory	Deletes the folder that you select.
Delete directory content	Deletes all of the files in the folder that you select.
Delete file	Deletes the file that you select.
Move directory	Moves the folder that you select to another location. (2)
Move file	Moves the file to another folder. (2)
Rename file	Renames the file to the new name that you enter.
Set Attributes	Is used to set the following attributes for the selected file: Hidden, read-only, archive and system.

Table 3-1 Operation options explained

(2)   You have to indicate what should happen if the file or folder already exists in the new location.

Destination And Source Connection Sections

The properties in these sections on the File System Task Editor are ones that you will use for operations. They are shown later in Figure 3-35. The options are explained below.

The **SOURCE CONNECTION** and **DESTINATION CONNECTION** properties are used to select an existing connection or create a new connection. The dialog box shown later in Figure 3-34 is used to set up a new connection. When these properties are used with the Copy file operation, a connection refers to selecting an existing file or folder or creating a new file or folder.

The **IS SOURCE PATH VARIABLE** property is used to select whether or not the path/location of the data source file or folder is stored in a string variable.

The **IS DESTINATION PATH VARIABLE** property is similar to the Is Source Path Variable property. The difference is that the destination would not include the file name in the variable, just the folder location. This property is used to select a connection manager or variable. If this property is set to false, the **DESTINATION CONNECTION** property is displayed. This lets you select the connection manager or create a connection for the file or folder (the path) that you need. If the Is Destination Path Variable property is set to true, the **DESTINATION VARIABLE** property is displayed instead of the Destination Variable and is used to select or create a variable that has the file or folder that you need.

When the Is Source Path Variable or the Is Destination Path Variable is set to true, the source connection and destination connection options, shown later in Figure 3-35, are replaced with the Source Variable and Destination Variable properties.

To create the variable, open the Source Variable property drop-down list, shown in Figure 3-32, (or the Destination Variable drop-down list) and select **<NEW VARIABLE>**, to display the Add Variable dialog box. [See Chapter 8 Figure 8-41] This dialog box is used to create a variable that the source or destination path will be stored in.

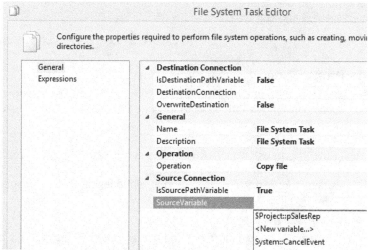

Figure 3-32 Source Variable property

Exercise 3.5: Create A Folder And Copy A File

In this exercise you will use the File System Task to create a new folder, then copy an existing file to the new folder.

1. Rename a new package to `E3.5 Create folder-copy file`.

2. Add the File System Task ⇒ Open the Task Editor.

   Figure 3-33 shows the types of operations that the File System Task can perform.

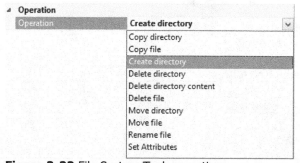

Figure 3-33 File System Task operations

 The option selected in the **OPERATION** field, shown above in Figure 3-33, changes the other options on the dialog box. It is a good idea to select this option first, then select the options for the other fields, on the editor.

3. Open the Operation drop-down list ⇒ Copy file.

4. In the Name field, type `Create folder and copy file`.

The **DESTINATION CONNECTION** property is used to select the folder that you want to copy the file to or to create a new folder.

The **OVERWRITE DESTINATION** property is used to select whether or not the file or folder on the Destination Connection property can be overwritten. If this option is set to False, the task will fail the second time that the package is run because the folder will already exist.

5. Open the Destination Connection drop-down list and select <New connection>.

6. Open the **USAGE TYPE** drop-down list ⇒ Create folder.

7. In the Folder field, type `C:\SSIS Book\Ch3 Exercise3-5`, as shown in Figure 3-34. This will be the name of the folder that will be created when this task is executed ⇒ Click OK.

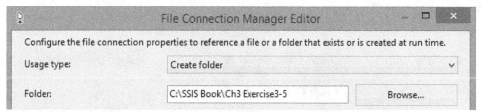

Figure 3-34 File Connection Manage Editor options to create the folder

8. Change the Overwrite Destination property to True.

9. Open the Source Connection drop-down list ⇒ <New connection>.

10. Click the Browse button ⇒ Navigate to your folder and select the Ch2 Customer data.txt file ⇒ Click Open. This is the file that will be copied to the folder that you created earlier in this exercise ⇒ Click OK. You should have the task editor options shown in Figure 3-35.

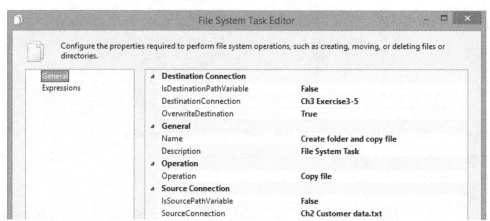

Figure 3-35 File System Task Editor options to copy a file

Run The Package And View The Results

1. Click the Start button on the toolbar. This is another way to run/execute the package. When you see a green check mark next to each task, it means that the package ran without a problem.

2. In Windows Explorer, in the folder for this book, you should see a folder named Ch3 Exercise 3-5. In this folder, you should see a copy of the Ch2 Customer data file.

SSIS Import And Export Wizard

The SSIS wizard is very similar to the SQL Server Import and Export Wizard that you used in Chapter 1. While the names of the wizards are similar, the biggest difference is where they are located. The other difference is that in the SSMS version, you have to select whether or not to save the options selected on the wizard as a package. Other then these differences, they have the same functionality.

Hopefully, by the time that you complete the wizard exercises in this chapter, you will see how easy the wizard is to use and how helpful it is for importing and exporting data. While there will always be people that prefer to write code manually for everything, I am more than happy to use a wizard to do some of the coding for me. <smile>

Exercise 3.6: Use The SSIS Import And Export Wizard

While the **BULK INSERT TASK** is known for being able to load very large data sets, it dawned on me to try the Import and Export wizard, to see if it could load a .txt file that had 2 plus million rows of data.

In this exercise, you will use the wizard to create a package that will load data in a text file to a SQL Server database. The SSIS version of the Import and Export wizard automatically creates a package that will load the data to the SQL Server database that you select.

1. Right-click on the SSIS Packages folder ⇒ SSIS Import and Export Wizard ⇒ Click Next on the Welcome page.

2. Open the Data Source drop-down list and select **FLAT FILE SOURCE**.

3. Click the Browse button ⇒ Select the FactSales.txt file in your folder. This file has over 2 million rows of data.

    You should have the options shown in Figure 3-36 ⇒ Click Next.

    The Columns page shown in Figure 3-37 is used to view all of the fields in the data source.

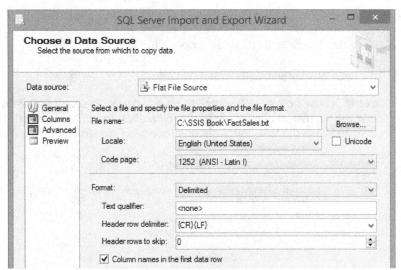

Figure 3-36 General page options on the wizard

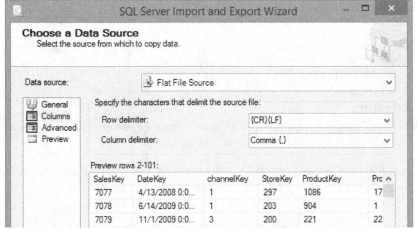

Figure 3-37 Columns page options

4. Click Next ⇒ Open the Destination field drop-down list and select the **SQL SERVER NATIVE CLIENT 11.0** option.

5. In the Server name field, type `localhost`.

6. Open the Database field drop-down list and select the AW database.

    The options shown in Figure 3-38 select the database that the data in the text file will be written to ⇒ Click Next.

    The **NEW BUTTON** displays the dialog box shown in Figure 3-39. The options are used to create a new SQL Server database.

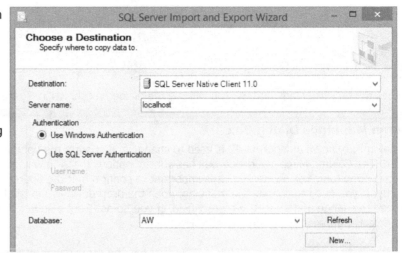

Figure 3-38 Destination options

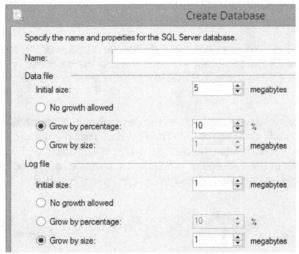

Figure 3-39 Create Database dialog box

The screen shown in Figure 3-40 displays the table that will be copied to the database.

If you needed to rename the destination table, you would change it on this screen.

If the data source had more tables, they would be displayed here and you could clear the check mark for the tables that you did not want to copy to the database.

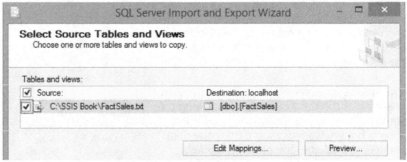

Figure 3-40 Source tables that will be copied

The **EDIT MAPPINGS BUTTON** opens the dialog box, shown later in Figure 3-42.

The **PREVIEW BUTTON** displays data in the selected table (on the Select Source Tables and Views screen), as shown in Figure 3-41.

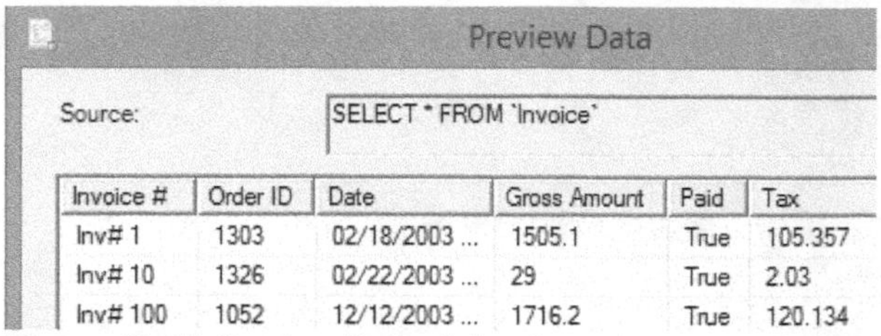

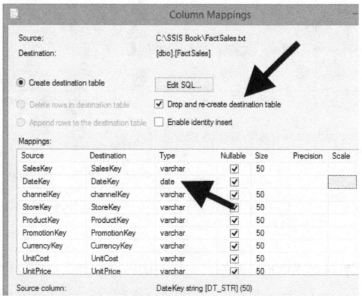

Figure 3-41 Preview Data dialog box

7. Click the Edit Mappings button. You will see the dialog box shown in Figure 3-42.

Column Mappings Dialog Box

The dialog box shown in Figure 3-42 is used to change and confirm the options for the destination table that will be created. The Column Mappings dialog box has a lot of options that you will probably use. As you can see, by default, the destination table will be created. It is important to confirm that the Source and Destination columns are mapped correctly. If you need to change the mapping, open the drop-down list, in the Destination column, for the field that you need to change and select the correct field. If you do not want a source field to be created in the destination table, select <ignore> in the drop-down list.

If the destination database already has a table that has the same name as the data source table, which in this exercise is the Fact Sales, the **CREATE DESTINATION TABLE** option would not be enabled. Instead, the options below it would be enabled. When this option is not enabled, a table with the same name already exists and the data will be appended to the existing table.

The **EDIT SQL BUTTON** displays the dialog box shown in Figure 3-43. You can edit the code for the creation of the table, if needed. For example, if you wanted to use a different name for the table that will be created in the database, you would replace "Fact Sales" on the first line of the code, with the table name that you want. You can also change the field name, data type or field length.

If checked, the **DROP AND RE-CREATE DESTINATION TABLE** option will delete the table in the destination SQL database and recreate it, each time that the package (that you are currently creating) is run. The first time that the package is run and the table name does not exist, you will not have a problem. After the destination table is created and you change the structure (for example, add or delete fields), either in the package or in SSMS, the package may need to be run again. If so, and this option is not checked, the package will fail. As it does not hurt to have the option checked, most of the time I check the option.

If I need to add or delete rows of data, I create another package using this wizard (save it as a package part), then add the package part to the original package.

As you will see, selecting the Drop and recreate option will create an **EXECUTE SQL TASK** in the package. This task is covered in more detail, later in this chapter.

If the **ENABLE IDENTITY INSERT** option is enabled, it means that the table that you are copying the data to already has an identity column. If this option is not enabled and you try to copy data to an identity column, the package will fail. [See Options Page, later in this chapter for more information]

Figure 3-42 Column Mappings dialog box

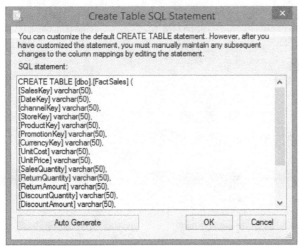

Figure 3-43 Create Table SQL Statement dialog box

 Changes made on the Column Mappings dialog box, are also automatically changed on the Create Table SQL Statement dialog box. This includes changing the Destination column names. If you need to map the destination column to a different column in the source, open the drop-down list, as shown later at the bottom of Figure 3-50. The one thing that cannot be changed on this dialog box is the destination table name. Click the **EDIT SQL BUTTON** (on the Column Mappings dialog box) to change the destination table name, or change it on the screen shown later in Figure 3-49.

8. Check the Drop and re-create destination table option.

While not obvious, the columns in the **MAPPINGS SECTION** (on the Column Mappings dialog box) can be changed. More than likely, you would not change the field names in the Source column. Changing the field names in the Destination column is a good idea, if the name would be confusing to the end user. For example, Store Key may not make sense to the person using the data, so changing it to Store Number, would be better.

Like the Flat File Connection Manager Editor that you used earlier in Exercise 3.2, the data type defaults to String for all of the fields. For example, the Date Key field is a date. The more that you can correct here before the data is imported, the fewer transformations you will have to create in the package. And truth be told, it is easier to change field names and data types on the Create Table dialog box, then it is to create the same functionality using transformations.

9. Open the Type drop-down list for the Date Key field and select Date. You should have the changed options illustrated, earlier in Figure 3-42 ⇒ Click OK.

10. Click Next on the Select Source Tables screen. If you get a warning that says that the data type conversion file cannot be located, click OK. I saw this warning on one laptop, but not the other one. Getting this warning did not keep the package from being saved or run.

11. Click Next on the Convert Types Without Conversion Checking screen.

    Figure 3-44 shows how the wizard will create the package.

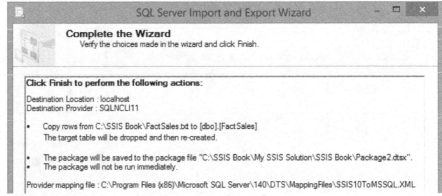

Figure 3-44 Options selected to create the package

Notice the third bullet in the figure lets you know that the package will not be run, as soon as it is created. That is a good thing because you can make changes to the package, like add transformations to the package before it is run.

12. Click Finish. The package will be created.

    You will see the dialog box shown in Figure 3-45. It lets you know that all is well. <smile>

    If there was a problem, you would see something in the Message column ⇒ Click Close.

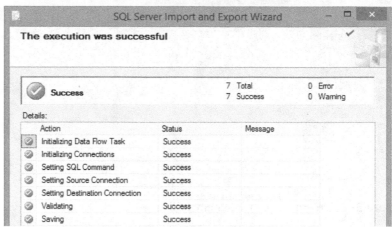

Figure 3-45 Wizard execution details

13. The package is automatically displayed on the workspace ⇒ Rename the package to `E3.6 Import a text file via the wizard`.

The left side of Figure 3-46 shows the Control Flow tab tasks that the wizard created.

The first two tasks on this tab are Execute SQL Tasks. The first task deletes the existing Fact Sales table in the AW database.

The second task uses the SQL query shown earlier in Figure 3-43, to create a new Fact Sales table in the destination database.

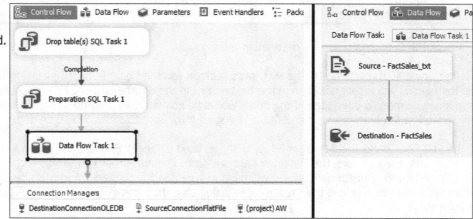

Figure 3-46 Tasks created by the wizard

The right side of Figure 3-46 shows the Data Flow tab tasks that the wizard created. They will connect to the source file and write data to the table in the destination file.

14. Right-click on the E3.6 package file ⇒ Execute Package.

    When finished, you should see the window shown in Figure 3-47.

    It shows that 2.2 million rows of data were added to the destination table (in this exercise, that is a table in the AW database).

    Do you think that this wizard will handle the large .txt and .csv files that you may need to work with?

Figure 3-47 Result of package created by the wizard

Exercise 3.7: Create A Query In The SSIS Wizard To Select Data

In the previous exercise, you learned how to use the SSIS Import and Export Wizard to load data into a SQL Server database. In this exercise, you will take those skills a step further by learning how to create a query to select the rows that will be added to a new table in a SQL Server database. The package that will be created in this exercise is based on the premise that it will be run on a regular basis, because the data source (a sheet in an Excel workbook) will be updated daily. The table that will be created in this exercise, will be used later in this book.

1. Open the SSIS Import and Export Wizard ⇒ Select Microsoft Excel, as the data source.

2. Select the ssis_data.xlsx workbook. The **FIRST ROW HAS COLUMN NAMES** option should be selected ⇒ Click Next.

3. Select the SQL Server Native Client 11.0 destination ⇒ In the Server name field, type `localhost` ⇒ Select the AW database ⇒ Click Next.

4. Select the **WRITE A QUERY OPTION** ⇒ Click Next.

5. In the SQL statement box, type the query below, as shown in Figure 3-48.
```
SELECT *
FROM [MissingData$]
WHERE YEAR(ShippedDate) = 2016
```

The **PARSE BUTTON** is used to stop checking the syntax (after you click Next), when the time exceeds 30 seconds and times out.

The **BROWSE BUTTON** is used to select a **.SQL FILE** that has the code to select the table, columns and rows.

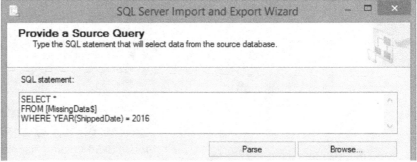

Figure 3-48 Query to select the data to import

What The Code In The Query Means

This query will select the rows in the Missing Data table, if the year in the shipped date field is 2016.

SELECT * selects all of the fields in the table (in this case a sheet in the workbook). If you only wanted to import some of the fields, you would type in the field names that you want to import, instead of the *.

The $ after the table name, on the FROM clause, indicates that it is a table, opposed to a named range, which does not use the $, as part of the name.

The WHERE clause contains the filter criteria that each row must meet, in order to be imported. It is not a requirement to have filter criteria. YEAR is a function that extracts the year from a date field.

It is not a requirement to type each clause (SELECT, FROM and WHERE) on separate lines. Doing so, just makes the code easier to read. You can type the code on one line, if you like.

6. Click Next ⇒ Change the Destination table name to `MissingData`, as shown in Figure 3-49.

The reason that the Source table name is Query, instead of a table name, like it was in the previous exercise, is because a query is being used to select the rows, instead of a table.

Figure 3-49 Destination table name changed

Configure The New Table

In this part of the exercise, you will change the data type of some fields, change the length of some fields and select to have the table re-created each time the package is run.

1. Click the **EDIT MAPPINGS** button.

2. Check the Drop and re-create destination table option.

3. Change the data type for the Order Date and Shipped Date columns to Date.

4. Change the size of each column that has 255 as the size, to 50, except for the State field ⇒
Change the State field to size 2, as shown in Figure 3-50.

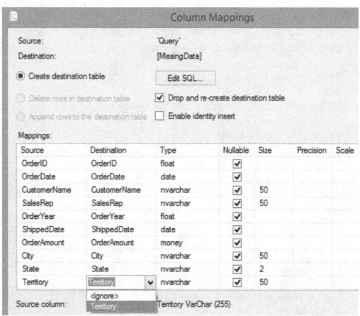

Figure 3-50 Column Mappings changes

 How To Set A Column To Not Be Imported
As shown at the bottom of Figure 3-50, select the **<IGNORE>** option for a column that you do not want to import.

5. Click OK, when you have made the changes ⇒ Click Next ⇒ Click OK, if you get the warning.

6. Click Next on the Conversion Checking screen ⇒ Click Finish.

7. You should see the success screen. It lets you know that the package was successfully created. Whether or not it will run, is a different story. <smile> ⇒ Click Close.

Finish The Package

On the Control Flow tab, you should see the tasks on the left side of Figure 3-51.

You should see the tasks on the right side of the figure on the Data Flow tab.

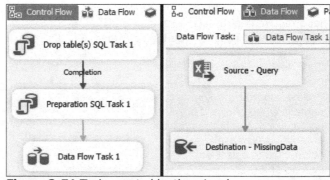

Figure 3-51 Tasks created by the wizard

1. Rename the package to E3.7 Create Missing Data table.

. . . .

2. Run the package. Over 9,000 rows will be written to the Missing Data table, in the AW database.

Changing The Wizard Options
While you cannot re-open the wizard to make changes to the options that were selected, the options can be changed on the editor for a task, just like any task that you create without using the wizard. Changes specific to the options selected on the wizard, like the data type and column length are changed on the Advanced Editor for the task. This editor is especially helpful when importing Excel data, because it is easy to incur data type errors, each time the package is run.

Bulk Insert Task

This task is used to load data from a flat file or text file directly into a table in an SQL Server database. By directly, I mean that the data cannot be transformed while it is being loaded into the database. As you will see, this task selects the source and destination connections. That is why the data can be loaded quickly.

In addition to being able to load data to a table that does not have any data, it can also be used to append data to a table in a database. This task works the same as the **BULK INSERT SQL STATEMENT** that you may have heard of or used. If you need to load a lot of data from a text or flat file and want to transform it before it is loaded to the database, use the previous two SSIS wizard exercises, as examples. Another option is to add a Data Flow task above the Bulk Insert Task that will perform the transformations that you need, then write the data to a staging file (a temporary file). When setting up the Bulk Insert Task, use the staging file instead of the original source file.

① If the table that you want to load the data into (in the Destination Connection section, shown later in Figure 3-53), does not exist in the database, you have to write a script to create it, put another task before this one that will create it, or create it manually before using this task. That is because this task selects the source and destination files.
② This task does not let you perform any data cleansing, validation or transformations during the load process.

Exercise 3.8: Use The Bulk Insert Task To Append Data

In Exercise 3.6, you learned how to use the SSIS Import and Export Wizard to import data into a new table. In that exercise, the Bulk Insert Task was discussed as being a way to append data. In this exercise you will learn how to append data using the Bulk Insert Task. Keep in mind that this task requires data being added to an existing table, to have the same format.

If you need records that cause an error to be added to a log file, use the Data Flow Task instead of the Bulk Insert Task, as the Bulk Insert Task does not have this functionality.

1. Rename a new package to `E3.8 Append using Bulk Insert`.

2. Add the Bulk Insert Task ⇒ Rename it to `Append Data`.

3. On the editors Connection page, select the following **DESTINATION CONNECTION** options.
   Connection ⇒ localhost.AW
   Destination Table ⇒ [dbo].[FactSales]

Format Options

The options in this section of the Bulk Insert Task Editor are used to specify if the format of the input data should be defined by the row and column delimiter properties, that are used in the input file (the file selected in the Source Connection section) or the ones that you select in this section.

Create A Connection To The Source File

The Source Connection is the file that has the data that will be appended to the table in the database that you selected in the previous part of this exercise. If a shared connection (a project connection) already exists for the input file that you want to use, it will be in the File field drop-down list.

1. Open the File field drop-down list ⇒ <New connection>.

2. Click the Browse button ⇒ In your folder, select the Append To Fact Sales.txt file. You should have the options shown in Figure 3-52. Figure 3-53 shows the Connection page options.

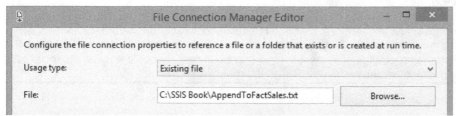

Figure 3-52 File Connection Manager Editor options

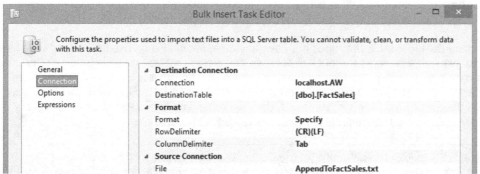

Figure 3-53 Connection page options

Options Page

Most of the time, the majority of options on this page (on the Bulk Insert Task Editor, shown later in Figure 3-55) do not have to be changed. The ones that you may want to change are explained below.

① **LAST ROW** Is used to select the last row of data in the data source file that you want to import or append. This is helpful if the source file has a lot of records and you do not need to import or append all of them. The default value is 0 (zero), which is the last row in the table.

② **FIRST ROW** Is used to select which row in the table, that the import should start on. The default value is 1, which is the first row in the table. Often, source files will have a header row. When appending data, the header row does not need to be imported because the destination table (hopefully) already has a header row or column names.

③ **OPTIONS** Figure 3-54 shows all of the options that are available. They are explained below.

    ☑ **CHECK CONSTRAINTS** Is enabled by default. It checks column and table constraints before each record is written to the destination table.

    ☑ **KEEP NULLS** Check this option to replace any fields in the source that are empty with the NULL value, when it is written to the destination table.

    ☑ **ENABLE IDENTITY INSERT** If the destination table has an identity column, check this option to avoid getting an error. An identity column is a field that has a unique value for each row in the table. You may know this as a **PRIMARY KEY** or **ID FIELD**.

    ☑ **TABLE LOCK** If checked, the destination table is locked and other people cannot use the table while the package is running. It also stops other updates and inserts from happening. This option basically gives the package exclusive rights to the table.

    ☑ **FIRE TRIGGERS** Check this option, so that the Bulk Insert Task will not ignore triggers that may be set for the table that you are adding records to.

④ **SORTED DATA** Is used to type in the name of the column that you want the data sorted on, when it is written to the destination table.

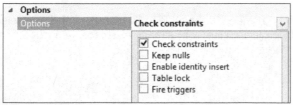

Figure 3-54 Options property values

Bulk Insert Task Code Page Property
RAW is the default option for this property, as shown below in Figure 3-55. It is also the fastest, in terms of loading the data. That is because no code page conversion is applied. The code page selected is based on the data that will be loaded to the SQL Server database.

Select The Options For The Source File

In this exercise, the table with the data that will be appended, has a header row.

1. Change the **FIRST ROW** option to 2.

2. Options drop-down list ⇒ Check the Keep Nulls option.

   You should have the options shown in Figure 3-55.

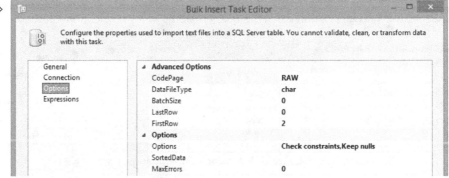

Figure 3-55 Options page options

3. Run the package. You will see the Debug mode window.

The **BULK INSERT TASK** tends to handle errors in an all or nothing way. If one row fails to be inserted, when this task is running, it is possible that the task will fail. This depends on the value that is set for the **MAXIMUM ERROR COUNT PROPERTY** on the Properties window.

Execute SQL Task

This task is one of the most used tasks. It is used to select, insert (add), update and truncate (delete) data in tables in an SQL database.

If you already know SQL, you will feel right at home using this task, because the task relies on SQL. This task requires a database connection to already be set up in the Connection Manager. Parameters, variables and stored procedures can be used with this task.

Figure 3-56 shows the General page of the Execute SQL Task Editor. The options displayed in the figure are for the Drop Table Execute SQL task that was created by the wizard used in Exercise 3.6.

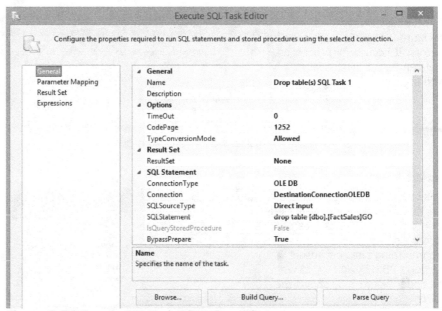

Figure 3-56 Execute SQL Task Editor General page

In addition to giving the task a descriptive name, selecting the correct option for the **CODE PAGE PROPERTY** is important. Code pages are based on the code page that is used on the SQL Server. The most used code page number used for the United States is Western European (1252) for the SQL Server. The number is the important part. The Code page property option is used with the following connection types: Excel, Flat File, OLE DB, ADO.NET and SQL Mobile.

When the **TYPE CONVERSION MODE** property is set to Allowed, this task will automatically convert data types when saving the variable. The SSIS variable data types do not exactly match the data types in SQL Server. [See Chapter 4, Table 4-1]

The **SQL SOURCE TYPE** property is used to select the source of the query. The options are explained below.

☑ Select **DIRECT INPUT** when you want to type in or paste the SQL query into the Execute SQL Task. While this option may appear to be the easiest to use, the downside is that the query cannot be modified outside of the package, making it more difficult to maintain.

☑ Select the **FILE CONNECTION** option when the query is saved in a file. This is the easiest way to maintain the query because access to the package is not needed. The query file can be modified and tested outside of SSIS.

☑ Select the **VARIABLE** option when the query is stored in a variable in the package.

The **PARAMETER MAPPING PAGE** is used to create parameters that will be passed to the SQL query. The page shown in Figure 3-57 is used to map parameters to the query.

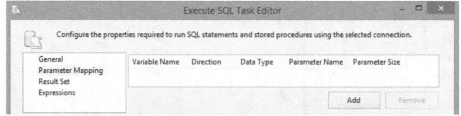

Figure 3-57 Parameter Mapping page

The **RESULT SET PAGE** shown in Figure 3-58, is used to map the result of the SQL statement to an existing or new variable.

Figure 3-58 Result Set page

The **EXPRESSIONS PAGE** shown in Figure 3-59, is in many task editors. It is used for properties that can be set dynamically with an expression, at run time.

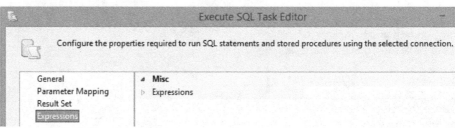

Figure 3-59 Expressions page

Script Task

This task is used when you need functionality that the built-in tasks cannot provide. This task can accomplish any .NET programming task, because it supports VB.NET and C# to write the code. Figure 3-60 shows the editor.

Clicking the **EDIT SCRIPT BUTTON** displays a workspace, based on the programming language that you select.

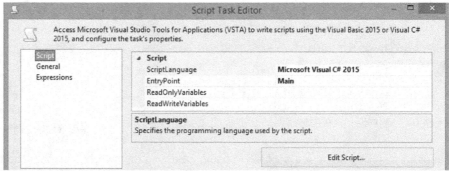

Figure 3-60 Script Task Editor

Execute Process Task

This task is designed to run an application, utility or command line program that is outside of SSIS, as part of the control flow of a package. Some of the utilities that you may want to use with this task are in the C:\Windows\System32 folder. This task is usually placed early (at or near the beginning) in the control flow sequence for the package. That is because the result that this task produces is often needed by other tasks later in the package.

A good use of this task is to extract files from a zip file, so that the data files can be loaded into a package. The Execute Process Task can automate this process for you, because SSIS does not have a task specifically for compressing or decompressing files.

Execute Process Task Editor

The General page is where you give the task a name and description.

Figure 3-61 shows the Process page. This is the page where the magic happens, as they say. <smile>

The first four properties explained below are the ones that you will probably use the most.

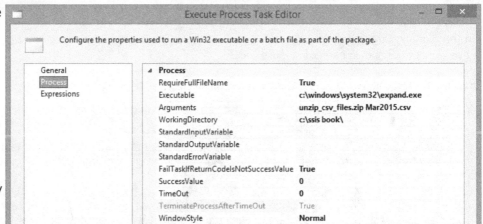

Figure 3-61 Process page properties

☑ **REQUIRE FULL FILE NAME** The default for this property is True. The option selected is used to let the task know whether or not it needs the full path to execute the command (the executable file on the Executable property). If the file is not found in the specified path, the task will fail. If the executable file is in the C:\Windows\System32 folder, using the full path is not required, because the path is known to a Windows system. For example, when you click the Start button in Windows and select Run, you can type Notepad or Regedit on the Run dialog box and the corresponding application will open, without having to type in the full path to the file.

☑ **EXECUTABLE** This property is used to type in or select the path and name of the executable file that you want this task to run. To select the executable file to run, click in the field, then click the button at the end of the field. Nothing else, like switches or parameters, should be added to this property. When needed, these items can be added to the Arguments property.

☑ **ARGUMENTS** This property is used to enter command prompts for the executable file. In Figure 3-61 above, the name of the zip file and the file in the zip file that will be extracted, are on this property. Arguments can be thought of as parameter values, because the options entered on this property are passed to or used by the executable file. Using arguments is not a requirement.

☑ **WORKING DIRECTORY** Type in or select the directory that the executable file will work in. This is the folder that the zip file on the Arguments property, is in and the folder that the file will be extracted to.

☑ **STANDARD INPUT VARIABLE** This property is used to select or create a variable that will be passed as an argument. This allows you to dynamically provide a parameter for the executable file.

☑ **STANDARD OUTPUT VARIABLE** This property is used to select or create a variable that will be used to capture the output of the process.

☑ **STANDARD ERROR VARIABLE** This property is used to select or create a variable that will be used to capture any errors from the executable.

While not required to use the Execute Process Task, errors that occur (from running the external program) in this task, can be stored in variables that are stored in the package. These variables can then be written to a log file.

 While the next exercise uses the Windows zip tool, you can use other tools like WinZip™ or 7-Zip™, to zip or unzip a file. To use one of these tools, change the path in step 3 below, to point to the executable file of the zip tool that you want to use.

Exercise 3.9: Unzip A File

In this exercise you will learn how to use the **EXECUTE PROCESS TASK** to unzip a file and place the file in a specific folder.

1. Rename a new package to `E3.9 Unzip a file`.

2. Add the Execute Process Task ⇒ On the General page on the editor ⇒ In the Name field, type `Unzip a file`.

3. Process page ⇒ In the Executable field, type `c:\windows\system32\expand.exe`, or select it by clicking the button at the end of the field. Expand.exe is the name of the Windows tool that zips and unzips files.

4. In the Arguments field, type `unzip_csv_files.zip Mar2015.csv`. There is a space after .zip. Mar2015.csv is the name of the file in the zip file that will be extracted.

5. In the Working Directory field, type `C:\SSIS Book\`. This is the folder where the zip file is located. You should have the options shown earlier in Figure 3-61.

6. Run the package ⇒ When finished, look in the folder for this book. You should see the Mar2015.csv file.

> **Options To Unzip Multiple Files**
> The zip file used in the exercise above, actually has three csv files in it. By default, the Execute Process Task will only extract one file from the zip file. I was way past shocked when I figured this out, as none of the documentation that I read mentioned this lack of functionality. I also could not find a way to select a folder for the file to be extracted to.
>
> When I started looking for a solution for what I thought I was doing wrong, I came across a lot of posts from people looking for "an easy" solution, meaning they did not want to or did not know how to write code to solve this problem. There are several options to unzip multiple files at the same time, as listed below.
> ☑ Create an Execute Process Task for each file in the zip file.
> ☑ Put the Execute Process Task in a Foreach Loop Container.
> ☑ Create variables to add to the Execute Process Task Editor.
> ☑ Use the Script Component Task to write a custom script.
> ☑ Use a third party SSIS component (free or not) or task to unzip a file.

Package Parts

This feature is used to create and save control flow tasks, including containers, that you need to use frequently. This keeps you from having to create the same task over and over again, in different packages. The tasks are saved as a package file, which can be used over and over, in as many packages as you need, just like project connection managers. A package part is like a template. Once created and saved, a "Package Parts" folder is automatically created in the Solution Explorer, for the package parts that you create. A Package Parts section is also automatically created in the toolbox.

An example that comes to mind is creating a package part for a connection to a data source or to a data source and a specific table in the data source. A connection to only a database data source, will let you select the table that you want or create a query for any table in the database, when the package part is added to a package.

Package parts are created the same way that packages are created and can have as many tasks as needed. They are created to save time and to keep from having to recreate the same steps/tasks in several packages. For example, in Exercise 3.8, you learned how to append data to an existing table in an SQL database. That package could be created as a package part and used as part of a bigger package that needs to append data to the same table, using the same source file every month.

Exercise 3.10: Create A Package Part For A Data Source Connection

In this exercise, you will learn how to create a package part that uses the Data Flow Task to connect to the AW database. A specific table will not be selected in the package part, so that the package part can be used for any table or view in the AW database.

1. In the Solution Explorer window ⇒
    Package Parts folder ⇒
    Right-click on the Control Flow folder ⇒
    New Control Flow Package Part, as shown in
    Figure 3-62.

    Notice that the workspace is the same as the
    package workspace, including the toolbox.

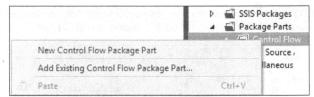

Figure 3-62 Control Flow folder shortcut menu options

2. Add the Data Flow Task ⇒ Rename it to `Connect to AW database`.

3. On the Data Flow tab, add the OLE DB Source task ⇒ Rename it to `AW database`.

4. On the editor, click the New button ⇒ Select the localhost.AW connection ⇒ Click OK.
    If a connection did not exist for the data source that you needed, you would create it now.

If you selected a table, view or created a query, it would be the default data that this package part would use.
Not selecting one of these options, lets you select the table, view or query, when the package part is used in a
package, thus making the package part more generic. On your own, you can select either option. Not selecting
an option will display a red circle with an X on the task on the Data Flow tab, which in this case is okay.

5. Click OK to close the OLE DB Source Editor.

6. Rename the package part to `E3.10 AW connection`.

View The SSIS Toolbox

The Package Parts section of the SSIS toolbox is only displayed when a package is open.

1. Open any package file.

2. Scroll to the bottom of the SSIS toolbox.
    You will see the Package Parts section, shown in
    Figure 3-63.

Figure 3-63 Package Parts section of the toolbox

When you create a package, the package part can be added to it,
just like any other task in the toolbox. For exercises in this book
that need a connection (source or destination) to the AW database,
you can use this package part.

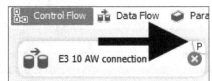

Figure 3-64 Package part added to a package

When a package part is added to a package, you will see a "P" in
the upper right corner, as illustrated in Figure 3-64. This indicates
that it is a package part.

 Control Flow Package Parts Limitations
A package part:
① Cannot be run or debugged in the designer.
② Can only have one top level task or container. If more than one top level task or container is needed, put all
of them in a Sequence Container.

 Like packages, package parts can be copied or duplicated, by right-clicking on it in the Solution Explorer and
selecting Copy.

Configure A Package Part

The control flow package part can be customized for each package that it is added to. To configure a package part,
it must be added to a package first. Once added, double-click on it or right-click on it and select Edit, to display the

dialog box shown below, in Figure 3-65. Changes made on this dialog box are only applied to the instance of the package part that you opened the dialog box from.

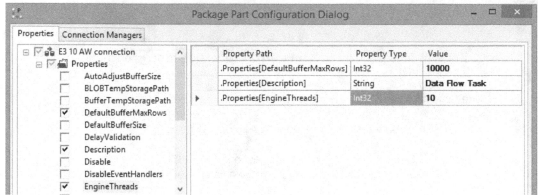

Figure 3-65 Package Part Configuration dialog box

 If you want the customization to be applied to every package that the package part will be added to, make the change in the original package part file.

Properties Tab

The left pane on this tab lists all of the package part properties. Clearing the check mark for a property means that the default value for the property (that was defined for the package part), will be used. In the figure, the three properties that are checked will override the default values that are set for the package part.

The right pane is where you change the properties, explained below.

The **PROPERTY PATH COLUMN** displays the name of the property.
The **PROPERTY TYPE COLUMN** displays the properties data type.
The **VALUE COLUMN** displays the properties current value. This is where you change the value. What is entered here, overrides the default value.

Connection Managers Tab

The options shown in Figure 3-66 are used to change the connection options for the package part.

The **SET COLUMN** is used to check the properties that you want to change.
The **PROPERTY NAME COLUMN** contains the connection options that can be changed.
The **VALUE COLUMN** displays the current property value. This is where you enter the value that you want to use for the property. What is entered here, overrides the default value.

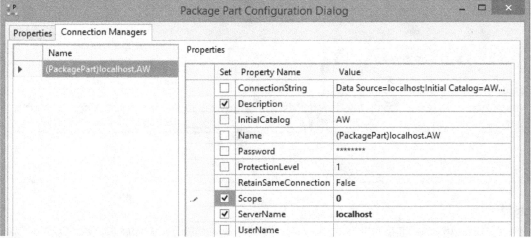

Figure 3-66 Connection Managers tab

Using A Package Part

When a package is saved, one of the things that is checked is whether or not it contains a package part. If the package has a package part, another **.DTSX** file is automatically created, which contains a copy of the package part.

The second file is saved with the same name as the original package and adds **.DESIGNER** to the end of the file name, as illustrated in Figure 3-67.

Figure 3-67 Package file saved that has a package part

Add An Existing Package Part To A Project

If there is a package part that is saved outside of the project that you want to use, it can be added to the project, by selecting the Add existing option, shown earlier in Figure 3-62.

The dialog box shown in Figure 3-68 is used to add an existing package part to a project.

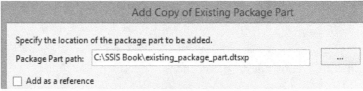

Figure 3-68 Add Copy of Existing Package Part dialog box

The **PACKAGE PART PATH** field is used to type in or select the path and file name of the package part file that you want to bring into the project or to use as a reference.

If checked, the **ADD AS A REFERENCE** option will add the package part as a reference to the project. This option is used when you want to reference (in this case use), the package part file in more than one project. If this option is not checked, a copy of the package part is added to the project.

Exercise 3.11: Add A Package Part To A Project

1. In the Solution Explorer, right-click on the Control Flow folder ⇒ **ADD EXISTING CONTROL FLOW PACKAGE PART**, as shown earlier in Figure 3-62.

2. Click the ellipsis (browse) button ⇒ Select the existing_package_part.dtsxp file in your folder. You should have the options shown above in Figure 3-68.

3. Click OK. You will see the package part in the Control Flow folder and in the Package Parts section of the toolbox, when you have a package open.

Exporting Data

As you will see later in this book, SSIS has tasks that will let you write data from one source to another source. The Import and Export Wizard is another way to write data to a different file. Because the wizard can create a package, you may find it easier to use the wizard to export data and then if needed, modify the package with any other functionality that may be needed.

Exercise 3.12: Export Data To A Text File

In this exercise, you will learn how to use the SSIS Wizard to create a package that exports data from a database to a text file.

1. Open the SSIS Import and Export Wizard.

2. On the Choose a Data Source screen, select the SQL Server Native Client 11.0 option ⇒ Type `localhost` in the Server name field ⇒ Open the Database drop-down list and select the AW database.

3. On the Destination screen, select the **FLAT FILE DESTINATION** option.

4. In the File name field, type `C:\SSIS Book\Ch3 ExportFromSSISWizard.txt`. This file will be created when the package is run. You should have the options shown in Figure 3-69 ⇒ Click Next.

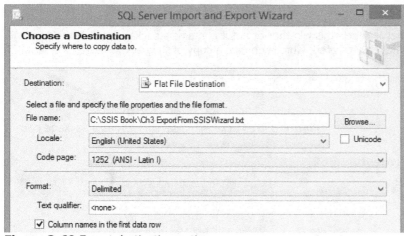

Figure 3-69 Export destination options

5. Select the Copy data option ⇒ Click Next.

6. On the Flat File Destination
    screen, select the Order Info
    table, as shown in Figure 3-70.

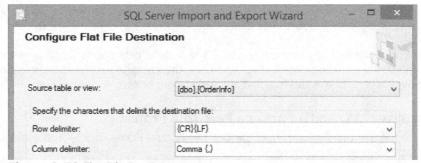

Figure 3-70 Flat File Destination options

7. Click the **EDIT MAPPINGS** button.

    Change the following Destination columns to
    <ignore>: Sales Rep ID, Shipped Via,
    City and State, as shown in Figure 3-71.
    These fields will not be exported ⇒
    Click OK.

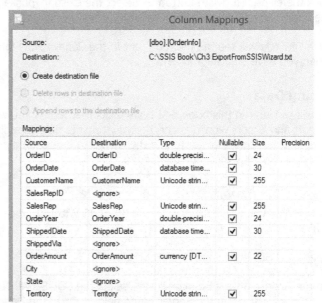

Figure 3-71 Column mappings options (for a text file)

8. Click Next ⇒ You will see the options that will be used to create the export ⇒ Click Finish.
    The package file will be created ⇒ Click Close, when you see the success screen.

9. Rename the package file to E3.12 SSIS Wizard export to a text file.

10. Run the package ⇒ When complete, look in your folder. You will see the Ch3 Export From SSIS Wizard.txt file.
    If you open the file, you will see 70,000 plus records.

Exercise 3.13: Export Data To Excel

In this exercise, you will export data from three tables in the AW database to sheets in an Excel workbook.

1. Open the SSIS Import and Export Wizard.

2. On the Choose a Data Source screen, select the SQL Server Native Client 11.0 option ⇒
    Type `localhost` in the Server name field ⇒ Open the Database drop-down list and select the AW database.

3. On the Destination screen, select the **MICROSOFT EXCEL** option.

4. In the Excel file path field, type `C:\SSIS Book\Ch3 Export3TablesFromSSISWizard.xlsx`.
    This workbook will be created when the package is run. You should have the options shown in Figure 3-72.

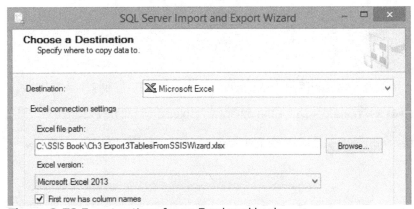

Figure 3-72 Export options for an Excel workbook

5. Click Next ⇒ Select the Copy data option ⇒ Click Next.

The Select Source screen is used to select the table(s) that you want to export (copy) to the Excel workbook. Each table that you select on this screen will be added to its own sheet in the workbook, with a sheet name that you can create or select from a list of sheets already in the workbook.

6. Check the following tables: Employee List, Financial Data and Order Info.

7. Click on the Financial Data name in the
    Destination column ⇒
    Change the name to `NetSales`,
    as shown in Figure 3-73.

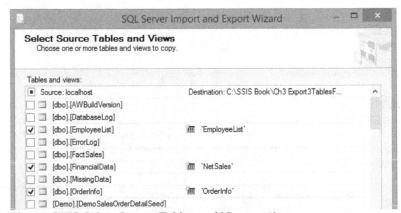

Figure 3-73 Select Source Tables and Views options

Column Mappings

When exporting to Excel, you have the same column mapping options that are available, for SQL databases.

1. Click on the Employee List row ⇒ Click the **EDIT MAPPINGS** button.

2. On the Column Mappings dialog box, check the Drop and re-create destination table option.

3. Change the settings so that the Employee ID, Birth Date and Salary fields will not be exported, as shown in Figure 3-74.

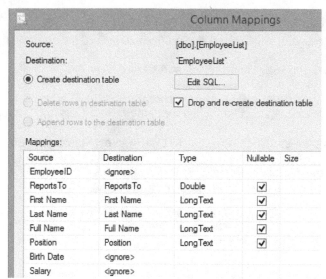

Figure 3-74 Column mappings for the Employee List table

4. Select the **DROP AND RE-CREATE DESTINATION TABLE** option for the other two tables that will be exported.

5. Click Next on the Select Source Tables and Views screen ⇒ Click Next on the Conversion checking screen ⇒ Click Finish.

Test The Package

1. Rename the package to `E3.13 SSIS Wizard export to Excel.`

Figure 3-75 shows the Data Flow tab of the package that you just created by using the wizard.

It shows that three tables will be written to in destination file(s). If necessary, you could add transformations to one or all of the data flows. Not bad for not creating each task individually. <smile>

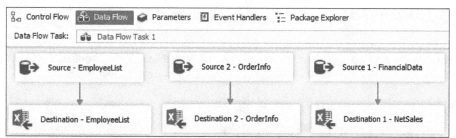

Figure 3-75 Data flows for the Excel export package

2. Run the package.

As you can see in Figure 3-76, the package ran successfully and wrote data to each of the tables. Also notice the error that starts on the second row of the figure. The error lets you know that the task failed because the Employee List table does not exist in the destination file. This is true because this is the first time that the package is being run and the destination table will be created in this package. If you open the workbook, you will see that three sheets were created and each has data.

Modifying Connection Information
This chapter has shown you how to create connections for several file types. More than likely, at some point, you will need to change some of the connection information. When that is the case, right-click on the connection on the Connection Managers tab and select Edit or right-click on the connection in the Connection Managers folder and select Open. This will display the connection manager information that was used to create the connection. You can select a different file, change the column mappings, change a data type and more.

```
Output                                                                          ▾ ☐ ✕
Show output from:  Debug                          ▾  ⬚ | ⬚ ⬚ ⬚ | ⬚ | ⬚
SSIS package "C:\SSIS Book\My SSIS Solution\SSIS Book\E3.13 SSIS Wizard Export To Excel.dtsx" starting.  ▲
Error: 0xC002F210 at Drop table(s) SQL Task 1, Execute SQL Task: Executing the query "drop table `EmployeeList`
" failed with the following error: "Table 'EmployeeList' does not exist.". Possible failure reasons: Problems with t
Task failed: Drop table(s) SQL Task 1
Information: 0x4004300A at Data Flow Task 1, SSIS.Pipeline: Validation phase is beginning.
Warning: 0x80047076 at Data Flow Task 1, SSIS.Pipeline: The output column "EmployeeID" (129) on output "OLE DB Sourc
Warning: 0x80047076 at Data Flow Task 1, SSIS.Pipeline: The output column "Birth Date" (135) on output "OLE DB Sourc
Warning: 0x80047076 at Data Flow Task 1, SSIS.Pipeline: The output column "Salary" (136) on output "OLE DB Source Ou
Information: 0x40043006 at Data Flow Task 1, SSIS.Pipeline: Prepare for Execute phase is beginning.
Information: 0x40043007 at Data Flow Task 1, SSIS.Pipeline: Pre-Execute phase is beginning.
Information: 0x4004300C at Data Flow Task 1, SSIS.Pipeline: Execute phase is beginning.
Information: 0x40043008 at Data Flow Task 1, SSIS.Pipeline: Post Execute phase is beginning.
Information: 0x4004300B at Data Flow Task 1, SSIS.Pipeline: "Destination - EmployeeList" wrote 22 rows.
Information: 0x4004300B at Data Flow Task 1, SSIS.Pipeline: "Destination 1 - NetSales" wrote 6944 rows.
Information: 0x4004300B at Data Flow Task 1, SSIS.Pipeline: "Destination 2 - OrderInfo" wrote 73595 rows.
Information: 0x40043009 at Data Flow Task 1, SSIS.Pipeline: Cleanup phase is beginning.
SSIS package "C:\SSIS Book\My SSIS Solution\SSIS Book\E3.13 SSIS Wizard Export To Excel.dtsx" finished: Success.  ▾
◀                                                                               ▶
Command Window  Call Stack  Breakpoints  Exception Settings  Immediate Window  Output
```

Figure 3-76 Output window in Debug mode

Shortcut To Creating A New Package

If you are like me, creating a new package seems to require a lot of scrolling, just to be able to rename the new package. If this bothers you also (keep in mind that this is only Chapter 3 in this book <smile>), follow the steps below for a shortcut that I came up with. This shortcut will keep a new empty package at the top of the SSIS Packages folder, so that you will not have to scroll down the list to rename a new package. If you aren't sure, just try the following steps to see what I am talking about. If you don't think it will be helpful, you can always delete the package file that will be created.

1. Create a new package ⇒ Rename it to `0 New Empty Package`. You can use whatever name you want. Just make sure that the first character of the file name is a zero. That is what will place the package file at the top of the SSIS Packages folder.

2. If you want, you can also add the Data Flow Task to the Control Flow tab, as it is used a lot in this book and will keep you from having to add it all the time. In the exercises that do not need it, you can delete it. Plus, at some point in the book, I stop saying to add the Data Flow Task to the Control Flow tab. <smile>

3. Save the changes to the package.

Now, when instructed to "Rename a new package to", make a copy of this package, instead of selecting the New SSIS Package option on the SSIS Packages folder shortcut menu, then having to scroll down to the "P" section of the files, to rename the new package. Actually, I will make several copies of the 0 New Empty Package at one time, to keep from having to do it each time that I need to create a new package.

The package that you just created and the copy of it will be at the top of the SSIS Packages folder, as shown in Figure 3-77.

The package with a "1" at the end of the file name is the one that you should rename for the exercise.

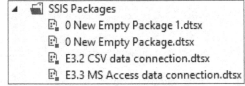

Figure 3-77 Empty package and a copy of it

Creating A Copy Of A Package

There may be times when an existing package or part of an existing package would be a good starting point for another package. Instead of manually recreating the existing package, you can create a copy of the package that you want to reuse. (This is similar to creating a new package, then renaming the new package.) When that is the case, follow the steps below.

1. Right-click on the package that you want to make a copy of ⇒ Copy.

2. If the solution has more than one project, right-click on the project or SSIS Packages folder that you want the copy of the package to be placed in ⇒ Paste. The copied package will have a number at the end of the file name.

3. Rename the copied package. You can add, modify or delete the tasks in the copied package. You can change the copied package however you need to.

Generating A New Package GUID

Each package that you create has a unique GUID number that is automatically generated. In the past, when you made a copy of a package, the GUID number was also copied. When one of the packages (with the same GUID) is run and generated an error, when looking in the log file at the Source ID field, it is difficult to know which package is causing the problem.

While I have not generated any errors in Visual Studio/SSDT 2015, I checked the GUID number of copied package files, which now automatically have a different GUID number, this bug may have been fixed. But just in case, the steps below show you how to generate a new GUID number, in case you run into this problem or something else causes you to need to generate a new GUID number. I have seen things like this fixed in one version of a software package, then in the next version it is broken again.

1. Display the properties for the copied package, or the package that you need to generate a new GUID number for ⇒ Scroll down to the Identification section in the Properties window.

2. Open the ID property drop-down list ⇒ <Generate New ID>, as illustrated in Figure 3-78.

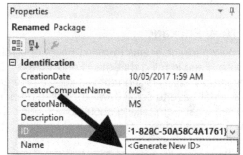

Figure 3-78 Option to generate a new GUID number for the package

3. Save the changes.

Saving A Package As A Template

If you create a package that you would like to use as a starting point for other packages (like a template), instead of making a copy of an existing package each time that you want to use it, the steps below show you how to create a template from an existing package.

You can include and configure connection managers, containers, tasks, variables and parameters that you use on a regular basis. You do not have to connect them. For example, if you need to use the same three tables in a database, on a regular basis, create a connection manager for each one. If you need to unzip files from the same zip file or append data from multiple files in the same folder on a regular basis, create the tasks and containers needed and save all of these items in the package. Then, when you use this template package, you can delete the items that you do not need and edit the ones you do need.

Doing this does not overwrite or replace the default empty template package that you see when you first create a new package file. Over time, you will probably need to add more tasks to the template. That is fine.

1. Create the package that you want to use as a template. I use "Template" as part of the file name so that a year from now, I stand a chance of remembering the purpose of the package. Doing this is optional.

2. Close Visual Studio ⇒ In Windows Explorer, find the package that you want to use as a template.

3. Click on the package file ⇒ Press CTRL+C.

4. Navigate to the location below.
    C:\Program Files (x86)\Microsoft Visual Studio 14.0\Common7\IDE\Private Assemblies\Project Items\ Data Transformation Project.

    The "14.0" in the folder name, changes with each version of Visual Studio. More then likely, you should select the folder that has the highest number. This is true for any numbers that are part of a folder name.

5. Click on the Data Transformation Items folder ⇒ Press CTRL+V.

6. Open Visual Studio ⇒ Right-click on a project folder ⇒ Add ⇒ New Item. On the dialog box shown in Figure 3-79, you should see the package that you want to use as a template, as illustrated in the figure.

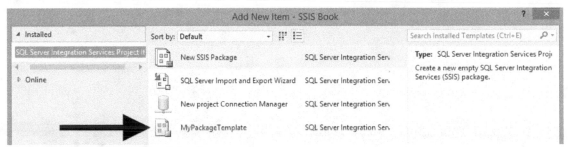

Figure 3-79 Add New Item dialog box

7. Select your package template file ⇒ Type in a name for the package ⇒ Click the Add button, as you would for the templates that come with SSIS.

USING THE DATA FLOW TAB TO EXTRACT AND LOAD DATA

Overview

After reading this chapter and completing the exercises you will:

☑ Have a better understanding of the Data Flow tab
☑ Know how to use the Source Assistant and Destination Assistant
☑ Know how to use an SQL query file to select the data to import
☑ Know how to append data to a csv file
☑ Know how to use the File System Task
☑ Be able to use the Data Conversion and Derived Column transformations
☑ Know how to set up a data viewer

CHAPTER 4

Overview

This chapter introduces you to the Data Flow tab. As you have learned in previous chapters, this tab is only available when the Data Flow Task is added to the Control Flow tab. In the previous chapter, when you added a task to the Control Flow tab, the task had an editor that was used to configure it. The Data Flow Task on the Control Flow tab does not have an editor. When you right-click on the Data Flow Task and select Edit, the Data Flow tab is displayed. In a way, the Data Flow tab is the Data Flow Tasks editor. While the primary focus of this chapter is the source and destination components on the Data Flow tab, some transformations are also covered.

Understanding The Roles Of The Control Flow And Data Flow Tabs

Some of this has been covered earlier in this book, but I want to briefly go over it again, now that you have had a chance to use both tabs, in hopes of providing additional information. I remember that when I first started using SSIS, I spent quite some time trying to understand the difference between the functionality of these tabs.

The first thing that I want to make clear is that even though the data sources used in this book, do not have tens of millions of rows of data, SSIS is designed to handle large amounts of data. Trying to put very large data files on your computers hard drive to learn how to use SSIS is not practical. As you saw in the previous chapter, I did include one data file that has over 2 million rows of data.

The Control Flow tab manages the workflow of the entire package. This includes tasks on the Data Flow tab and all of the default tabs on the workspace. This tab also controls the order that the tasks are executed in. As you saw in the previous chapter, all of the tasks on the Control Flow tab have their own editor to configure the task, except for the Data Flow Task, which is configured on the Data Flow tab.

Workflow tasks also control other (outside of SSIS) applications and processes. Examples of workflow tasks are the Execute SQL Task, Execute Package Task and the Send Mail Task. Workflow tasks are used to send email, open software like Excel, zip and unzip files.

A **SOURCE** is used to select the location of the data that you want to use. As you have seen, most sources point to a connection manager, which has the location of a data file. Most of the time, a **DESTINATION** receives the data from the source, whether or not it has been transformed. Source and destinations use connection managers. A destination can also be a folder, as you learned in Chapter 3, Exercise 3.5.

Creating Data Flows

Previous chapters covered what is known as the **CONTROL FLOW**, which showed you how to create the layout, flow and direction of the package. This chapter and the next chapter cover the basics of using the Data Flow Task that is added to the Control Flow tab. Each Data Flow Task that is added to the Control Flow tab creates a new **DATA FLOW** on the Data Flow tab.

The **DATA FLOW TASK** is used to transfer the data from the source to a destination and in between this transfer, transform the data as needed. The source and destination can be the same file type or different file types. For example, the source could be an Excel file and the destination can be a new table in an SQL database. This task can also be used to copy data from one database to another.

This chapter covers the components that are used to get data from a file (the source) and transfer it to another file (the destination). The primary focus of the Data Flow tab is to transform the source data before it gets to the destination file. This process is known as the Data Flow portion of a package.

After a connection (when one task is connected to the next task) is created, **METADATA** (data about the columns and their data types) is also created and passed to the next component in the flow. A data flow also allows you to save data from a source to multiple destinations at the same time. This improves performance when saving data.

Transformations

Data flow transformations (also known as **TRANSFORMS**) are used to make changes to the data before it is written to a destination. Common transformations include sorting data, deciding what to do with rows of data that are missing data in one or more fields, pivoting data and selecting rows that meet specific criteria. An example would be an input file that has rows that do not have zip codes. You can send rows without a zip code to a path that looks up the zip code, before writing the row to the destination. Rows where a zip code could not be found, could be sent to a different destination file to have someone manually look up the zip code and update the file. Fixing things like this prior to writing the data to the destination file keeps you for having to create and run data validation updates to the destination file later.

Transformations run in memory, which can be faster than reading the data from a database, then performing the transformation, then writing the data back to the database. This reading and writing to the same database is what makes the process slow, when compared to using transformations in SSIS.

Data Flow Tab

The Data Flow tab is used to select what happens to the data that is retrieved from the Data Flow Task (on the Control Flow tab) before it is sent to the destination. The options on the toolbox for the Data Flow tab are used to clean, transform and manipulate the data, in addition to selecting the source and existing destination or creating a new destination. This tab is only available and used with the Data Flow Task.

Keep in mind that each transformation task added to this tab changes the data in some capacity, be it filter the data, add a new (derived) column or aggregate data. As the data flows from one task to the next, the data that is passed, is the result of previous tasks. This means that if the second task for example, filters the data to only keep records from one year, the data for the other years in the data source are not available for the third task or any other task after the second task.

Initially, the Data Flow tab is not enabled until a Data Flow Task is added to the Control Flow tab. If you click on the Data Flow tab without a Data Flow Task being added, the Data Flow tab displays a link, letting you know this, as shown at the bottom of Figure 4-1. Clicking on this link will add a Data Flow Task to the Control Flow tab.

The Data Flow tab has the component types explained below, as shown in Figure 4-2. Collectively, these components make up the **FOUNDATION OF ETL**.

- ☑ **SOURCE** (The last word of these tasks is "Source"). The source tasks are used to import data from a variety of data sources, including Excel, flat files, XML and a variety of databases that are ODBC or OLE DB compliant. These are the options in the "Other Sources" section on the toolbox.
- ☑ **DATA TRANSFORMATION** tasks are used to clean and change the data that is imported from the source. This includes combining data from two or more fields (using a derived column), filling in missing data values or making data standard (using the **FUZZY LOOKUP TASK**).
- ☑ **DESTINATION** (The last word of the majority of these tasks is "Destination"). The destination tasks are used to write (load) data into a variety of file formats. The majority of destinations are the same as the Source options discussed above. The following are unique to destinations:
  - ☑ The **DATA READER DESTINATION** is used to send data to an application that supports the Data Reader interface, like an application developed in C#.
  - ☑ The **RECORDSET DESTINATION** is used to create and populate an ADO recordset that is available outside of the data flow.

As you will see, several sources have an equivalent destination. This means that for example, you can load data from one Excel file, perform transformations and write the data out to the same or different Excel file. The purpose of creating SSIS packages is to copy data from one file/table to another and clean the data.

Data Flow Tab Tips

① A **SOURCE COMPONENT** can only read data. A **DESTINATION COMPONENT** can only write data. The source and destination components are not interchangeable.

② Transformations create the changes and hold them until the data is written to a destination file. If the flow gets the data from a database and writes the data to an Excel file, the modified data from the transformations is only in the Excel file. If you also want the changes applied to the database, you also have to add a destination component for the database.

③ A connection to a file can be used as a source connection and as a destination connection. Using the same data file for the source and destination in a data flow, lets you read and write to the same data file. This is known as **UPDATING IN PLACE**.

Figure 4-1 Data Flow tab without a Data Flow Task on the Control Flow tab

In addition to the source and destination connection options shown in Figure 4-2, don't forget that additional options are on the **ADD SSIS CONNECTION MANAGER DIALOG BOX**. [See Chapter 3, Figure 3-4]

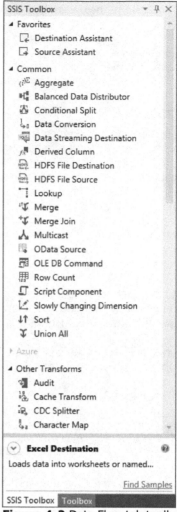

Figure 4-2 Data Flow tab toolbox

Data Flow Paths

While the arrows on the Data Flow tab look like the precedence constraint arrows on the Control Flow tab, they do not have the same functionality. The **BLUE ARROW** represents the flow of good data between the components on the Data Flow tab. It points to the next task that should be executed, if the data is good. The **RED ARROW** represents the flow of data that has errors (bad data). It points to the task that should be processed if the data is bad or data that has an error. For example, send the rows with bad data to a different destination file, then the good data will be sent to, or data that triggers an event on the **ERROR OUTPUT PAGE** on the source or destination editor, when the redirect row value is selected on the editor.

> **Precedence Constraints vs Data Flow Paths**
> Both of these features use arrows to direct the flow and order of tasks.
>
> ☑ **PRECEDENCE CONSTRAINTS** are used on the Control Flow tab. They represent the workflow, meaning that they determine what tasks should be run and in what order. The previous chapter covered precedence constraints in detail.
> ☑ **DATA FLOW PATHS** are used on the Data Flow tab. They use blue and red arrows to direct the flow of data, by defining which transformations and destinations the data should be routed to.

Understanding Connection Managers

Chapter 2 covered creating connections to different types of data sources. As you saw, different file types use different options to connect to the file. All of the options for each file that a connection is created for, is stored in its own connection manager. That is why it is a good idea to give connections unique and meaningful names, especially if they will be used in more than one package.

If you are familiar with **CONNECTION STRINGS** in other software development tools, connection managers in SSIS provide the same functionality. Once a connection manager is created for a specific data source, it can be used to as a source or destination connection.

Differences Between Data Sources

If the majority of your source data is not from a database, you will probably spend a lot of time using options on the Data Flow tab. While some people consider transforming data a tedious job, it is necessary, in particular, when the data does not come from a database. When a database is designed, data validation is part of the design, or at least it is suppose to be. Making fields required is also part of the database design. Often, when transformations are used with data from a database, it is to update or enhance the data, opposed to clean the data. Data created in text files or spreadsheets do not have data validation functionality, which is what makes it critical to use the transformation options, when the data from these file types will be added to a database.

For example, in a spreadsheet, you can type the first and last name in the same cell. Most databases use one field for the first name and another field for the last name. Data coming into a database must match the layout of the database. In this scenario, that means that the first and last name that are in the same cell in the spreadsheet would have to be separated, before it could be added to the database.

While the same transformations can be accomplished at the database level, they run faster in SSIS, because SSIS performs the transformations in memory before writing the data to the database. Reading from and writing to the same database is labor intensive and can cause performance issues. During the transformation process, you have the option of selecting which records are added to the output (destination) file. Records that do not pass the validation transformation can be written to a different destination file.

Source Assistant And Destination Assistant

These components are designed to make it easier to create a connection to a source or destination. It is not a requirement to use both assistants in the same package. They do not include the functionality that the task editors have. They are in the Favorites section of the toolbox. New connections can be created from these dialog boxes.

Initially, the drivers that you see on these dialog boxes are the ones that are already installed on your computer. That is because the **SHOW ONLY INSTALLED** option is checked, by default. Removing the check mark for this option will display other providers that are currently not installed.

Connections stored in the Connection Managers folder are displayed on these dialog boxes. All of this is done to make it easier to select the appropriate connection manager for the data source that you need to connect to. The most frequently used connection types (OLE DB, Excel and Flat File) are covered in more detail in this chapter.

 I find it easier to use the source and destination assistants when I need to connect to a source that is in the Connection Managers folder, because it does save time. It also keeps you from having to select the file that you want to connect to. In general, the key to creating useful connections, in addition to making them a project connection, is giving them names that will make sense today and a year from now.

 Both assistants will create a **CONNECTION MANAGER** to the selected source type if one does not already exist. [See Figure 4-3, the Select Connection Managers list]

Creating A Connection Using An Assistant

When you need to create a new connection for a source or destination, follow the steps below.

1. Open the Source or Destination Assistant ⇒ Select the type of connection (Excel, OLE DB, etc.).

2. Double-click on the **NEW** option, on the right side of the dialog box.

 As covered earlier, connections created from the **SOURCE ASSISTANT** and **DESTINATION ASSISTANT** are not project level connections. If you want a connection that is created by an assistant to be a project level connection, you have to convert the connection to a project connection. To me, it would be helpful is these dialog boxes had an option to let you select whether you want the connection to be a project connection.

Once the connection is created, you will see the corresponding source or destination task. At that point, you have to open the editor to configure the connection, like you have in previous chapters.

Source Assistant

Figure 4-3 shows the Source Assistant. As shown, the SQL Server source type (an OLE DB connection), currently has one connection.

You may see additional source types, depending on the drivers that are installed on your computer.

The bottom of the dialog box shows the options used to configure the selected connection.

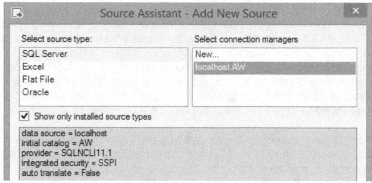

Figure 4-3 Source Assistant

OLE DB Source

This source is popular because it supports any OLE DB compliant database. It is used to connect to databases like SQL Server, Oracle and Access. Figure 4-4 shows the Connection Manager. The **PROVIDER** drop-down list, at the top of the dialog box, displays a list of drivers to select from, to connect to the database that you want to use, as shown in Figure 4-5. The provider that is selected determines the options that are displayed on the Connection Manager dialog box.

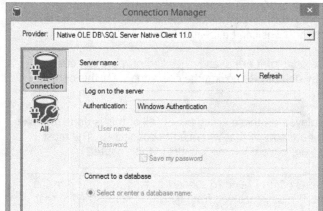

Figure 4-4 OLE DB Connection Manager dialog box

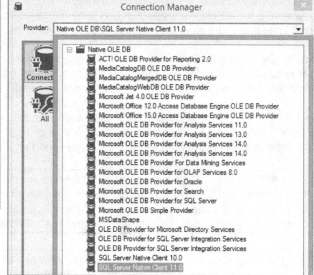

Figure 4-5 OLE DB providers

OLE DB Source Editor And Data Access Mode Field

Figure 4-6 shows the OLE DB Source Editor. The **DATA ACCESS MODE** field is used to select how you want to select the data. The options shown in Figure 4-7 are explained below.

- ☑ **TABLE OR VIEW** Is used to select a table or view in the data source. This option is used when you want to initially select all of the fields in the table or view. The **COLUMNS PAGE** on the editor, will let you select which fields to send to transformations and the destination file.
- ☑ **TABLE NAME OR VIEW NAME VARIABLE** Is used to select a variable that has the table or view name.
- ☑ **SQL COMMAND** Is used to create or import a query that will select the data to retrieve. The SQL command options are used when you want to use an SQL query or stored procedure to select specific records or filter the data before it is imported into the package. In addition to being able to type in, paste or import the SQL code to create a query, the SQL command option also provides an option to use the **QUERY BUILDER**, to create the SQL query.

☑ **SQL COMMAND FROM VARIABLE** Is used to select a variable that has the SQL query.

It is best to use one of the query options to select the data for the following reasons.

☑ The query provides better performance. All of the rows and columns do not have to be imported. The processing done by using the Columns page to remove columns is done after the data has been loaded into memory.

☑ The Source Editor cannot filter the data. A query can filter the rows before the data is loaded into memory.

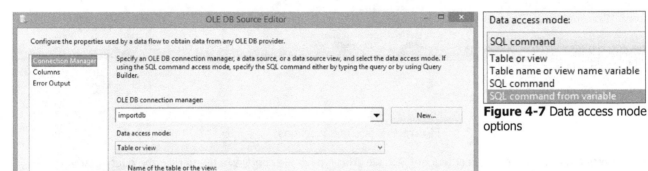

Figure 4-7 Data access mode options

Figure 4-6 OLE DB Source Editor

 Which Access Mode Is Better, Table Or SQL Command?
While the Table data access mode is the easiest to use, most of the time, you will not need or use all of the fields and rows in a table. From a performance perspective, the table option is slower because more data has to be read into memory, then is actually needed. Yes, the Columns page can be used to uncheck columns that you do not need to use, but what may not be obvious, is that all of the data is still read in first, then the columns that are not checked are deleted.

Creating a query allows you to only select the rows and columns that are needed. This creates a smaller data set, which makes the performance much better. That is because the rows of data are run through the query as they are being read into memory.

 Exercise Tips
① When using a new package as the starting point for an exercise, add the **DATA FLOW TASK** to the Control Flow tab, unless stated otherwise.
② For exercise in this book, you may want to add the following source and destination tasks to the Favorites section of the toolbox. Excel, Flat File and OLE DB.
③ When using a Flat File Destination, make sure that the Delimited option on the Flat File Format dialog box is selected, then click OK on the dialog box.

Exercise 4.1: Use The Source Assistant

In this exercise you will learn how to use the Source Assistant to create a connection using an existing connection. You will also learn how to use a query file to select the records to import from the data source.

Use The Source Assistant To Create A Connection

1. Rename a new package to `E4.1 Use an SQL query to select data`.

2. On the Data Flow tab, add the Source Assistant ⇒ Select SQL Server ⇒ Select the AW connection, as shown earlier in Figure 4-3.

3. Rename the OLE DB Source connection to `AW Source`.

Use An SQL Query File To Select The Data

1. On the editor, change the Data access mode to **SQL COMMAND**.

2. Click the Browse button ⇒ In your folder, select the 2014orders.sql file. You should have the options and query shown in Figure 4-8.

The **PARAMETERS BUTTON** is enabled when the Data access mode is set to one of the SQL command options. The dialog box that opens is used to select the parameter that will pass a value (to the question mark) to the query. [See Chapter 8, Figure 8-16]

The **BUILD QUERY BUTTON** opens the Query Builder.

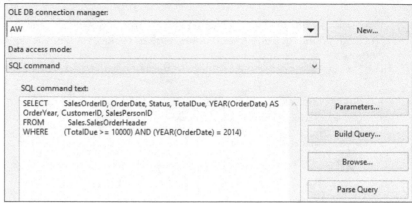

Figure 4-8 SQL query options

The **BROWSE BUTTON** is used to select a query SQL file. This type of file contains a query (like the query that you created in Chapter 2, Exercise 2.2) that is used to select the records to retrieve from the source. This query file can also be created in SSMS.

The **PARSE QUERY BUTTON** is used to verify the queries syntax.

As shown above in Figure 4-8, there are two sets of criteria that the data must meet, to be selected. The criteria is explained below.

① The value in the Total Due field must be greater than or equal to 10,000.
② The Order Date year must be 2014. The table has data for several years.

The **SELECT STATEMENT** lists the fields that will be retrieved. This statement is also used to rename a column.
The **FROM CLAUSE** contains the table name that has the fields on the SELECT statement.
The **WHERE CLAUSE** is the equivalent of a filter. It is the criteria that records in the data source must meet in order to be retrieved and used in the package.

Rename A Field On The Columns Page
The Columns page can be used to view the columns in the source and rename columns. In this exercise, the only columns shown are the ones selected by the query, even though the table has more columns.

1. On the Columns page, click in the Total Due Output Column cell ⇒ Change the name to `TotalOrderAmount`, as shown in Figure 4-9.

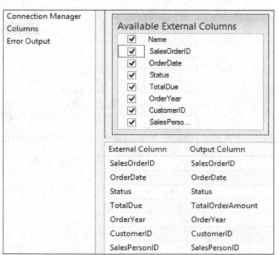

Figure 4-9 Column name changed

Error Output Page

The options in the drop-down list, illustrated in Figure 4-10, are used to decide on a field by field basis, what to do if the field has an error or if the data in the field will be truncated.

The options in the drop-down list are the same for a truncation column.

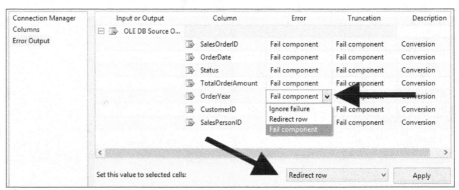

Figure 4-10 Error Output page

Truncation occurs when the incoming field has more data then the corresponding field in the destination source is set up to accommodate. Truncation usually occurs more frequently with string fields.

Another example of when using the options on this page are helpful, would be deciding what to do with data that is not compatible with the corresponding field in the destination table. You could send records with this error to a different destination table. To do that, you would select the **REDIRECT ROW OPTION** in the drop-down list, for each field that you want the redirect option applied to.

You can select the entire Error or Truncation column by clicking in the first cell in the column and then drag the mouse down to the last cell. You can also click in a cell in either column ⇒ Press and hold down the CTRL key and click on each cell that you want to apply the same option to ⇒ Change the **SET THIS VALUE TO SELECTED CELLS** option to Redirect row, as illustrated at the bottom of Figure 4-10 ⇒ Click Apply. The values in all of the selected cells will be changed to Redirect row.

Rows that are redirected will be handled by the task connected to the red arrow of the source component or transformation task. Usually, a connection to a new destination table would be added to the red arrow.

The **IGNORE FAILURE** option will change the value in the field to NULL.

> **Which Option Should I Use?**
> If all of this is too much to digest now, redirect all rows with an error to a different output file. That will let you view the rows that generated an error, then decide what should be done with the data. This will also give you a better understanding of how the error options work. Also keep in mind, the data flow will fail, if there is a truncation or data type error and you have not selected what to do when there is an error with the data.

2. Click OK ⇒ Save the package. This package will be modified later in this chapter, to export data to Excel.

Excel Source

This component is used to import data from an Excel workbook. The Excel Source component works similar to the OLE DB source component, including being treated like a database, because it is able to use an SQL query to select the data.

While Excel data types are supported in SSIS, sometimes it can be problematic adding Excel data to an SQL Server database. This is because the format of cells in Excel are set to General. SSIS interprets the General format (used in Excel), as a Unicode string data type. SSIS translates this data type into the **NVARCHAR DATA TYPE**, which is usually not a data type found in databases. Additionally, the nvarchar data type may be slower and use twice as much space. Trying to insert this data type into a **VARCHAR DATA TYPE**, which is what SSIS supports, can fail. A solution is to add the **DATA CONVERSION TRANSFORMATION** to the package to change the data type, before the destination task is run.

Flat File Source

This component is used to import data from a text based file. This file type usually has the extension .txt or .csv, but other text file types can be used. Text files are most often tab or comma delimited. Some are fixed-width or what is known as **RAGGED-RIGHT**, meaning that all rows do not have the same number of columns. Creating a flat file source is similar to creating an OLE DB source.

As shown in Figure 4-11, the field delimiter of the file is displayed in the **COLUMN DELIMITER FIELD**. Make sure that the delimiter displayed, is the correct one for the file that you are using.

Like an Excel file, the data type for all fields in a flat file are set to String. By default, the Flat File Connection Manager sets each column to a String field with a length of 50 characters.

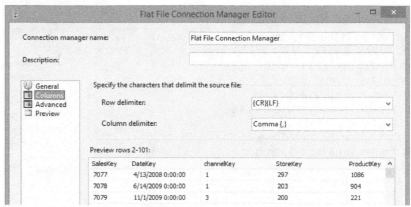

Figure 4-11 Flat File Connection Manager Columns page

The data type of the fields that will be used in the import, should have the data type changed on the Advanced page or use the Data Conversion transformation, to select the appropriate data type.

Advanced Editor

This editor has additional options that can be configured for components used on the Data Flow tab. It is accessed by selecting the **SHOW ADVANCED EDITOR** option on the components shortcut menu. This editor is available for most components that have their own editor.

It can also be used to configure components that do not have their own editor. Properties can be configured at the following levels: Input and output level, input and output column level, and the component level.

The Advanced Editor has the common and custom properties for the selected component. The tabs and properties on the dialog box shown in Figure 4-12, are based on the component that is selected. All components do not have all of the tabs discussed below.

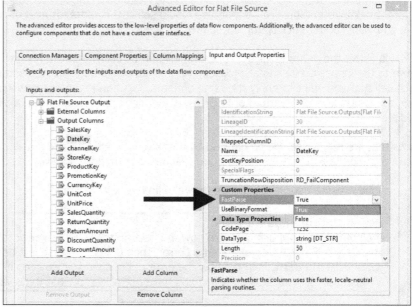

Figure 4-12 Advanced Editor For Flat File Source dialog box

☑ **CONNECTION MANAGERS** is used to view and change the connection manager options.

☑ **COMPONENT PROPERTIES** is used to view and change the common component level properties. This includes the components, name and data source.

☑ **COLUMN MAPPINGS** is used to view and change the mapping for the output columns. An example would be if there are fields that are not needed, they can be set to ignore.

☑ **INPUT COLUMNS** is used to view and change the input columns and change the Output Alias column names. The **USAGE TYPE** property can also be changed from read only, to read write.

☑ **INPUT AND OUTPUT PROPERTIES** is used to set properties for the input and output columns. Properties that can be changed include the column name, data type and length. Columns can be added or deleted.

Use The Fast Parse Property To Improve The Performance Of A Flat File Source
By default, SSIS requires a Flat File source to validate the data in date and numeric fields. The data in a date field must be in a valid date range. For example, 09/99/2017 has the correct date format, but 99 is not a valid day. This data would not pass the validation. The data in a numeric field cannot have any character data in it.

However, the validation of the date and integer data types, adds additional processing time. Setting the Fast Parse property to True, for a integer (numeric) or date field, bypasses this processing for the field that the property is changed on. Doing this improves the packages performance. When this property is set to True, the validation and verification for the column is turned off. When this property is set to True, it is a good idea to ensure that the data in the column is consistent and trustworthy. By default, the Fast Parse property is set to False for each field. This means that to disable this property for the entire table, you have to manually change the property for every date and numeric field in the table.

The Fast Parse property is also available for the DATA CONVERSION TRANSFORMATION, which is covered later in this chapter. Before you rush off and change this property, keep in mind that .txt and .csv files use the Flat File Source connection. These source files do not have any data validation built in, like tables in a database do.

For example, the following dates can be typed in the same field, in a flat file, 9/19/15 and Sept 19, 2015. In this example, setting the Fast Parse property to True for the date field would allow both date formats to be accepted and you would not know it, until the destination task failed because data could not be written to the destination file.

My suggestion would be to find out how the flat file was created. If the file is the result of an export from a database that has validation for numeric and date fields enabled, then setting the Fast Parse property to True, should not be an issue. Otherwise, consider leaving this property set to False.

The steps below show you how to change the Fast Parse property.
1. Right-click on a Flat File Source or Data Conversion component on the canvas ⇒ Show Advanced Editor.
2. Click on the Input and Output Properties tab ⇒ In the Output Columns folder, click on a numeric or date field.
3. In the CUSTOM PROPERTIES section on the right, change the Fast Parse property to True, as illustrated earlier in Figure 4-12.

Destinations

A destination connection is created to accept data from a data source or from a transformation. This biggest difference between the Source and Destination editors is the Mappings page, shown later in Figure 4-18. The destination connection cannot be completely set up until it is linked to a source or transformation task.

Destination Assistant

Figure 4-13 shows the Destination Assistant. It has the same options as the Source Assistant.

Like the Source Assistant, the purpose of the Destination Assistant is to help you create a connection manager.

Also like the Source Assistant, the most popular connection types are OLE DB, Excel and Flat File.

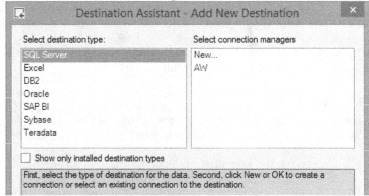

Figure 4-13 Destination Assistant

OLE DB Destination

This destination will write data to an OLE DB compliant database.

Figure 4-14 shows the Connection Manager page of the editor, with the default options selected. The options are explained below.

KEEP NULLS option [See Chapter 3, Options Page]

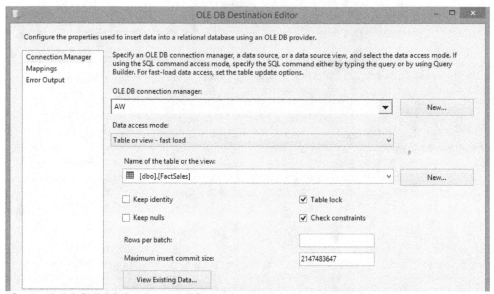

Figure 4-14 OLE DB Destination Editor - Connection Manager page options

 Creating A New Table
Clicking the New button next to the Name of the table or the view field, shown above in Figure 4-14, allows you to create a table in SSIS like you did when you used the wizard. On my own, I have a test package with a connection to the database that I am using. For the most part, I only use the test package to create new tables in the database, as needed. Remember, that once you click OK on the Create Table dialog box, the table is created, whether or not the package is run.

Data Access Mode

The OLE DB Destination has similar data access mode options, that the OLE DB Source has. Figure 4-15 shows the options. The options that are different from the ones on the OLE DB Source Editor covered earlier in this chapter, are explained below.

These options make the connections dynamic and enables the **BULK LOAD OPTION** instead of the default row-by-row load option. [See OLE DB Source Editor And Data Access Mode Field, earlier in this chapter]

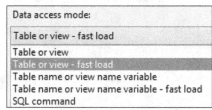

Figure 4-15 Data access mode options

TABLE OR VIEW - FAST LOAD is used to load data in bulk, into the destination table.

TABLE NAME OR VIEW NAME VARIABLE - FAST LOAD is used to select a variable that has the table or view name of the data that will be loaded in bulk, into the destination table.

Fast Load Options

The options below are only available if one of the fast load options, discussed above is selected and the destination is a SQL Server database. When this option is selected, the options explained below, can be used to configure the fast load.

☑ If checked, the **KEEP IDENTITY** option, is used to add data to a column that has the identity property enabled. [See Chapter 3, Options Page - Enable Identity Insert Option]
☑ The **TABLE LOCK** option does just that. It prevents other people and processes from accessing the table, while the package is writing to it. Checking this option allows the data to be written to the table faster. That is because it enables a bulk load option instead of a row-by-row operation. The option is only available for SQL Server databases.
☑ The **ROWS PER BATCH** field is used to select how many rows (records) you want in each batch that is sent to the destination.

☑ The **MAXIMUM INSERT COMMIT SIZE** field is used to select how large the batch size should be before records are written to the destination file. The suggested rule of thumb is 10,000, because this size or smaller, usually increases performance.

Selecting The Destination Table

There are two destination table options, as explained below.

① Use an existing table by selecting one in the Name of the table or the view drop-down list.
② Create a new table in the destination database.

Create A Destination Table

Clicking the **NEW** button across from the table or view drop-down list, opens the dialog box shown in Figure 4-16. It works like the Create Table SQL Statement dialog box in the Import and Export Wizard. The difference is that it does not have the Auto Generate button. [See Chapter 3, Figure 3-43]

As you can see, most fields have the string varchar (50) default data type. If any of the fields that have numeric, date or currency values will be used in a transformation, the data type will have to be changed first. When a new table is created, the Name of the table or the view field (on the OLE DB Destination Editor dialog box) changes, based on the name that you give the table.

OLE DB Destination
On the first line of the code in Figure 4-16, is the default name of the new table that will be created. You should replace that with a table name that is appropriate for the data that it will store. Once you click OK on this dialog box, an empty table will be created in the database. If you change your mind, typed the name incorrectly or do not need the table, open the database in SSMS and delete the table that you do not need.

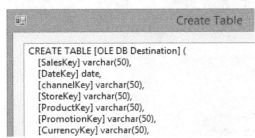

Figure 4-16 Create Table dialog box

Mappings Page

The biggest configuration difference between source and destination connections is that destination connections have a Mapping page, as shown in Figure 4-17.

By default, the Input Column table is created based on the field names in the source or transformation. If there is no match in the destination table, you have to match the fields manually by dragging a field in the Input Column table to the matching field in the Destination Column table.

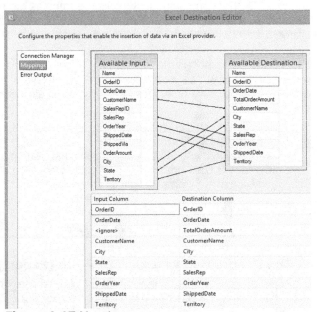

Figure 4-17 Mappings page

Source fields that are not mapped to a destination field will not be written to the destination file. As shown earlier in Figure 4-14, the destination editor does not have a Columns page (like source editors do).

Notice the following about the tables on the Mappings page:

☑ The fields are not in the same order in both tables, but were still mapped.

☑ The Total Order Amount field in the destination table, was not automatically mapped. If you look at the field across from it, in the grid at the bottom of the figure, you will see <ignore>. This lets you know that SSIS did not find a match for the field, based on the field name. Without changing <ignore> to a field, the Total Order Amount field will not contain any data, when the data is exported to the destination table.

In this scenario, the Total Order Amount field should be mapped to the Order Amount field. To make this change, open the drop-down list for the <ignore> field and select the Order Amount field. This will automatically add the link between the fields in the tables at the top of the dialog box. You could also drag the Total Order Amount field in the table and at the top of the dialog box, to the Order Amount field to map them.

Below are some tips for mapping fields.

☑ It is not a requirement that all fields in the source be mapped to a field in the destination file.

☑ Fields do not have to be in the same order in the source and destination tables.

☑ Configuring a destination should be done after a source or transformation is configured, otherwise an error will be generated saying that the component does not have any available input columns, as shown in Figure 4-18. Configuring a destination should also be done after the transformation tasks are created, because the output of the transformation tasks contain the data that will be sent to the destination file.

☑ The preferred order of creating tasks on the Data Flow tab is source ⇒ transformations ⇒ destination. One reason is because some transformation information comes from the source, which is automatically filled in on the transformation editor for you. Other data can be created in a transformation that is not in the source.

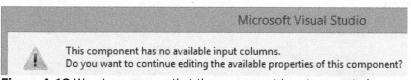

Microsoft Visual Studio

⚠ This component has no available input columns.
Do you want to continue editing the available properties of this component?

Figure 4-18 Warning message that the component is not connected

Excel Destination

For the most part, the Excel Destination component works the same as the Excel Source component, which was covered earlier in this chapter. Like the Flat File destination that has the ability to create a new file, the Excel destination has the same functionality.

While the Excel Destination component has the functionality to create workbooks and sheets, I created a workbook named Exported Exercise Data that will be used to write data to, in several exercises, to keep from having to create a table for each exercise, which will save time. Don't worry, you will also learn how to create tables, in an Excel workbook.

 Excel .xls vs .xlsx File Type Differences
There is a difference between these file type extensions that you need to be aware of when using the Excel Destination. The difference is the number of rows that can be written to the file. .xls files have a limit of 65,536 rows per sheet. .xlsx files have a limit of 1,048,576 rows per sheet. If you select .xls as the file type and there are more than 65,536 rows that need to be written to the sheet, the package will fail, when it is run. If at all possible, use the .xlsx file type all of the time. That way you will not have to worry about this. Just make sure that the people that will use the workbook, have a version of Excel that supports .xlsx files.

Exercise 4.2: Use The Destination Assistant To Write (Export) Data To An Excel Workbook

In Exercise 4.1, you created a package that connects to the AW database. You also learned how to use a query file that selects the records that will be processed and written to another data source. In this exercise, you will make a copy of that package and add a destination to it.

Create A Connection To An Excel Workbook Using The Destination Assistant

1. Rename a copy of the E4.1 package to `E4.2 Export to Excel`.

2. On the Data Flow tab, add the Destination Assistant to the canvas.

3. On the Destination Assistant dialog box, select the Excel destination type ⇒ New ⇒ Click OK.

4. Click the Browse button ⇒ Select the Exported Exercise Data workbook.

5. On the Connection Managers tab, rename the Excel Connection Manager to `Excel exported exercises data`.

6. Right-click on the Excel Connection ⇒ Convert to Project Connection ⇒ Rename the connection to `Ch4 Destination Assistant`.

7. Rename the Excel Destination to `Exported exercises data`.

8. Connect the blue arrow from the AW source to the Exported exercises data destination.

Configure The Excel Destination File

In this part of the exercise, you will learn how to create a new table in the Excel workbook that the Order Header table will be written to.

1. Open the editor for the Excel destination file ⇒ Click the New button across from the Name of the Excel sheet field ⇒ Click OK when you see the warning shown in Figure 4-19.

   This is what I was talking about earlier when I referenced using Excel as the destination of data from a SQL Server database. The way to prevent this warning is to convert the fields.

   When you see this warning, click OK to complete the exercises in this book.

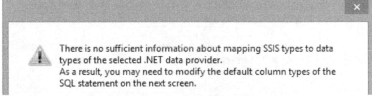

There is no sufficient information about mapping SSIS types to data types of the selected .NET data provider.
As a result, you may need to modify the default column types of the SQL statement on the next screen.

Figure 4-19 Mapping and column type warning

2. On the Create Table dialog box, change the table name to `E4.2_OrderHeader_Table`, as illustrated in Figure 4-20.

   This will be the name of the tab in the Excel workbook that will be created, for the data to be written to.

   Be careful not to delete the quotes around the table name ⇒ Click OK.

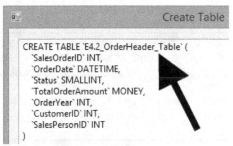

Create Table

```
CREATE TABLE `E4.2_OrderHeader_Table` (
    `SalesOrderID` INT,
    `OrderDate` DATETIME,
    `Status` SMALLINT,
    `TotalOrderAmount` MONEY,
    `OrderYear` INT,
    `CustomerID` INT,
    `SalesPersonID` INT
)
```

Figure 4-20 Layout for the new table in the workbook

 If you use table names with spaces or a period, you will get a warning saying to select a table name from the drop-down list. Instead of spaces, the standard is to use an underscore, as shown above in Figure 4-20. You can also use a dash.

3. Open the drop-down list and select the E4.2 table name with the dollar sign, as shown in Figure 4-21.

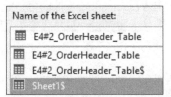

Name of the Excel sheet:

▦ E4#2_OrderHeader_Table
▦ E4#2_OrderHeader_Table
▦ E4#2_OrderHeader_Table$
▦ Sheet1$

Figure 4-21 Sheets to select from

Sheets that have a $ at the end of the name is a sheet in the workbook. Sheet names without a $ are a **NAMED RANGE**, on a sheet. A sheet can have more than one named range.

Check The Column Mappings

1. On the Mappings page, you should see that all of the fields have been mapped, as shown in Figure 4-22 ⇒ Click OK.

   If the Excel Destination button has a red circle with an X, in the upper right corner, there is a problem on the editor. Go back and check the options because the package probably will not run successfully.

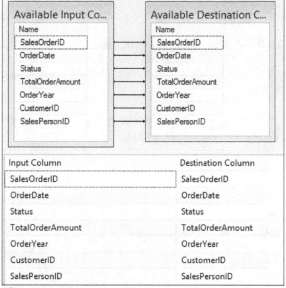

Figure 4-22 Mappings page

2. Run the package. You should see that 284 rows were written to the Excel workbook. Figure 4-23 shows the first few rows that were written to the table in the Excel workbook.

	A	B	C	D	E	F	G
1	SalesOrderID	OrderDate	Status	TotalOrderAmount	OrderYear	CustomerID	SalesPersonID
2	65152	2014-01-29 00:00:00	5	13183.2788	2014	29592	277
3	65154	2014-01-29 00:00:00	5	30071.8855	2014	30113	282
4	65155	2014-01-29 00:00:00	5	36923.8462	2014	29579	281
5	65156	2014-01-29 00:00:00	5	34047.5926	2014	29714	289

Sheet1   **E4.2_OrderHeader_Table**   ⊕

Figure 4-23 Data exported to Excel

Keep in mind that packages that write to an Excel destination do not drop (delete) the table before writing to it. This means that records are appended to the sheet, opposed to overwriting the existing data, each time the package is run. While many exercises in this book use the same Excel workbook as the destination file, on your own, this probably should not be done. I did it in this book to make it easier for you to find the table created in each exercise. When each package has it's own workbook, you can use the File System Task, to drop (delete) the workbook file, before running the tasks on the Data Flow tab. This lets you recreate the workbook each time the package is run.

Creating Connections
While this book has you creating (source and destination) connections, as they are needed, on your own, you will probably know most, if not all of the data files that will be used in the packages in a project. You will probably find it much easier and faster if you create them all as project level connections before creating any of the packages. Just remember to include the file or database name as part of the connection name. Doing this means that all of the connections will be on the Source and Destination Assistant dialog boxes, which saves you a step or two when selecting connection options.

Flat File Destination

A benefit that the Flat File Destination has is that you can select whether or not to overwrite data in the selected file. You can also create a custom header row. The flat file can be a delimited or fixed-width file. A delimited file uses special characters to define rows. Columns are usually delimited by a comma, but other characters can be used. A fixed-width file uses width measurements to define the columns.

Exercise 4.3: Export To A New CSV File

In this exercise, you will modify a package so that it writes data to a csv file.

1. Rename the copy of the E4.1 package to `E4.3 Write to a new csv file`.

2. Add the Flat File Destination component to the Data Flow tab ⇒ Rename the component to `Export to new csv file` ⇒ Connect it to the AW source.

3. On the Destination Editor, click the New button ⇒ In the Connection manager name field, type `Connect to order header csv file`.

4. In the File name field, type `C:\SSIS Book\Ch4 Orderheader.csv`. This is the name of the new csv file that will be created.

5. Check the Column names option.

   You should have the options shown in Figure 4-24 ⇒ Click OK.

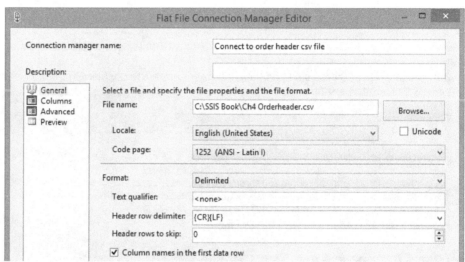

Figure 4-24 Flat File Connection Manager Editor

Figure 4-25 shows the editor. In this exercise, the **OVERWRITE DATA IN THE FILE** option should be checked because if the package will be run more than once (which it probably will), you want the data replaced with the latest data.

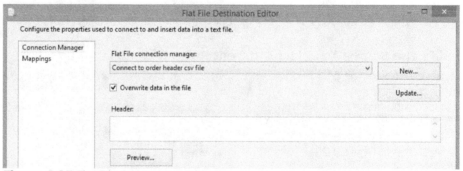

Figure 4-25 Flat File Destination Editor

If you are creating a package that you want to append the new data to the data already in the flat file, clear the check mark for this option.

The **UPDATE BUTTON** is used to create a package that will update (append records to) an existing data source. It also updates the meta data for a flat file.

The **HEADER FIELD** is a string field that is used to add text to the top of the flat file. What is entered in this field is written to the file before the data is written to the file. You could enter text like a report heading or column names if the source does not have them. You can create more than one row in this field.

The **PREVIEW BUTTON** displays the Data View dialog box. It displays some of the data that will be written to the destination table.

6. On the Mappings page, the columns should have automatically been mapped, as shown in Figure 4-26.

   This is because the destination table in this exercise is new. When updating an existing file, you may have to map fields.

   For example, if the field names in the source do not match the names in the destination file, or if new fields were created in a transformation and need to be written to an existing destination file.

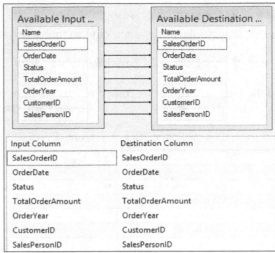

Figure 4-26 Column mappings

7. Run the package. 284 rows should have been written to the csv file. Figure 4-27 shows some of the records that were written to the csv file.

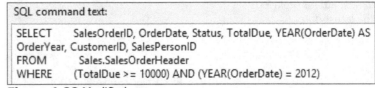

Figure 4-27 Records written to the csv file

Exercise 4.4: Append Rows To A CSV File

In the previous exercise, you learned how to configure a package to create a new csv destination file. In this exercise, you will create a package that will append rows of data to the csv file created in the previous exercise. To make things more interesting, you will modify the query for the source, to select rows of data for a different year.

Modify The Source To Select Different Rows Of Data

1. Save a copy of the E4.3 package as `E4.4 Append rows to a csv file`.

2. Open the Source Editor ⇒ In the SQL command text field, change the Year criteria on the last line to `2012`, as shown in Figure 4-28.

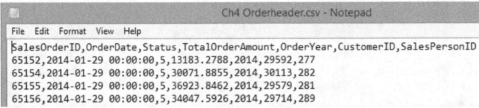

Figure 4-28 Modified query

Modify The Destination To Append Rows Of Data

1. Rename the Flat File destination component to `Append data to a csv file`.

2. On the destination editor, click the **UPDATE** button.

3. Clear the check mark for the Column names in the first data row option. The reason that you are clearing this option is because you do not want the column header row to be appended to the table. The first row of the table that the records will be written to, already has the headings. Well, at least it should have them. <smile> The File name field stays the same because it is the file that you want to append records to.

4. Click OK ⇒ Clear the check mark for the **OVERWRITE DATA IN THE FILE** option.

Map The Columns

Because this package will not write out the column names, the columns have to be mapped manually. As you will see, the destination table will not have column names. This is what should happen when appending data.

1. On the Mappings page, open the first drop-down list in the Input Column and select the Sales Order ID field. You will see that this is automatically mapped to Column 0.

2. Repeat the previous step for all of the fields in the drop-down list.

    Make sure to select the fields in the order that they are in.

    When finished, the Mappings page should look like the one shown in Figure 4-29.

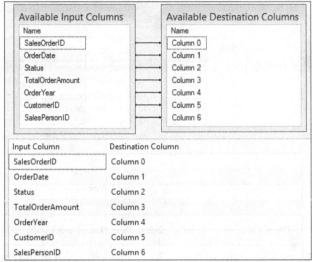

Figure 4-29 Mapping options when appending data

Preserve The Original File

In this part of the exercise, you will use the File System Task to create a folder and place a copy of the csv file that will be append to, in this exercise, in the new folder. Doing this will preserve the original file.

Create The Folder

In this part of the exercise, you will select the options to create a new folder. This is the folder that the file will be copied to.

1. On the Control Flow tab, add the File System Task ⇒ Place it above the Data Flow Task.

2. Rename the task, `Copy csv file to folder` ⇒ Connect the task to the Data Flow Task.

3. On the File System Task Editor, select the Copy file operation.

4. Open the Destination Connection drop-down list and select <New connection>.

5. Open the **USAGE TYPE** drop-down list and select Create folder.

6. In the Folder field type `C:\SSIS Book\Ch4 Exercise 4.3 destination file`, as shown in Figure 4-30. This is the exercise that the file was originally created in ⇒ Click OK.

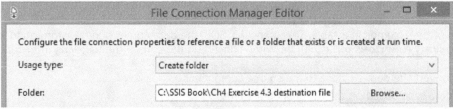

Figure 4-30 Options to create a new folder

7. Change the Overwrite Destination property to True.

Select The File To Copy To The New Folder

1. Open the Source Connection drop-down list and select <New connection>.

2. Click the Browse button ⇒ Navigate to your folder and select the Ch4 Orderheader.csv file ⇒ Click OK.
    You should have the options shown in Figure 4-31. The File System Task (Copy csv file to folder) needs to run
    before the records are appended to the destination file.

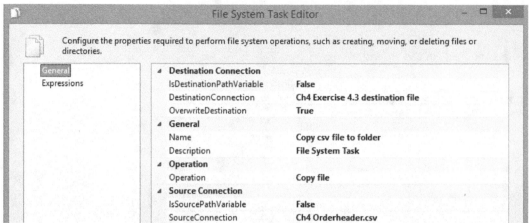

Figure 4-31 Options to create a new folder and copy an existing file to the new folder

3. Run the package. 618 rows should be appended to the csv file. To confirm, open the Ch4 Orderheader.csv file.
    At the top of the file you should see the header row and records with a date in 2014. Scroll down the file.
    You should not see another header row. The rows at the bottom of the file should have the year 2012.
    These are the records that were just appended to the file.

Transforming Data

So far, you have learned how to get data from one location to another. Often, you will have the need to reformat the
data before it is written to the destination file. The solution is to transform the data. For example, the data written to
a spreadsheet in Exercise 4.2 displays the date and time in a field and the currency data is displayed as a numeric
value. [See Figure 4-23] These are common types of transformations that need to be addressed.

Other types of transformations include, creating a new column in the destination table to store more data, sorting data
and combining data from multiple columns.

Understanding Data Types

Without a doubt, being able to select the appropriate data type in SSIS is one of the most used transformations for
data that is not from a database. Sadly, it is probably the most frustrating type of transformation, because if you get
it wrong, it can take a while to figure out. This web page has more information about Integration Services data types.
http://msdn.microsoft.com/en-us/library/ms141036.aspx.

Data Conversion

The Data Conversion transformation may be the most popular transformation, especially when the source data is not
in a database. That is because data that is not stored in a database is pretty much free form. This transformation is
used to change the columns data type. The good thing is that only one Data Conversion component is needed for a
table because it allows you to convert all of the fields in the table that need to be converted at the same time. It is
not a requirement to convert all of the columns in a table. If you know T-SQL, the data conversion transformation is
the equivalent of the **CAST** or **CONVERT FUNCTIONS** for a column. When converting data, keep the following in mind:

☑   As much as possible, convert the data as close to the source component as possible.
☑   Select the conversion data type based on the destination file type.
☑   Only convert columns that will be used in a calculation or written to the destination file.

SSIS Data Types

One thing that can be annoying (at least to me) is how SSIS handles SQL Server data types. Table 4-1 shows some data types and their SQL Server equivalent.

SSIS Data Type	Variable & Parameter Date Type	SQL Server Data Type
[DT_BOOL]	Boolean	Bit
[DT_DBTIMESTAMP]	Database time stamp	DateTime
[DT_I4]	Four-byte signed integer	Int
[DT_NUMERIC]	Numeric	Numeric or decimal
[DT_STR]	String	varchar
[DT_TEXT]	Text	Text
[DT_WSTR]	Unicode string	nvarchar

Table 4-1 SSIS data types

Exercise 4.5: Change The Data Type

Earlier, two fields in Exercise 4.2 were discussed as needing to be transformed. In this exercise, you will learn how to use the Data Conversion transformation to change the data type of a date field.

1.   Rename a copy of the E4.2 package to E4.5 Data conversion.

2.   Data Flow tab ⇒ Delete the destination task (Exported exercises data).

3.   Add the Data Conversion transformation ⇒ Rename it to Change the data type.

4.   Connect the AW database source to the Change the data type task.

Configure The Data Conversion Transformation

By default, the **OUTPUT ALIAS** name given to a column is "Copy of", plus the column name, as shown below in Figure 4-32. You could rename the column, but it is not a requirement. I do not rename these columns because I consider this a staging or intermediate task. That is because the columns in this task will be mapped to columns in the destination task. The column names in the destination task are the ones used to write the data to the destination file.

When columns are selected to be converted, SSIS will automatically select a data type. It may or may not be the data type that you need. You should confirm the data type, especially for the columns that you will use, and change the data type as needed.

The columns on the Data Conversion Transformation Editor explained below are used to further configure columns that are being converted.

The **LENGTH**, when used with the string data type, is used to list the maximum number of characters that can be stored in the field. When used with a numeric data type, it is used to enter the total bytes that are needed to store the number.

PRECISION is the total number of digits in a number, including the digits after the decimal point.

SCALE is used to enter the number of digits to store after the decimal point. For example, the number 12.345 has a scale of 3. If you only wanted to store two digits after the decimal point, change the Scale to 2.

CONFIGURE ERROR OUTPUT BUTTON Clicking this button opens a dialog box with the same name. It works the same as the one shown earlier in Figure 4-10.

1.   On the Data Conversion Transformation Editor, check the following fields: Sales Order ID, Order Date and Total Order Amount. The data type selected for the Sales Order ID and Total Order Amount fields is correct. On your own, you would probably convert all of these fields.

2.   Open the Data Type drop-down list for the Order Date field and select the **DATABASE DATE [DT_DBDATE]** option. This date data type will format the date without the time. You should have the options shown in Figure 4-32 ⇒ Click OK.

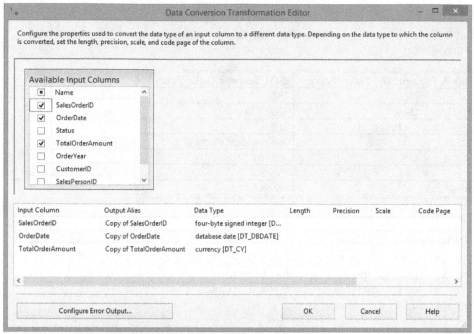

Figure 4-32 Data Conversion Transformation Editor options

Create The Destination Table

In this part of the exercise, you will create a new table in the destination file and map the fields that are used in the Data Conversion transformation. This exercise will create a new sheet in the Exported Exercise Data.xlsx file that you used in Exercise 4.2.

1. Add the Excel Destination component ⇒ Rename it to `Write out converted data`.

 By default when creating a destination table, the default name used is the name of the Excel Destination component. To keep from having to rename the table on the Create Table dialog box, you can use the name of the table that you want to create, as the component name. For example, in this exercise, the table name will be E4.5_ConvertedData. In step 1 above, this is what you would rename the component to.

2. Link the Data Conversion transformation to the Excel Destination. On the Excel Destination Editor, the Excel exported exercises data connection manager should be selected. This is the file that the new table will be created in.

3. Click the Excel sheet New button ⇒ Click OK on the Mapping warning dialog box ⇒ On the Create Table dialog box, change the table name to `E4.5_ConvertedData` ⇒ Leave the dialog box open to complete the remaining steps in this part of the exercise.

 Just like the Create Table dialog box on the Import and Export Wizard creates the table immediately, when the OK button on the Create Table dialog box, in the Excel destination is clicked, the table is also created immediately.

As you can see on the Create Table dialog box, the data types for two of the three fields that were selected to be converted in the previous part of this exercise are the same data type, as the original field. The only data type that changed was the Order Date field, which is the one that you manually changed. This is the field that will have to be mapped.

4. On the Create Table dialog box, delete the "Copy of" fields. The reason to delete fields is so that they will not be created in the destination table. Leaving the fields in this table, will create them in the destination table, but they would not have any data, in this exercise. That is because they will not be mapped to an input field.

5. Delete the comma after the Sales Person ID field.

6. Click OK twice ⇒ Open the Excel sheet drop-down list and select the E4.5 table with the dollar sign at the end of the name.

Change The Mappings

1. On the Mappings page, in the Input Column, change the <ignore>, to Copy of Order Date.

   The reason that this field is being mapped to the Order Date field is because it has the correct data type. You should have the mappings shown in Figure 4-33.

   I find modifying the table on the Create Table dialog box easier then making changes on the Mappings page.

   Hopefully, as you become more familiar with using the Create Table dialog box, you will see the benefits of using it, also. Figure 4-34 shows the original table that would have been created. (This is the table that you modified in the previous part of this exercise.)

   If you know what the data type should be, you can change it on the Create Table dialog box instead of using the Mappings page to remove fields and a transformation to change the data type. Figure 4-35 shows the modified table. Below are the changes that were made.

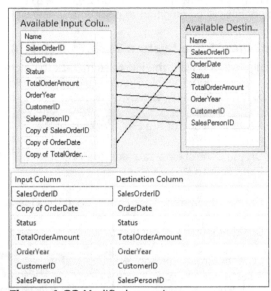

Figure 4-33 Modified mappings

☑ The data type of the Order Date field was changed to Date.
☑ The three "Copy of" fields were deleted.

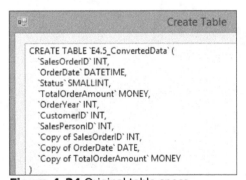

Figure 4-34 Original table specs

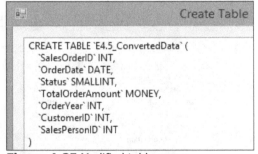

Figure 4-35 Modified table specs

2. Click OK ⇒ Run the package. You will see that 284 records went into the Data Conversion transformation and that 284 records were written to the new table.

Keep in mind that if this package is run again, the data will be appended to the E4.5 table (sheet) in the workbook. The Excel Destination component does not have an option to overwrite the existing table, like the Flat File Destination component has. The options are to use a Flat File Destination component to delete the sheet or the Script component to write a script that deletes the sheet.

An option if the destination file is only used for one package is to add the File System Task to the beginning of the Control Flow tab, to delete workbook. Then attach the File System Task to the Data Flow Task. This control flow will delete the Excel file, then complete the tasks on the Data Flow tab.

If the destination table was in an OLE DB data source, two Execute SQL Tasks could be created, one to drop (delete) the table and one to recreate the table, like the wizard did in Chapter 3 Exercise 3.6.

Exercise 4.6: Use The File System Task To Delete And Copy An Excel File

Earlier, you learned that the Excel Destination component does not have functionality to delete a workbook or sheet in a workbook. One solution is to use the File System Task to delete a workbook at the beginning of the control flow. Doing this will allow the destination Excel file to be written to without appending the data. The Excel Destination component will be modified to point to the new workbook.

Configure A File System Task To Delete A File

The file that you want the File System Task to delete must already exist. If it doesn't already exist, create it before trying to configure the File System Task. The Excel workbook that will be used in this exercise has already been created. It is an empty Excel workbook.

1. Rename a copy of the E4.5 package to `E4.6 Delete destination workbook`.

2. On the Control Flow tab, add the File System Task above the Data Flow Task ⇒
    Rename it to `Delete Excel Workbook`.

3. On the File System Task Editor, open the Operation drop-down list and select **DELETE FILE**.

4. Use the Source Connection property to create a new connection.

5. Click the Browse button ⇒
    Select the Ch4 File System
    Task Exercise.xlsx file.

    You should have the options
    shown in Figure 4-36.
    Figure 4-37 shows the task
    editor options ⇒ Click OK.

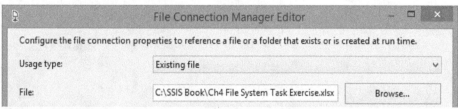

Figure 4-36 File Connection Manager

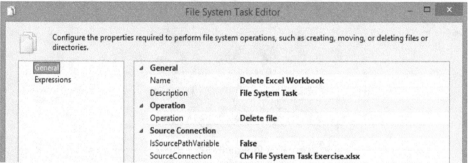

Figure 4-37 File System Task Editor delete file options

Configure A File System Task To Copy A File

Several options for resolving the issue of an Excel destination connection not being able to create a new file were discussed, at the end of the previous exercise. What you may not realize is that using the File System Task to delete the workbook only resolves part of the problem. There is no task that will create an excel workbook. While not the best solution, you could store a copy of the workbook in a different folder. After the File System Task that you created in the previous part of this exercise runs, you could use another File System Task to copy the copy of the workbook that is in another folder (In this exercise C:\SSIS Book\More Files\) to the C:\SSIS Book folder. Like I said, this is probably not the best solution, but it would work. The best solution is to write a script to drop the workbook, then recreate it.

1. Add a File System Task below the one created in the previous part of this exercise ⇒
    Rename it to `Copy Excel Workbook`.

2. Connect the Delete Excel Workbook task to the Copy Excel Workbook task.

3. On the File System Task editor for the Copy Excel Workbook task, open the Operation drop-down list and select Copy file.

4. Open the Destination Connection drop-down list and select <New connection> ⟹ Open the Usage type drop-down list and select Existing folder.

5. Click the Browse button and select the SSIS Book folder. This is the folder that the file will be copied to.

6. Change the Overwrite Destination property to True.

7. Open the Source Connection drop-down list ⟹ Select <New connection> ⟹ The Existing file option should be selected. Select the SSIS Book\More Files folder. This is the folder that has the file that will be copied to the destination folder selected in step 5. ⟹ Select the Ch4 File System Task Exercise workbook. You should have the options shown in Figure 4-38 ⟹ Click OK.

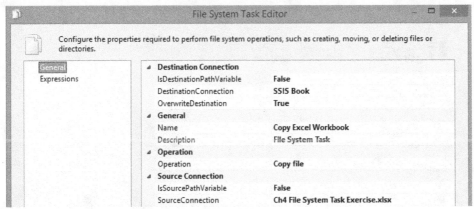

Figure 4-38 File System Task copy file to folder options

8. Connect the Copy Excel Workbook to the Data Flow task.

Modify The Excel Destination

In this part of the exercise, you will learn how to modify the destination so that it points to the workbook shown above in Figure 4-38.

1. On the Data Flow tab, open the editor for the Excel destination component.

2. Click the New button to create a new connection manager ⟹ Click the Browse button ⟹ Select the Ch4 File System Task Exercise workbook in the SSIS Book folder ⟹ Click OK.

3. Click the New button to create a new sheet (table) in the workbook ⟹
    Make the following changes, as illustrated in Figure 4-39.

    ☑ Change the table name to E4.6_ConvertedData.
    ☑ Change the data type of the Order Date field to Date.
    ☑ Delete the three "Copy of" fields. [See the bottom of Figure 4-34] Make sure that you delete the comma at the end of the Sales Person ID field.

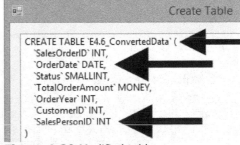

Figure 4-39 Modified table

4. In the Excel sheet drop-down list, select the E4.6 sheet.

   You should have the options shown in Figures 4-40 and 4-41 ⇒ Click OK.

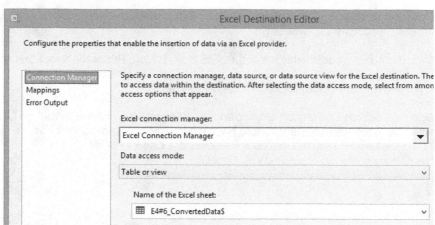

Figure 4-40 Connection Manager page options

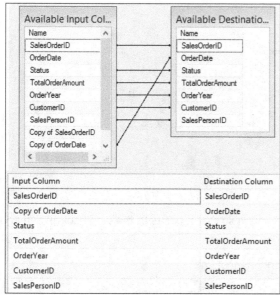

Figure 4-41 Mappings page options

5. On the Connection Managers tab, rename the Excel connection manager connection to Ch4 File System Task data connection.

6. Run the package.

Derived Column Transformation

In Chapter 2, you used this transformation to combine the data from two fields to create a new field. This transformation has a lot more functionality and is one that you will probably use a lot, especially if you do not know T-SQL. It is used to create what is known as a **CALCULATED COLUMN**. This transformation can be used to replace data in an existing column or create new columns of data.

It can also be used to add today's date to the column, fill in the column when it is NULL (does not have data) or to create a calculation and store the result in the new column. In addition to creating new data, this transformation can also replace data (also known as an **IN PLACE UPDATE**), in an existing column.

The Derived Column transformation has math, string, data and null functions. If you click on a function, a description of what the function does is displayed on the Derived Column Transformation Editor. Table 4-2 shows some functions and expressions and explains what they do.

Function/Expression	Description
YEAR([Order Date])	Extracts the year from the date field and puts the year in the derived column. You saw this in use, earlier in Figure 4-28.
DATEDIFF("dd", [Order Date], [Shipped Date])	Calculates the difference between the two date fields and places the difference in the derived column. "dd" returns the difference between the dates in days. "mm" returns the difference between the dates in the number of months.
ISNULL([Zip Code]) ? "None" : Zip Code	If the Zip Code field is null (empty), replace the null value with the word None, otherwise, keep the existing data.
ROUND([Sales Tax], 2)	Rounds the value in the Sales Tax field to only have two decimal places.
SUBSTRING([First Name], 1,1) + " " +[Last Name])	Extracts the first letter from the First Name field, then adds a space and the contents of the Last Name field. For example, the column would have C Brown.
GETDATE()	Returns the current date.
DATEPART("dd", GETDATE()) = 1	This boolean expression checks to see if the current day is the first day of the month. This expression is often used to run certain tasks on the first day of the month.

Table 4-2 Functions and expressions explained

Function Differences Between T-SQL And SSIS
If you have used T-SQL, there are some differences in how some of the functions work.
① In T-SQL, creating an expression that uses string fields are created by using single quotes. In SSIS, double quotes are used, as shown above in Table 4-2.
② In SSIS, the **DATEPART FUNCTION** is required to extract any part of the date, except the month, day or year.

ISNULL Function Differences In SSIS
① The ISNULL function returns true or false, when testing for a null value.
② While this function tests an expression for a null value, it does not allow for a default value, like it does in T-SQL.

A common use of the **ISNULL FUNCTION** in the Derived Column transformation is to fill in fields that do not have data.

The **REPLACE NULL FUNCTION** provides the same functionality as the ISNULL function, shown above in Table 4-2. You may find it a littler easier to use. The syntax is REPLACE NULL (<<expression>>, <<expression>>). The first expression is the value to check for. The second expression is the value to use to replace it with, if the value is null. REPLACENULL ([Zip Code], None) accomplishes the same functionality as the ISNULL expression in Table 4-2.

Type Casts Functions

The functions in this category are used to convert values in an expression, so that they are compatible with the columns data type. This is known as **CASTING**, which is the process of defining the data type for an expression or value. For example, the **DT_WSTR** function converts the month number to a string.

Expression Operators

In addition to functions, the editor also has the operators shown in Figure 4-42. I find it easier to type them in, opposed to dragging them into the Expression column on the editor.

The **CONDITIONAL OPERATOR** was used with the ISNULL function, above in Table 4-2.

You may have used the operators in Table 4-3, but used different characters to create the expression. These operators are also used in the **CONDITIONAL SPLIT TRANSFORMATION**, that is covered in the next chapter.

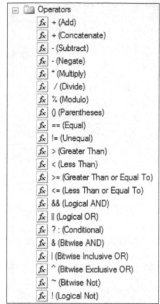

Figure 4-42 Operators

Operator	Description
||	The vertical bars are used between conditions to create an **OR** expression.
&&	The ampersands are used between conditions to create an **AND** expression.
==	Compares the values to see if they are equal. (1)
!=	Compares the values to see if they are not equal.
?:	Is used to create a conditional expression. This operator works like an If . . . Then . . . Else statement.

Table 4-3 Expression operators explained

 (1)   Not typing two equal signs when using a variable in the expression, will cause the value in the variable to be overwritten. This will not generate an error and the task will continue to run.

Derived Column Transformation Editor

Figure 4-43 shows the editor. The expression language that the editor uses is C# based syntax, but there are some differences. The sections of the editor are explained below.

The upper left section has the variables, parameters and columns that you can use to create expressions. The Columns folder has the fields in the data source. I tend to keep the Columns folder open so that I can type in the field names correctly or drag a field to the Expression column.

The upper right section contains the functions and operators that can be used to create an expression.

The lower section is where you create the expressions. You can create as many expressions (for the table) that you need. If you need to copy or delete an expression, right-click on the row and select the option.

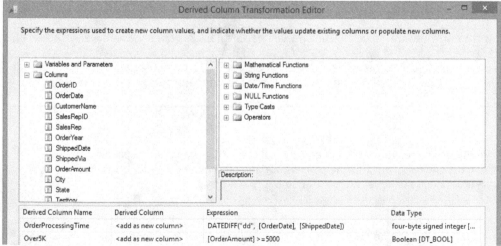

Figure 4-43 Derived Column Transformation Editor

    The font color of expressions are displayed in red until it meets the syntax requirements and you click in another column. Keep in mind that even though an expression meets the syntax requirements, it may not produce the result that you are expecting, when the package is run.

The Derived Column Transformation Editor does not have functionality to let you test the expressions that you create. This is because data is not available. You have to run the package to test expressions. When possible, a work around is to create the expression outside of the Derived Column Transformation Editor, then use the expression as a variable in the Derived Column Transformation Editor.

Exercise 4.7: Create Derived Columns

In this exercise, you will learn how to use the Derived Column transformation to calculate the difference in days between the Order Date and Shipped Date and find the largest orders based on the Order Amount.

Create A Date Expression To Calculate The Order Processing Time

In this part of the exercise you will create an expression to find out how long it is between the day an order is placed and the day the order was shipped. This is known as the order processing time. The result of this expression can be used to let you know if the expected number of days orders need to be shipped in, is met. For example, if all orders need to be shipped in three days, any order with an order processing time greater than three days in the derived column, indicates that the order was not shipped within the expected time frame.

1. Rename a copy of the E3.4 package to E4.7 Derived columns.

2. On the Data Flow tab, add the Derived Column transformation ⇒ Connect it to the Excel Source.

3. On the Derived Column Transformation Editor, type OrderProcessingTime in the Derived Column Name field. Accept the default new column option.

When creating new data, it is not a requirement to use the corresponding name in the table that the data will be added to. Just remember the name that you used, so that you can map it correctly.

4. In the Expression column, type DATEDIFF("dd", [OrderDate], [ShippedDate]).

Find The Largest Orders Based On The Order Amount

In this part of the exercise, you will create an expression to find the orders that have an amount over $5,000. The orders that meet this criteria will have the word True added to the derived column, otherwise False will be written to the column. For example, an expression like this is often done to create a customer mailing or email list for the marketing department to create a promotion for. This type of expression is a **BOOLEAN EXPRESSION**. This means that the expression created must evaluate to true or false.

1. On the next row, type Over5K in the first column. Accept the new column option.

2. Drag the Order Amount field from the Columns folder to the Expression column.

3. Click after the Order Amount field ⇒ Type >=5000. You should have the expressions shown earlier, at the bottom of Figure 4-43.

 Add As New Column Option
What may not be obvious is that the **<ADD AS NEW COLUMN>** name is somewhat misleading. It does not actually create a new column in the destination table, unless you are creating a new table in the destination file. The option is used to create an expression, that creates the new data for an existing column in a table. This means that you have to create the column in the destination table, if it does not already exist, to use this feature. Otherwise, the package will run, but the new data will not be added to the table.

Set Up The Destination

In this part of the exercise, you will create the destination table that will include the fields created in the derived column transformation.

1. Add the Excel Destination component ⇒ Rename it to Write to exported exercises data.

2. Connect it to the Derived Column transformation.

3. On the editor, in the Excel connection manager drop-down list, select the Excel exported exercises data connection.

4. Click the Excel sheet New button ⇒ Change the table name to `E4.7_Derived Data`.

5. Select the E4.7 Derived Data sheet in the last drop-down list on the editor.

6. On the Mappings page, confirm that the derived columns are mapped. If not, map them now.

7. Run the package. When complete, you should see the output shown in Figure 4-44, on the Debug mode window.

    If you look in the Exported Exercise Data workbook, you will see the data shown in Figure 4-45, on the E4.7_Derived Data sheet.

    If you scroll down the sheet, you will see different values in the Order Processing Time column. I hid some columns to make it easier to see the columns of interest, for this exercise.

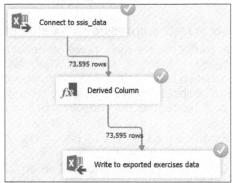

Figure 4-44 Output from the package

	A	B		D	F	G	H	I
1	OrderDate	CustomerName	SalesRep	ShippedDate	OrderAmount	OrderProcessingTime	Over5K
234	01/03/2013	Wingtip Toys (Homer City, PA	Kayla Woodcock	01/04/2013	15992.74	1	True
235	01/03/2013	Wingtip Toys (Mauldin, SC)	Lily Code	01/04/2013	8.04	1	False
236	01/03/2013	Svetlana Todorovic	Amy Trefl	01/04/2013	612.14	1	False
237	01/04/2013	Tailspin Toys (Maple Shade, N	Sophia Hinton	01/07/2013	77.32	3	False
238	01/04/2013	Wingtip Toys (Bethel Acres, C	Jack Potter	01/07/2013	15.45	3	False
239	01/04/2013	Tailspin Toys (Howells, NE)	Archer Lamble	01/07/2013	30.14	3	False
240	01/04/2013	Wingtip Toys (Goodings Grove	Taj Shand	01/07/2013	6.94	3	False
241	01/04/2013	Tailspin Toys (Caselton, NV)	Kayla Woodcock	01/07/2013	8773.68	3	True

Figure 4-45 Derived Column data written to the spreadsheet

Excel Files
If you are running a package that uses an Excel file for the source or destination, make sure that Excel is closed. If it is open when the package is run, the package will display errors in the Output window. If Excel is closed and you still get the file locked error, close and reopen Visual Studio.

Data Viewer

This tool is used to look at the data during the execution phase of a package. Data viewers are used to view data as the package is running. A package can have more than one data viewer. As you have seen, the Data Flow Task moves the data in the source to a transformation, then to a destination. If you had anything go wrong with the exercises that write data to a table, so far in this book, you may find it helpful to be able to see the data before it was written to the table.

It is not uncommon for a package to have two or more transformations. Wouldn't you like to see why a field in the destination table does not have any data? It would be helpful to see which transformation is not working as expected. Being able to see the data when it is moving through the package would be helpful. This is where data viewers come in. When they are added to a package, a window will open, in the debug mode, that displays the data.

Setting Up A Data Viewer

Data viewers are added to the blue or red arrows between tasks on the Data Flow tab, by double-clicking on the arrow. Doing this displays the dialog box shown in Figure 4-46. The content on each page is explained below.

The **GENERAL PAGE** displays the common data flow properties.

The **METADATA PAGE** shown in Figure 4-47, displays the metadata for each column that is in the flow, at that point. Metadata is data about other data. As shown in the figure, the characteristics for each field are displayed. Often, the value in one of these columns can be the reason why a package is not running as expected.

The **DATA VIEWER PAGE** shown in Figure 4-48, is used to display the data viewer in the debug mode window, when the package is run. The Columns to display section is used to select which columns will appear on the data viewer and in what order the columns will be displayed on the viewer. You do not have to display all of the columns in the data viewer.

After you have selected the options on the Data Flow Path Editor, a button with a magnifying glass is displayed on the data flow arrow, as illustrated in Figure 4-49.

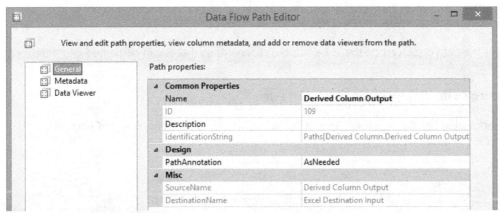

Figure 4-46 Data Flow Path Editor

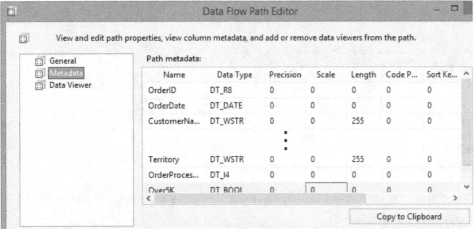

Figure 4-47 Metadata page

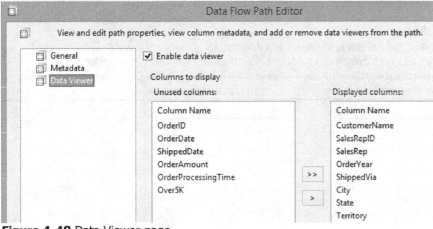

Figure 4-48 Data Viewer page

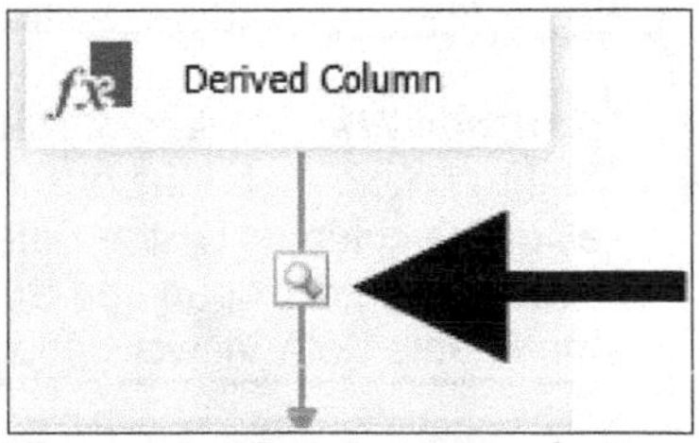

Figure 4-49 Data Viewer button

How The Data Viewer Works

When the package is run, the Data Viewer stops the processing at approximately 10,000 rows of data and displays the window shown in Figure 4-50. This is so that you can view the data. The number of rows will change, if the buffer size of the data flow has been changed, or if the table does not have 10,000 records.

Clicking the **ARROW BUTTON** will display more data.

The **DETACH BUTTON** separates the data viewer from the debugging process and allows the package to continue running without viewing any more data in the data viewer. Clicking this button does not close the viewer.

The **COPY DATA BUTTON**, copies the data displayed on the viewer to the clipboard, so that it can be pasted into a file, like Excel.

You can sort the data by clicking on the **COLUMN HEADINGS** on the viewer.

Figure 4-51 shows that the processing has been paused. The circles on the in the upper right corner of each task actually spin when the processing is paused.

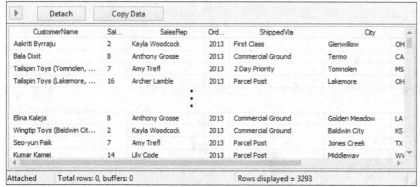

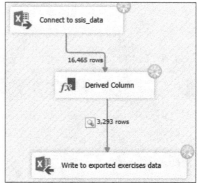

Figure 4-50 Data Viewer window   **Figure 4-51** Processing paused

How To Remove The Data Viewer

When you are finished using a Data Viewer, you should remove it from the package.

1. When the process has finished, display the Data Flow tab in design mode (click on the package execution link).

2. Double-click on the Data Viewer button to open the Data Flow Path Editor.

3. On the Data Viewer page, clear the check mark for the Enable data viewer option.

Another Way To Add A Data Viewer
Right-clicking on a blue or red arrow and selecting **ENABLE DATA VIEWER**, as shown in Figure 4-52, will display all of the columns on the Data Viewer. This option does not initially allow you to select any options on the editor. The **EDIT** option on the shortcut menu, opens the Data Flow Path Editor. If the Data Viewer is enabled, the Enable Data Viewer option on the shortcut menu changes to **DISABLE DATA VIEWER**.

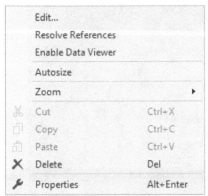

Edit...	
Resolve References	
Enable Data Viewer	
Autosize	
Zoom	▶
✂ Cut	Ctrl+X
📋 Copy	Ctrl+C
📋 Paste	Ctrl+V
✕ Delete	Del
🔧 Properties	Alt+Enter

Figure 4-52 Data flow line shortcut menu

 Data viewers should be removed before putting a package into production. When a package is in production, it will not stop at a point where a data viewer is. Instead, the Data Viewer is loaded into memory, which will use additional memory, thus slowing down the processing in the package.

Exercise 4.8: Use A Derived Column To Date Stamp Rows Of Data

In Exercise 4.3 you created the Ch4 Orderheader.csv destination file. Initially, it only had rows written to it if the Order Date year was 2014. In Exercise 4.4, you modified the query to only write/append rows that had an order year of 2012. In this scenario, there is no way to know what rows were written to the csv file when.

When data can be appended to a table at different times, it is a common practice to also write today's date, for each row that is written to the file. This is often done for auditing purposes.

In this exercise, you will modify the E4.4 package to include a derived column that will have today's date in the field. To add this new column, a new table in the database will be created. On your own, you may want to use the source table as the destination table. If that is the case, the new field has to be added to the source table.

Create The Date Derived Column

1. Save a copy of the E4.4 package as `E4.8 Date added derived column`.

2. On the Data Flow tab, delete the destination.

3. Add the Derived Column transformation ⇒ Connect it to the source.

4. On the Derived Column transformation editor, in the Derived Column name field, type `DateRowAdded`.

5. In the Expression field, type `GETDATE()`, as shown in Figure 4-53. This function retrieves today's date from your computers operating system.

Derived Column Name	Derived Column	Expression	Data Type
DateRowAdded	<add as new column>	GETDATE()	database timestamp [DT_DBTIMESTAMP]

Figure 4-53 Expression to get today's date

Create The Destination Table

1. Add a destination connection to the OLE DB AW database (Hint: You can use the Destination Assistant) ⇒ Connect it to the Derived Column transformation.

2. On the OLE DB Editor, click the second New button (across from the Table name drop-down list).

3. Change the table name to `TrackDateAdded`, as shown in Figure 4-54 ⇒ Click OK.

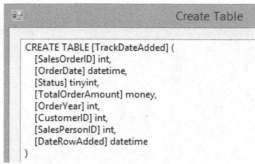

Figure 4-54 Table name changed

4. On the Mappings page, confirm that all of the fields have been mapped ⇒ Click OK.

5. Add a data viewer after the derived column.

6. Run the package ⇒ The last column in the data viewer should have today's date, as shown in Figure 4-55. The next time the package is run, you will see the current date and time in the Date Row Added column for the new rows that are written to the table.

SalesOrderID	OrderDate	Status	TotalOrderAmount	OrderYear	CustomerID	SalesPersonID	DateRowAdded
45266	2012-01-01 ...	5	27605.6261	2012	29955	275	2017-11-19 15:21:14.649
45270	2012-01-01 ...	5	32394.8687	2012	29888	279	2017-11-19 15:21:14.649
45273	2012-01-01 ...	5	45754.8749	2012	29717	283	2017-11-19 15:21:14.649
45274	2012-01-01 ...	5	75434.2741	2012	29818	276	2017-11-19 15:21:14.649

Figure 4-55 Date Row Added column updated with today's date

Copy Column Transformation

This transformation creates a copy of the data in a column. This is helpful when you need to keep the original data intact and want to create a complex calculation.

While the data from a column can be copied to a new column using the Derived Column transformation, the Copy Column transformation is easier to set up. Figure 4-56 shows the editor.

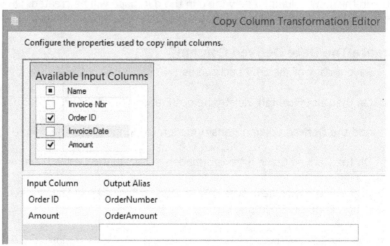

Figure 4-56 Copy Column Transformation Editor

USING THE DATA FLOW TAB TO CLEAN AND TRANSFORM DATA

After reading this chapter and completing the exercises, you will know how to use the following transformations:

- ☑ Character Map
- ☑ Sort
- ☑ Aggregate
- ☑ Conditional Split
- ☑ Pivot
- ☑ Unpivot
- ☑ Audit

CHAPTER 5

Transformations

The previous chapter covered some of the transformations that are available. This chapter picks up where that chapter left off. Hopefully, you are starting to see some of the power that transformations add to getting the data the way that you need it to be. While the majority of exercises only cover one transformation, it is done on purpose.

The reason is that when first learning a software package, it is easier to focus on one task (no pun intended) at a time. Then, when you are familiar with several tasks, you can determine which ones you need to use in one package to accomplish the goal of the package. So, to answer the questions, yes, multiple tasks can be used in the same package.

Quiet as it's kept, there are two categories of transformations, as explained below.

① **ASYNCHRONOUS TRANSFORMATIONS** There are two types of asynchronous transformations:

PARTIALLY BLOCKING creates new memory buffers for the output of the transformation. The Union All transformation is an example.

FULLY BLOCKING reads all of the data into memory before any processing occurs. The transformations in this category can and often do slow down the processing of data in the package. That is because this type of transformation often requires a lot of memory. The Aggregate and Sort transformations are examples. The reason that these transformations require a lot of memory is because they have to read the entire data set into memory before any processing can occur. In order to sort the records, all of the records have to be available to reorder them. The larger the data set, the longer the processing time will be and the more the amount of memory required increases.

While these transformations exist, on your own, it may be a good idea to create this type of processing outside of SSIS. For example, creating queries to sort or aggregate large data sets, in SSMS and writing the data to a temporary table, then use the temporary table in SSIS to complete the other tasks in the package.

② **SYNCHRONOUS TRANSFORMATIONS** The transformations in this category process much faster then asynchronous transformations because the data is processed one row at a time. This means that much less memory is required, because the rows of data are only held in memory for a short period of time. Synchronous transformations do not block the pipeline while it is running.

Using the Data Viewer tool illustrates this concept. By default, it reads in approximately 10,000 rows at a time, process those rows, releases them, then processes the next batch of rows. Because of the speed that they are processed, synchronous transformations are preferred. Data Conversion and Derived Columns are examples of synchronous transformations.

Transformations are mini applications that have pre-written code to accomplish a task. This keeps you from having to write all of the code and testing it yourself. This allows you to focus on the package requirements, without having to write and maintain a lot of code.

> **Order Of Transformations**
> While not a requirement, it is a good idea to put transformations that remove or filter out rows of data immediately after the source component. Doing this reduces the number of rows of data that the other transformations have to process, thus allowing the package to process faster.

Character Map

This transformation is used to change character data by using string functions. Some of the options are the same as ones that are available in the Derived Column transformation. The difference is that the Character Map transformation does not have expression functionality. Like the Derived Column transformation, the Character Map transformation has options to change the data in an existing column (in-place change) or save the data changes in a new column. When creating a new column of data, type in the new column in the **OUTPUT ALIAS** column.

The two operations that you may find the most helpful are: **LOWERCASE**, which converts the text to all lower case letters and **UPPERCASE**, which converts the text to all capital letters.

Exercise 5.1: Convert Data To Upper Case

In this exercise, you will learn how to use the Character Map transformation to convert the data in a column to all upper case letters. You will also learn how to update the data in place. **IN-PLACE** means that the transformation will change the current data in the column. Do this with caution because you are over writing the existing data. The benefit of updating data in place is that you do not have to create a destination component to write the data out to.

1. Rename a new package to `E5.1 Convert string data`.

2. Use the Data Flow Task to create a source connection to the AW database, which already has a project connection manager set up.

3. On the OLE DB Source Editor, select the Order Info table.

4. Add the Character Map transformation ⇒ Connect it to the source connection ⇒ Rename the transformation to `Change city to capital letters`.

5. On the editor, check the City column.

6. Change the Destination to **IN-PLACE CHANGE**.

7. Check the Uppercase operation, as shown in Figure 5-1 ⇒ Click OK twice.

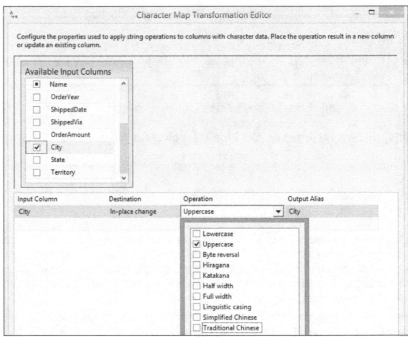

Figure 5-1 Character Map Transformation Editor

8. Add the Union All transformation and connect it to the Character Map transformation.

9. Add a Data Viewer after the Character Map transformation.

10. Run the package.

    You should see that the City field is all capital letters, as shown in Figure 5-2.

OrderDate	CustomerName	OrderAmount	City	State
2013-04-19 ...	Tailspin Toys (Ward Ridge...	30.14	WARD RIDGE	FL
2013-04-19 ...	Wingtip Toys (Athol Sprin...	6551.01	ATHOL SPRINGS	NY
2013-04-19 ...	Wingtip Toys (Gilford, NH)	36.94	GILFORD	NH
2013-04-19 ...	Gasper Havzija	622.07	SHELL KNOB	MO
2013-04-19 ...	Tailspin Toys (Heilwood, PA)	33.14	HEILWOOD	PA

Figure 5-2 City field converted to uppercase

Sort

Surprisingly, this transformation is used to sort data, in ascending or descending order, on as many columns as you need. <smile>

Figure 5-3 shows the Sort Transformation Editor. As stated earlier, this transformation will slow the performance of the package. If you are using an OLE DB source, it is more efficient to create a query and use an ORDER BY clause to sort the data.

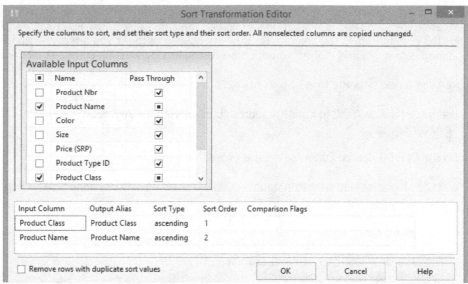

Figure 5-3 Sort Transformation Editor

 While the Sort transformation is discouraged, the Merge and Merge Join transformations, require data to be sorted. If the data source that you are using is not an OLE DB source, you will probably have to use the Sort transformation.

The **PASS THROUGH** option is used to select whether or not a column should be passed to the next task in the package. By default, all columns are checked, which means that every column would be sent to the next task. As you check the field(s) that will be sorted on, the Pass Through check mark is automatically removed.

The **OUTPUT ALIAS** column is used to give a column being sorted on, a different name. Doing this is optional.

The **SORT ORDER** column is used to indicate the order that the columns should be sorted in, when more than one column is being used to sort on.

If checked, the **REMOVE ROWS WITH DUPLICATE SORT VALUES** option prevents other rows with the same value in the column(s) being sorted on, from being passed to the next task in the package. This option can be used to remove the row from the sort process, meaning duplicate rows (based on the values, in columns being sorted on) will not be available for transformations or destinations that come after the Sort transformation. The duplicate rows are not deleted from the source file.

Exercise 5.2: Sort On Two Columns

In this exercise, you will use the Sort transformation to sort on two columns. The data will be sorted on the Product Class and Product Name columns, in ascending order.

1. Rename a copy of the E3.2 package to `E5.2 Two column sort`.

2. Add the Sort transformation ⇒ Rename it to `2 column sort` ⇒ Connect it to the Flat File source.

3. On the transformation editor, check the Product Class column ⇒ Check the Product Name column. You should have the options shown earlier in Figure 5-3 ⇒ Click OK.

4. Set up a Data Viewer after the Sort transformation.

 It will be easier to see if the Sort is working as expected, if the columns are displayed (from left to right) in the order that the data is sorted on. It is not a requirement to do this for a sort. It just makes it easier to see the records sorted. It may also help you determine if the table has duplicate rows of data, if the Remove rows option is **NOT** checked.

5. Run the package.

   The data should be sorted, as shown in Figure 5-4.

   As you can see, some of the products have a numeric class, while the majority of rows have a name in the class. This means that the data needs to be cleaned.

Product Class	Product Name	Size	Price (SRP)
1	Descent	15	"$2
1	Descent	15	"$2
1	Descent	20	"$2
1	Mozzie	15	"$1
1	Mozzie	20	"$1
1	Mozzie	17	"$1
1	Mozzie	22	"$1
1	Mozzie	18.5	"$1
Accessory	"Guardian ""U"" Lock"		$17.50
Accessory	"Guardian XL ""U"" Lock"		$19.90
Accessory	Active Outdoors Crochet Glove	lrg	$14.50
Accessory	Active Outdoors Crochet Glove	med	$14.50
Accessory	Active Outdoors Crochet Glove	xsm	$14.50

Figure 5-4 Data sorted on two columns

Exercise 5.3: Use A Query To Sort The Data

The previous exercise showed you how to use the Sort transformation, which at best, should only be used for small data sets. This exercise will show you how to use the ORDER BY clause in a query, to sort the data. Don't worry. If writing code is not your thing yet, I will show you how to create the sort criteria using the Query Builder.

In this exercise, you will learn how to use the ORDER BY clause to sort on the Year column in ascending order, then sort the Total Due column in descending order. This sort criteria will display the data by year, with the orders with the largest Total Due amounts displayed at the beginning of each years data.

1. Rename a copy of the E4.5 package to E5.3 Sort using ORDER BY.

2. Delete the Data Conversion and destination components.

3. On the editor, delete the WHERE clause.

4. On a new line at the end of the query type ORDER BY OrderYear, TOTALDUE DESC.

DESC is short for descending. This is how the data in the TOTAL Due field will be sorted. The default sort order is ascending. You do not have to type anything after a field name, to sort in ascending order.

The query should look like the one shown in Figure 5-5.

```
SELECT      SalesOrderID, OrderDate, Status, TotalDue, YEAR(OrderDate) AS OrderYear,
CustomerID, SalesPersonID
FROM        Sales.SalesOrderHeader
ORDER BY  OrderYear, TotalDue DESC
```

Figure 5-5 Query to sort on two fields

You have to admit, creating the sort criteria was not that bad. Order Year is the alias name for the Year(OrderDate) formula. It is not a requirement to use an alias name when creating a query. You could type YEAR(OrderDate) on the Order BY clause and get the same result. As shown on the first line of code in the figure, the alias name is shown.

Truth be told, it takes longer to create the sort on the Query Builder, then it does to type in the ORDER BY statement, but it will do, until you learn T-SQL. <smile>

If you click the Build Query button, you will see the grid shown in Figure 5-6.

The options selected in the Sort Type and Sort Order columns, are the options that you would have to select to create the ORDER BY clause from scratch.

Column	Alias	Table	Outp...	Sort Type	Sort Order
SalesOrderID		SalesOrder...	✔		
OrderDate		SalesOrder...	✔		
Status		SalesOrder...	✔		
TotalDue		SalesOrder...	✔	Descending	2
YEAR(OrderDate)	OrderYear		✔	Ascending	1
CustomerID		SalesOrder...	✔		

Figure 5-6 Query Builder options to create a sort for two fields

If you click the Preview button on the source editor, you will see the dialog box shown in Figure 5-7.

If you look at the values in the Total Due column, you will see that they are in descending order. The preview only displays the first 200 records. If you ran the query in the Query Builder, you could scroll down the results area and be able to see that rows for the new year are also in descending order, by the Total Due value.

Preview Query Results

Query result (up to the first 200 rows):

SalesOrderID	OrderDate	Status	TotalDue	OrderYear
44518	10/01/2011 ...	5	142312.2199	2011
43875	07/01/2011 ...	5	137343.2877	2011
43884	07/01/2011 ...	5	130416.4829	2011
44528	10/01/2011 ...	5	122500.6617	2011

Figure 5-7 Preview Query Results dialog box

Now that the data is sorted, on your own, you would add the other transformations that are needed to complete the package.

OLE DB Source And Sorting

As briefly covered earlier, an OLE DB source can sort the data, instead of using the Sort transformation. Creating a query to sort the data here is best, especially when another transformation requires the data to be sorted. What is interesting, is that SSIS is not aware of **ORDER BY STATEMENTS**. To make SSIS aware of an Order By statement, meaning that the data is already sorted, you have to complete the steps below. You do not have to complete these steps now. On your own, you would.

1. Create the query, including the ORDER BY clause in the OLE DB source.

2. Open the Advanced Editor for the OLE DB source.

3. On the Input and Output Properties tab ⇒ Click on the OLE DB Source Output option ⇒ Change the **IS SORTED PROPERTY** to True, as illustrated in Figure 5-8.

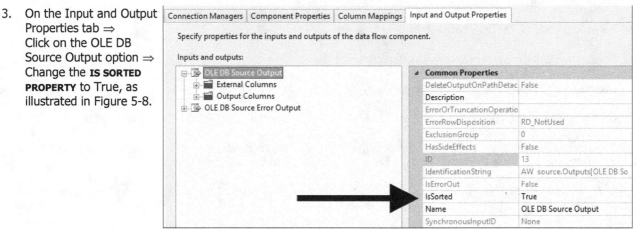

Figure 5-8 OLE DB Source Output option to change

4. Expand the **OUTPUT COLUMNS FOLDER**, shown above in Figure 5-8 ⇒ Click on the column that you sorted on, in the ORDER BY line in the query ⇒ Change the **SORT KEY POSITION PROPERTY**, illustrated in Figure 5-9, as follows:

    ☑ Type 1, if you are only sorting on one column, in ascending order.

    ☑ Type –1, if you are only sorting on one column, in descending order.

    ☑ If sorting on two or more columns, type in the number that corresponds to the position of the column in the ORDER BY statement. For example, if the statement is ORDER BY Customer Name, Order ID, Order Date, you would type in the following:
    Customer Name 1
    Order ID 2
    Order Date 3
    If any columns are sorted in descending order, type a - (a dash) before the number above.

    ☑ If the column is not sorted, the value of the Sort Key Position property should be zero.

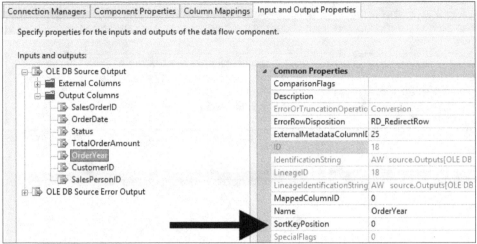

Figure 5-9 Sort Key Position property illustrated

Aggregate Transformation

This transformation is often used with a large data set. The groups that are created, create a summary of the data based on the rows used to create the group. Each group will display one row of data after the data is transformed. If you have used the a **GROUP BY CLAUSE** in T-SQL, you are familiar with the Aggregate transformation. Like a Group By clause, only columns that are being grouped on or aggregated are returned (displayed). Any columns that are not used are not sent to the next task in the data flow.

This is a popular and powerful transformation and is better suited for data that is not in a database. This transformation takes sorting one step further by creating a summary (a total) for rows that have a common value in the field(s) being grouped on.

This transformation will remind you of a **PIVOT TABLE** and the **PIVOT TRANSFORMATION** covered later in this chapter. Creating a SQL Group BY statement, is a better solution for data in a database. Figure 5-10 shows a Group BY query. Figure 5-11 shows the output from the query.

```
SELECT  Application.People.FullName AS SalesRep, YEAR(Sales.Orders.OrderDate) AS OrderYear,
        COUNT(DISTINCT Sales.Orders.OrderID) AS [# of orders for the year]

FROM Sales.Orders INNER JOIN
      Application.People ON Sales.Orders.SalespersonPersonID = Application.People.PersonID

GROUP BY YEAR(Sales.Orders.OrderDate), Application.People.FullName

ORDER BY OrderYear
```
Figure 5-10 Group BY query

	SalesRep	OrderYear	# of orders for the year
1	Amy Trefl	2013	1942
2	Anthony Grosse	2013	1936
3	Archer Lamble	2013	1986
4	Hudson Hollinworth	2013	1908
5	Hudson Onslow	2013	1945
6	Jack Potter	2013	1969
7	Kayla Woodcock	2013	2014
8	Lily Code	2013	1862
9	Sophia Hinton	2013	1966
10	Taj Shand	2013	1922
11	Amy Trefl	2014	2083
12	Anthony Grosse	2014	2130

Figure 5-11 Result of the Group By criteria shown in Figure 5-10

Keep in mind that when a Aggregate transformation is used, each field must either be grouped or summarized by. Fields that do not use an aggregate function are included after the fields that you aggregate on.

 The Aggregate transformation can be very memory intensive because each row in the table is read into the transformation before the first row is sent out. If the table has millions of rows, this could cause the package to run slow. As much as possible, filter out rows and columns before sending the data to this transformation. Because of this, like the Sort transformation, a query should be used instead of the Aggregate transformation, to allow the package to run more efficiently.

Aggregations Tab

Figure 5-12 shows the options on this tab. They are used to create groups and aggregate calculations.

The operations explained below are used to create a group and aggregate values. These are only applied to the fields that will be the output of the transformation.

Except for the Group BY operation, the others discussed below are functions that you may already be familiar with.

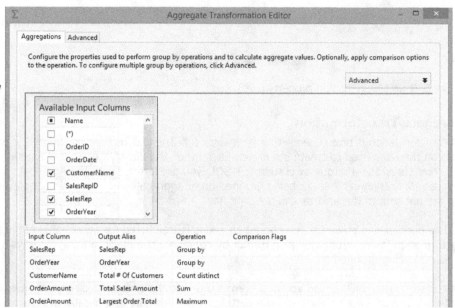

Figure 5-12 Aggregations tab

GROUP BY Select this operation for the fields that you want to group on. This option works the same as the Group By clause covered earlier in this chapter.
AVERAGE calculates the average of the values in the field. (1)
COUNT creates a count of the number of records in the group.
COUNT DISTINCT creates a count of the number of unique values in the specified field. Null values are not counted.
MINIMUM returns the lowest value in a field, in the group. (1)
MAXIMUM returns the largest value in a field, in the group. (1)
SUM calculates a total for the values in a column. (1)

(1) This function can only be used with numeric values.

 The functions only include rows that are in the group. While not a requirement, often, to make the data more meaningful, the aggregate columns are renamed.

 The functions that are in the **OPERATION FIELD** drop-down list are based on the columns data type.

The **ADVANCED BUTTON** displays the grid shown in Figure 5-13.

The options are used to create more aggregations as needed.

You can check different columns to create a different aggregation transformation, which gives you the opportunity to create another view of the data, if you will.

Type the name for the new aggregation in the Aggregation Name field, then check the fields that are needed to create the new aggregation in the Available Input Columns list.

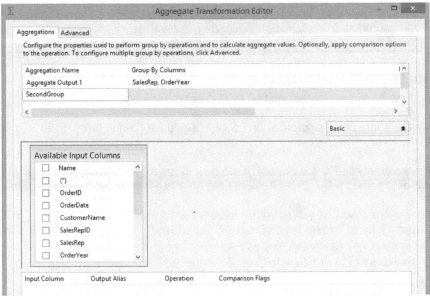

Figure 5-13 Advanced button options

Advanced Tab

The options shown in Figure 5-14 are used to configure multiple outputs for the transformation. Each output needs its own name.

The options are explained below.

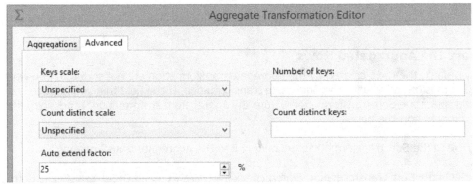

Figure 5-14 Advanced tab

The **KEY SCALE** option is used to set the approximate number of keys. This is done to optimize the transformations cache. Most of the time I think the default "Unspecified" value is okay.

The **COUNT DISTINCT SCALE** option is used to set the number of distinct values that can be written by the transformation. The default is Unspecified.

The **AUTO EXTEND FACTOR** option is used to select how much the memory can be extended by. The default is 25%.

The **NUMBER OF KEYS** field is used to enter an estimate of how many distinct groups will be created from the transformation. This will help optimize the transformation for the number of distinct values.

Exercise 5.4: Use The Aggregate Transformation

In this exercise, you will learn how to use the Aggregate transformation to group on the sales rep name and order year fields. Aggregate values will be created for the following fields: A count of customers, a sum of the order amount and the order with the largest order amount.

1.   Rename a new package to E5.4 Aggregate transformation.

2.   Add a source connection using the Excel ssis_data connection manager ⇒
     Name the connection Connect to Orders table.

3.   On the Excel Source editor, select the Orders table.

On your own, you should use the Columns page to clear the check mark of the fields that will not be used by the Aggregate transformation, or create a query to select the fields that are needed. This will allow the package to run faster, because fewer columns and/or rows will have to be processed.

Create The Aggregate Calculations

1. Add the Aggregate transformation ⇒ Connect it to the Excel source.

2. On the Aggregate Transformation Editor, check the following fields: Sales Rep, Order Year, Customer Name and Order Amount.

3. On the empty line at the bottom of the grid, in the Input Column, select the Order Amount field. Two calculations will be created for the Order Amount field, so it needs to be added twice.

4. Change the following values in the Output Alias column.
    Customer Name - Change to `Total # of Customers`
    Order Amount - Change to `Total Sales Amount`
    Order Amount (1) - Change to `Largest Order Total`

5. Change the following operations.
    Order Year - Change to Group by
    Customer Name - Change to Count distinct
    Largest Order Total - Change to Maximum

6. When complete, you should have the options shown earlier in Figure 5-12 ⇒ Click OK.

Sort The Aggregated Rows

By default, the rows created by the Aggregate transformation are not sorted. If you want the data sorted, add the Sort transformation after the Aggregate transformation. If the field that you need to sort on, is not an aggregated field, place the Sort transformation before the Aggregate transformation. If possible, the best solution is to create a query to sort the data.

1. Add the Sort transformation ⇒ Connect it to the Aggregate transformation.

2. On the Sort Transformation Editor, check the Sales Rep and Order Year fields. Both should be in ascending order, in the Sort Type column.

Create The Destination File

1. Add the Flat File Destination ⇒ Rename it to `Ch5 Aggregate transformation exercise.`

2. Connect it to the Sort transformation.

3. On the Flat File Destination Editor, click the New button ⇒ Accept the Delimited option ⇒ In the Connection manager name field, type `Ch5 Aggregate exercise.`

4. In the File name field, type `C:\SSIS Book\Ch5 Aggregate transformation.txt.`

5. Check the Column names option ⇒ Click OK.

6. In the Header box, type `* Rows From Aggregate Transformation Exercise *.`

7. On the Mappings page, click OK.

8. Run the package.

   When complete, you should see that 40 rows were created from the 73,595 rows that were read, as shown in Figure 5-15.

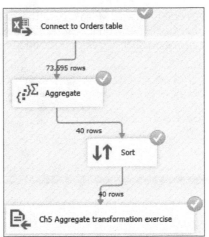

Figure 5-15 Number of rows created by the Aggregate transformation

Figure 5-16 shows the first few rows in the output file. As you can see, there is a row of data for each sales rep for each year, that they have data. The reason that they are grouped together is because the data was sorted before being written to the destination file. Not sorting the data, would display it as shown in Figure 5-17.

```
* Rows From Aggregate Transformation Exercise *
SalesRep,OrderYear,Total# Of Columns,Total Sales Amount,Largest Order Total
Amy Trefl,2013,578,4060354.51,130907.05
Amy Trefl,2014,607,5406647.89,126514.99
Amy Trefl,2015,630,5851754.62,101382.71
Amy Trefl,2016,472,957058.4,2838.66
Anthony Grosse,2013,586,1139290.92,3953.99
Anthony Grosse,2014,610,18755524.97,142312.22
Anthony Grosse,2015,624,21412636.8,170512.67
Anthony Grosse,2016,469,8548366.6,113231.02
Archer Lamble,2013,590,5642372.69,101382.71
```

```
Kayla Woodcock,2015,621,17205599.13,113231.02
Lily Code,2016,472,3688364.39,121823.19
Kayla Woodcock,2016,485,8692591.02,187487.83
Hudson Onslow,2013,586,7539603.9,145454.37
Amy Trefl,2013,578,4060354.51,130907.05
Hudson Onslow,2014,612,5879386.42,130249.26
Amy Trefl,2014,607,5406647.89,126514.99
```

Figure 5-16 Result of the aggregate transformation   **Figure 5-17** Result of aggregate data not sorted

Conditional Split

This transformation is used to separate data in a source, based on a condition (filter). Each condition is then used to send data to another transformation or to a destination. If you are familiar with **IF THEN ELSE STATEMENTS** or **CASE STATEMENTS**, you understand how this transformation works. This transformation allows you to send the data from one source to multiple output destinations as needed.

An example would be replicating the query used in Chapter 4, Exercise 4.5, that selects rows that have a specific value in the Year and Total Due columns. Rows where the Year equals 2012 and the Total Due value is >=10000 would be split off and sent to Path A. Path B could be all orders in 2015. The remaining rows in the source file could be sent to a third output file. This third file would be the equivalent of the **ELSE PORTION** of the If Then Else statement. Path A could be another transformation and Path B could be writing the data to a file.

Figure 5-18 shows the editor. The top section is the same as the Derived Column Transformation Editor, that was covered in Chapter 4.

The **ORDER** column is used to change the order of the expressions. By default, the order that the conditions will be processed in, is the order that they are created in. This gives you the flexibility to add conditions later and reorder them as needed, without having to delete some conditions to make room where needed, then enter them again.

The **OUTPUT NAME** column is used to give each condition its own name.

The **CONDITION** column is used to create the expression. More than one set of criteria can be created in one cell in this column. For example, the first condition shown in Figure 5-18 checks to see if the value in the Shipped Via column is Next Day or 2 Day Priority.

The vertical bars (| |) between the expressions represent an **OR CONDITION**, meaning that if the value in the Shipped Via column is Next Day or 2 Day Priority, the row of data will be routed to the Shipped Fast path.

Two ampersands (**&&**) between expressions represent the **AND CONDITION**, meaning that both conditions, on the second row shown in Figure 5-18, have to be met, for the row of data to be routed to the 2015 SW Orders.

The **DEFAULT OUTPUT NAME** field is used to enter a name for that data that did not meet any of the conditions that were created. I tend to use Good Data for the default output name. While not obvious, this is another path of data that can be connected to another transformation or to a different destination, from any of the conditions on the grid.

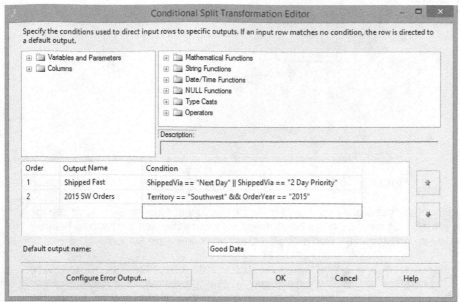

Figure 5-18 Conditional Split Transformation Editor

This transformation can also be used to find missing data (also known as **DIRTY DATA**). An example of this is whether or not rows have data in a specific column. Rows that do not have data in the column that is checked, could be written to a file, so that someone (not you) can fill in the missing data.

Order Of Conditions Tips
By default, the conditions are processed in the order that they are displayed in on the editor. Below are some tips to help you put the conditions in the best order to reduce the number of conditions that rows of data need to be checked against.

① A good rule of thumb, when using multiple conditions for the same column, is to put the condition that most rows of data will meet, at the top of the list. Rows that meet the first condition are not fed to the other conditions on the editor, to be checked. Doing this reduces processing time, which is a good thing. <smile>

② If you are familiar with Select Case statements, like the one shown in Figure 5-19, this tip will be familiar. Each line that starts with the word Case is the equivalent of a condition on the Conditional Split Transformation Editor. Notice the order that the values in the Order Amount field is being checked against. The values are in descending order. Why? Because you are trying to reduce the number of times each row of data is checked. The secret to this is knowing if the data set has more low or high values in the Order Amount field. In this example, it was determined that there were more high values then low values. This means that the first Case statement will select more of the rows of data and send them to a path. If the majority of Order Amount values were less than 25000, each row would have to be checked three times. In this example, that would increase processing time significantly, especially if the table had hundreds of thousands or millions of rows of data. The solution in that case would be to reverse the order of the three case statements.

```
Select {Orders.Order Amount}
   Case Is >= 10000: "10% discount"
   Case Is >= 5000: "15% discount"
   Case Is >= 2500: "20% discount"
   Default: "25% discount"
```
Figure 5-19 Case statement

Connecting The Conditional Split Transformation

Each condition that is created on the editor will usually have its own destination file or go to another transformation. In the example shown earlier in Figure 5-18, three blue arrows would be available from the Conditional Split transformation.

. . . .

When the Conditional Split transformation is connected to the next transformation or destination file (using a blue arrow), the dialog box shown in Figure 5-20 is displayed.

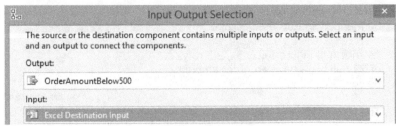

It displays the conditions created on the Conditional Split Transformation Editor in the **OUTPUT FIELD** drop-down list.

Figure 5-20 Input Output Selection dialog box

The Input field displays the list of options where the rows of data that meet the criteria for the condition will be sent to.

Exercise 5.5: Less Than Value Conditional Split

In this exercise, you will learn how to use the Conditional Split transformation to write records that have an order amount that is less than $500, to a file.

1. Rename a new package to `E5.5 Low order amount conditional split`.

2. Create a source connection for the AW database ⇒ Select the Order Info table.

Configure The Conditional Split Transformation

In this part of the exercise, you will create an expression to select records that have an order amount that is less than $500.

1. Add the Condition Split transformation ⇒ Connect it to the source.

2. On the editor, in the Output Name field, type `OrderAmountBelow500`.

3. In the Condition field, type `[OrderAmount] < 500`.

In this exercise, the only records that will be written to a file are the ones that meet the condition that you just created.

Therefore, there is no value in changing the Default output name field.

You should have the options shown in Figure 5-21.

Figure 5-21 Expression to find rows with an order amount below $500

Create A Destination

1. Add an Excel Destination ⇒ Rename it to `Below 500`.

2. Connect the Conditional Split transformation to the destination ⇒ Open the **OUTPUT FIELD** drop-down list and select Order Amount Below 500, as shown earlier in Figure 5-20. This is the flow for the conditional expression that you created.

3. On the Excel destination editor, select the Excel exported exercises data connection ⇒ Select the Ch5 Order Amount Below 500 sheet.

4. On the Mappings page, five columns should be mapped ⇒ Run the package.

As shown in Figure 5-22, 31,245 rows out of 73,595 rows have an order amount below $500.

The rows that meet the condition are written to the destination file.

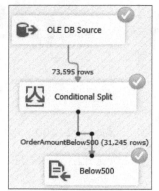

Figure 5-22 Rows that meet the conditional split criteria

Exercise 5.6: Missing Data Conditional Split

In this exercise, you will learn how to create a conditional split, based on a field that does not have data in every row. Rows that meet this criteria will be written to an Excel file.

1. Rename a new package to E5.6 Conditional split missing data.

2. Create a source connection named Missing Data for the AW database.

3. On the editor, select the Missing Data table.

Configure The Conditional Split Transformation

In this part of the exercise, you will create an expression to see if the order date is missing (null).

1. Add the Conditional Split transformation ⇒ Connect it to the Missing data source.

2. On the editor, type OrderDateMissing in the Output Name cell.

3. In the Condition field, type or create the following expression, by dragging the options to the field.
   ISNULL([OrderDate])

4. Change the Default output name field to GoodData. The rows that have a date in the Order Date field will go to this flow and will be written to a different destination file, then the rows that meet the condition. Figure 5-23 shows the conditional criteria ⇒ Click OK.

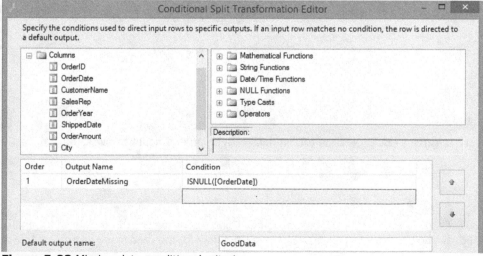

Figure 5-23 Missing data conditional criteria

Create And Connect The Destination Files

To link to the Conditional Split transformation, the destination files need to at least be on the canvas. At this stage of creating the package, there is no point in completely setting up the destination files, because you cannot confirm that the fields are mapped correctly.

1. Add two Excel Destinations ⇒ Rename one to `Missing Order Date` ⇒ Rename the other one to `Good Data.`

2. Connect the Missing Order Date destination to the Conditional Split transformation ⇒ Open the Output drop-down list and select Order Date Missing, as shown in Figure 5-24.

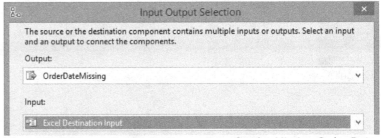

Figure 5-24 Input Output Section options for the Missing Order Date destination

3. Connect the Good Data destination to the Conditional Split transformation.

Finish Setting Up The Destination Files

1. On the Missing order date destination editor, select the Excel exported exercises data connection manager.

2. Select the Ch5 Missing Data sheet ⇒ On the Mappings page, all of the columns should be mapped.

3. On the Good Data destination editor, select the Excel exported exercises data connection manager.

4. Select the Ch5 No Missing Data sheet ⇒ On the Mappings page, all of the columns should be mapped.

5. Run the package.

   As shown in Figure 5-25, there are 130 rows that do not have an order date.

   If you look at the Ch5 Missing Data sheet, in the Exported Exercises Data workbook, none of the rows have an order date, which is correct.

   All of the rows on the Ch5 No Data Missing sheet have an order date.

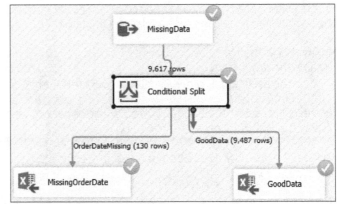

Figure 5-25 Conditional Split transformation

Exercise 5.7: Conditional Split With Multiple Conditions

In this exercise, you will learn how to create **OR CONDITIONS** to route the data to different tables.

1. Rename a new package to `E5.7 Multiple OR conditions.`

2. Create an Excel source connection using the Excel ssis_data connection manager ⇒ Name the connection `Orders table ssis data.`

3. On the editor, select the Orders sheet.

On your own, if there are columns that are not needed for the conditional split or do not need to be written to the destination table, remove them on the Columns page, on the source editor, or create a query that does not include the fields that are not needed.

Configure The Conditional Split Transformation

1. Add the Conditional Split transformation ⇒ Connect it to the source.

2. On the editor, create the following condition.
    Output Name - `NorthEastTerritory`
    Condition - `Territory == "Mideast" || Territory == "New England"`

3. Create the following condition.
    Output Name - `TheWest`
    Condition - `Territory == "Far West" || Territory == "Southwest"`

4. Type `All Other Territories` in the Default output name field.

    You should have the options shown in Figure 5-26.

Order	Output Name	Condition
1	NorthEastTerritory	Territory == "Mideast" || Territory == "New England"
2	The West	Territory == "Far West" || Territory == "Southwest"
Default output name:		All Other Territories

Figure 5-26 OR expressions

Create The Destination Files

1. Add three Excel Destination components.

2. Modify one of the destinations as follows:
    Rename the destination to `Send to North East table` ⇒
    Connect the destination to the Conditional Split transformation ⇒ Select the North East Territory output option.

3. On the editor, select the Excel exported exercises data connection manager ⇒ Select the Ch5 North East sheet ⇒ Display the Mappings page, to enable the OK button.

4. Modify one of the blank destinations as follows:
    Rename the destination to `Send to the West table` ⇒
    Connect the destination to the Conditional Split transformation ⇒ Select The West territory output option.

5. On the editor, select the Excel exported exercises data connection manager ⇒ Select the Ch5 West sheet ⇒ Display the Mappings page.

6. Rename the last new destination to `All other territories` ⇒ Connect the destination to the Conditional Split transformation.

7. On the editor, select the Excel exported exercises data connection manager ⇒ Select the Ch5 All Other Territories sheet ⇒ Display the Mappings page.

8. Run the package.

    You should see the row counts shown in Figure 5-27.

    If you created the 0 New Empty Package file that I discussed at the end of Chapter 3, I hope that you see the benefit of it.

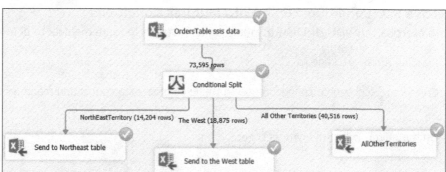

Figure 5-27 Row counts for each table

Row Count Transformation

While in debug mode, you can see the row count at each step (task) in the package, as shown above in Figure 5-27. When the package is deployed (in production), you will not be able to view the package to see what the number of rows processed is. There may also be a need to use these counts in a part of the package. When that is the case, use the Row Count transformation.

Not surprising, this transformation counts the rows of data. More than one row transformation can be used in a package. The result must be stored in a variable. This count can be used to store how many records were written to the bad data table. Then the bad data variable could be checked in a task on the Control Flow tab, to see if the value is greater than zero (meaning at least one row in the package has bad data), if it is, send an email to someone letting them know. Another example would be using the row count value as a condition to determine whether or not another task in the package should be run.

Pivot Transformation

This transformation is used to change rows into columns, which creates a **PIVOT TABLE**. The technical terminology for this is converting normalized data into denormalized data. Data displayed in a pivot table is summarized, just like the **AGGREGATE TRANSFORMATION** does. Figure 5-28 shows the data that will be used to create the pivot table shown in Figure 5-29. Some of the columns in Figure 5-28 have been hidden on purpose. What you cannot tell by the data shown in Figure 5-28, is that there is data for multiple years.

	B	C	E	F	I	L
1	OrderDate	CustomerName	SalesRep	OrderYear	OrderAmount	Territory
2	01/01/2013	Aakriti Byrraju	Kayla Woodcock	2013	$23,153.23	Great Lakes
3	01/01/2013	Bala Dixit	Anthony Grosse	2013	$55.24	Far West
4	01/01/2013	Tailspin Toys (Tomnolen, MS)	Amy Trefl	2013	$132.56	Southeast
5	01/01/2013	Tailspin Toys (Lakemore, OH)	Archer Lamble	2013	$835.74	Great Lakes
6	01/01/2013	Sara Huiting	Hudson Onslow	2013	$1,149.19	Plains

Figure 5-28 Order Info table

The pivot table was created in SSRS because SSIS does not have report design functionality. In the pivot exercise, you will be able to see the table created that was used to create the report, in Figure 5-29.

Sales Rep	2013	2014	2015	2016
Amy Trefl	$3,035,727.25	$4,298,653.93	$4,498,921.62	$419,348.47
Anthony Grosse	$508,897.51	$13,521,050.50	$16,811,285.55	$7,283,569.21
Archer Lamble	$4,445,712.14	$561,847.81	$4,620,125.50	$2,210,310.06
Hudson Hollinworth	$11,524,327.17	$8,762,211.18	$5,285,056.94	$2,737,804.07
Hudson Onslow	$6,436,939.53	$5,109,132.82	$7,027,596.55	$403,245.22
Jack Potter	$3,607,622.26	$3,651,279.09	$3,077,665.91	$1,892,863.38
Kayla Woodcock	$13,565,560.31	$16,700,480.71	$13,742,436.01	$7,437,229.44
Lily Code	$4,429,780.20	$4,534,501.87	$2,500,702.75	$3,380,356.90
Sophia Hinton	$4,531,686.12	$2,453,166.26	$3,730,559.95	$3,323,499.84
Taj Shand	$3,633,086.27	$3,053,909.75	$4,325,983.62	$434,741.18

Figure 5-29 Order Info table data in a pivot table layout

Aggregate Transformation vs Pivot Transformation
What may not be obvious is that both transformations can be used to create the data set that would be used to create the report shown above in Figure 5-29. If the data is in the correct layout, meaning that the rows do not have to be changed to columns, it is easier to use the Aggregate transformation that was covered earlier in this chapter to create the pivot table shown above in Figure 5-29.

A benefit that the Aggregate transformation has over the Pivot transformation is that it can use more than three fields to summarize the rows of data. As covered earlier in this chapter, the Aggregate transformation is more flexible. For example, it is not a requirement that the data is sorted. If you do sort the data, you can select the field(s) to sort on. You can also sort on fields that are not used in the Aggregate transformation.

Behind The Scenes Of Using The Pivot Transformation

I have used several software packages that have pivot table functionality and I will admit, the one in SSIS requires the most work. Because of that, I decided to use a different approach to explaining how the Pivot transformation works, then I have used for the other transformations. I will explain how to use the Pivot transformation in steps, before you actually create a pivot table. Hopefully, this will help you on your own, to create the data set for the pivot tables that you need.

The pivot table exercise that you will create, will display sales reps totals per year. The data needs to be grouped and sorted on the Sales Rep and Order Year columns. The steps below explain the process.

Step 1: Select The Fields Needed To Create The Pivot Table

Figure 5-29 shown earlier, shows a pivot table created with data generated from the Pivot transformation. Three fields are needed to display data in a pivot layout, as explained below.

   ① The field down the left column will be used to group the data on. While it is suggested that this field not have a lot of unique values, the transformation can handle as many values as you need to use.
   ② The field to create the columns across the top of the table.
   ③ The field to summarize (aggregate) on. This is the field that displays the values in the middle of the pivot table.

Step 2: Create The Query

A query needs to be created that includes the following criteria.

   ① The data must be sorted by the Set Key field, which is explained later. The Set Key field is the one displayed in the left column. If the data is not sorted, the Pivot transformation can create multiple records for each set key value.
   ② The data must be grouped on.
   ③ Summarize the field that will display the data in the middle of the pivot table.
   ④ While not a requirement for the Pivot transformation to process the data, duplicate rows of data should be removed or filtered out before the package is run.

Using Months As The Pivot Key Field
It is common to display a years worth of data in a pivot table. This is usually done by displaying the month names as the column headings. For example, in Figure 5-29 shown earlier, the years would be replaced with month names. This transformation will not extract the month names from a date field. You will have to do that in a query or create a derived column to convert the month number to the corresponding month name.

Step 3: Configure The Pivot Transformation

Figure 5-30 shows the dialog box used to transform the data from the query. Notice that the three fields used to create the pivot table data are in the location where their data will be displayed, when the pivot table report is created.

I think that this is done to help people visualize where the data will be displayed. The pivot fields and options used in this transformation are explained below.

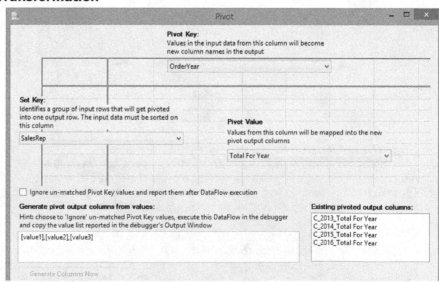

Figure 5-30 Pivot transformation dialog box

The **PIVOT KEY** field is used to select the field that will be used to create the unique column headings across the top of the pivot table. Usually, the field selected is one that would be grouped on. The field selected should not have a lot of unique values. For example, you would not select the Product ID in a Products table that has 20 or more products.

The **SET KEY** field is used to select the field that will be displayed down the left column of the pivot table. This is the field that the data must be sorted on.

The **PIVOT VALUE** field is used to select the field that will be aggregated. This field that will display the data in the middle (also known as the matrix) of the pivot table.

When checked, the **IGNORE UN-MATCH PIVOT KEY . . .** option will cause any rows that have values that are not recognized (in the Pivot Key field), to be ignored.

The **GENERATE PIVOT OUTPUT COLUMNS FROM VALUES BOX** is used to type in or paste the values that will be used to create the column headings. In the scenario discussed in this example, you would type in each of the distinct years in the data source. The hint lets you know how to have them automatically generated, when you run the package. This is one of those times when knowing the data is helpful because you could type in the values. [See How To Generate The Pivot Output Values]

Once you type or paste in the values, the **GENERATE COLUMNS NOW BUTTON**, is enabled. When this button is clicked, the values will be added to the **EXISTING PIVOTED OUTPUT COLUMNS BOX**, on the right.

Step 4: Select The Destination

This step is used to select what type of file you want the output from the Pivot transformation to be sent to. This file would then be used to create the actual pivot table shown earlier in Figure 5-29. Hopefully, this walk thru made it a little easier to understand the tasks that needs to be completed, to use the Pivot transformation.

Pivot Transformation Limitation
What I discovered is that the Pivot transformation only allows one field to be used for each of the drop-down fields, shown above in Figure 5-30. Other pivot table tools that I have used, allow multiple values to be used for the equivalent of the Set Key and Pivot Key options. For example, I can add the Territory field as the second field in the Set Key field, then the Sales Rep field. Doing that would take the yearly totals and sub divide them by territory for each sales rep. This is similar to the second group (the Order Year) that was used in the aggregate exercise earlier in this chapter. [See Figure 5-12] If you know SQL Server Reporting Services (SSRS), you can create a more elaborate pivot table.

Creating The Output Columns
I will admit that the process for creating the output columns through me for a loop, the first time that I used the Pivot transformation. Mainly because the process is manual. To me, the values should be retrieved from the data source and then let you select if you want to use all of the values or just some of them.

Then it dawned on me that in this scenario, what happens next year when the query retrieves data for another year? Figure 5-29, shows data through 2016. What happens in 2017, when that years data needs to appear on the pivot table. Sadly, the answer is that you will have to modify the transformation to include another year of data, otherwise the Pivot transformation will fail. No thank you. I will stick to creating pivot tables on my own in SSRS, as it does not have this limitation. Can you imagine if the columns used for the Pivot value option is a field in the data source that has values added to it monthly? Again, no thank you. <smile>

The reason the Pivot transformation will work for months, year after year, is because the months, as discussed earlier, do not change. The underlying query will need a parameter, so that whoever is running the package will be prompted to enter which years data to select for the transformation.

Another Way To Get The Pivot Key Values
Earlier in step 3 above, I discussed one way to get the unique values for the Pivot Key field. This tip explains another way, that you may find easier. On your own, if you have the need to get these values, the query shown in Figure 5-31 will give you the list of unique values. Follow the steps below to learn how to create this type of query.

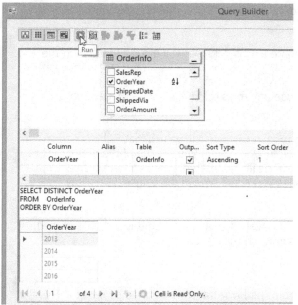

Figure 5-31 Query to create the list of unique values

1. Complete steps 1 and 2 in the first section of the exercise below.

2. Use the query shown in Figure 5-31, as the template. You have to change the Order Info table to the table that you are using ⇒ Change the Order Year field to the field that you would select in the Pivot Key field, (in the table that you are using), shown earlier in Figure 5-30.

3. Click the **RUN** button, shown above at the top of Figure 5-31.

4. Write down the values or take a screen shot of them, so that you do not have to memorize them.

Exercise 5.8: Use The Pivot Transformation

This exercise will show you how to use the Pivot transformation to create the output file needed to create the pivot table shown earlier in Figure 5-29.

Create The Query To Select The Data For The Pivot Table

1. Rename a copy of the E4.1 package to `E5.8 Pivot table`.

2. On the OLE DB Source Editor, delete the query.

3. Paste in the query in the Pivot Query.txt file.

 On your own, you can click the Build Query button to see how this query was created, or you could create a query.

4. Click the Preview button to see the data retrieved by the query, as shown in Figure 5-32.

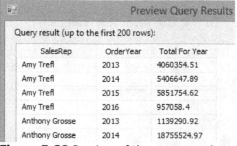

SalesRep	OrderYear	Total For Year
Amy Trefl	2013	4060354.51
Amy Trefl	2014	5406647.89
Amy Trefl	2015	5851754.62
Amy Trefl	2016	957058.4
Anthony Grosse	2013	1139290.92
Anthony Grosse	2014	18755524.97

Figure 5-32 Preview of the query result

Configure The Pivot Transformation

1. Add the Pivot transformation ⇒ Connect it to the data source.

2. On the Pivot dialog box, select the fields listed below. When finished, you should have the options shown earlier, at the top of Figure 5-30.

   Pivot Key - Order Year
   Set Key - Sales Rep
   Pivot Value - Total For Year

3. Replace the [value] place holders in the Generate pivot output section of the dialog box, with the ones shown below, as shown in Figure 5-33. [2013], [2014], [2015], [2016]
   These are the unique values in the Pivot Key field.

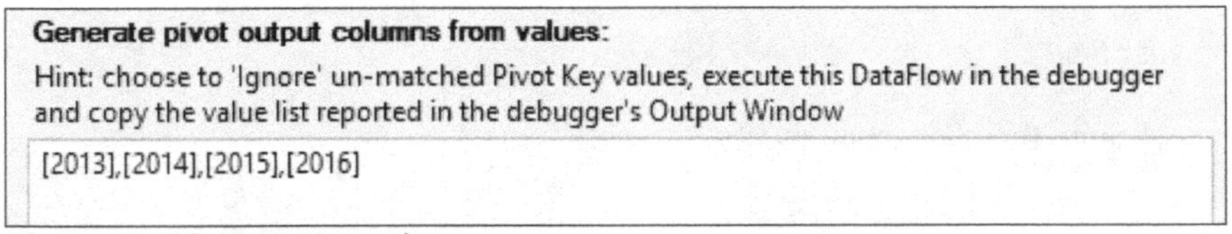

Generate pivot output columns from values:

Hint: choose to 'Ignore' un-matched Pivot Key values, execute this DataFlow in the debugger and copy the value list reported in the debugger's Output Window

[2013],[2014],[2015],[2016]

Figure 5-33 Pivot Key values

4. Click the **GENERATE COLUMNS NOW** button. The dialog box shown in Figure 5-34 lets you know what output columns were created. Why SSIS appends the Pivot Value field name to the column name is beyond me. <smile> ⇒ Click OK. You should have the options shown in Figure 5-35 ⇒ Click OK.

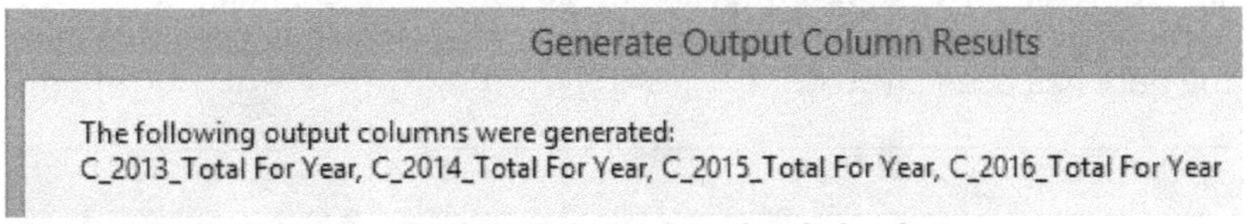

Generate Output Column Results

The following output columns were generated:
C_2013_Total For Year, C_2014_Total For Year, C_2015_Total For Year, C_2016_Total For Year

---

Figure 5-34 Generate Output Column Results dialog box

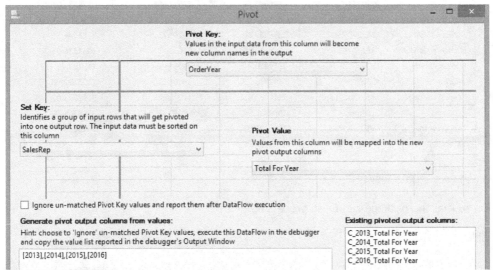

Figure 5-35 Options selected to create the pivot table data

 Once you click OK on the Pivot dialog box, the values in the **EXISTING PIVOTED OUTPUT COLUMNS** box cannot be changed or deleted on this dialog box. I tried things to change the Output column values and finally just gave up and decided that it was just easier to create the names I want in the destination file.

Create The Destination File

In this part of the exercise, you will create an Excel file that has column headings that only display the year.

1. Add an Excel Destination ⇒ Rename it Ch5 PivotTableData ⇒ Connect it to the Pivot transformation.

. . . .

2. On the editor, click the first New button ⇒ In the Excel file path field,
   type `C:\SSIS Book\Ch5 Pivot table data.xlsx.`

3. Click the Excel sheet New button ⇒
   Click OK on the warning message dialog box ⇒
   On the Create Table dialog box, change each of the Year
   headings to just the year number, as shown in Figure 5-36.

   Because the data is being written to a spreadsheet, it is ok
   to leave the Sales Rep field length as is, for this exercise.

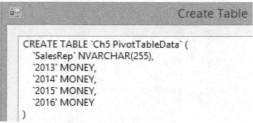

```
Create Table

CREATE TABLE `Ch5 PivotTableData` (
    `SalesRep` NVARCHAR(255),
    `2013` MONEY,
    `2014` MONEY,
    `2015` MONEY,
    `2016` MONEY
)
```

Figure 5-36 Pivot table layout

4. Open the Excel sheet drop-down list and select the table that you just created.

5. On the Mappings page, map the year fields.

6. On the Connection Managers tab, rename the connection to `Ch5 Pivot data.`

Test The Pivot Transformation

1. Add a Data Viewer after the Pivot transformation.

2. Run the package. You should see the windows shown in Figure 5-37.

Notice that the data source sent 40 rows of data to the Pivot transformation and 10 rows were created in the Pivot transformation, based on the 40 rows, that the Pivot transformation received. This is what should happen, meaning there should be fewer rows of data after the data has been pivoted.

AW Source

40 rows

Pivot

10 rows

Ch5 PivotTableData

	Detach	Copy Data		
SalesRep	C_2013_Total For Year	C_2014_Total For Year	C_2015_Total For Year	C_2016_Total For Year
Amy Trefl	4060354.51	5406647.89	5851754.62	957058.4
Anthony Grosse	1139290.92	18755524.97	21412636.8	8548366.6
Archer Lamble	5642372.69	1306853.93	5919660.25	2568349.92
Hudson Hollinworth	14314748.96	10381825.91	6183897.9	3051386.96
Hudson Onslow	7539603.9	5879386.42	7901688	762182.77
Jack Potter	4550210.14	4692736.75	4408003.73	2335127.48
Kayla Woodcock	18917300.02	21162633.36	17205599.13	8692591.02
Lily Code	5154549.97	5620935.06	3804989.96	3688364.39
Sophia Hinton	5545219.97	3545803.08	5017759.27	3629638
Taj Shand	4604308.37	4188487.98	5634364.25	916815.46

Figure 5-37 Package running with a Data Viewer

3. Click the Detach button so that the package can finish processing.

4. Open the Ch5 Pivot table
   data workbook.

   You should see the data
   shown in Figure 5-38.

	A	B	C	D	E
1	SalesRep	2013	2014	2015	2016
2	Amy Trefl	4060354.51	5406647.89	5851754.62	957058.4
3	Anthony Grosse	1139290.92	18755524.97	21412636.8	8548366.6
4	Archer Lamble	5642372.69	1306853.93	5919660.25	2568349.92
5	Hudson Hollinworth	14314748.96	10381825.91	6183897.9	3051386.96
6	Hudson Onslow	7539603.9	5879386.42	7901688	762182.77
7	Jack Potter	4550210.14	4692736.75	4408003.73	2335127.48
8	Kayla Woodcock	18917300.02	21162633.36	17205599.13	8692591.02
9	Lily Code	5154549.97	5620935.06	3804989.96	3688364.39
10	Sophia Hinton	5545219.97	3545803.08	5017759.27	3629638
11	Taj Shand	4604308.37	4188487.98	5634364.25	916815.46

Figure 5-38 Pivot data written to an Excel workbook

Unpivot Transformation

If you completed the previous exercise, it should come as no surprise, that the Unpivot transformation works the opposite of the Pivot transformation. The Unpivot transformation creates rows from columns. This transformation will take data that is in a non tabular format or the data that is in a pivot table layout, as shown in Figure 5-39 and transform it to a flat file (unpivoted layout), so that it looks like the data shown later on the right side of Figure 5-42. This process is known as changing the DATA STRUCTURE.

	A	B	C	D	E	F
1	Store	FY 2013	FY 2014	FY 2015	FY 2016	FY 2017
2	Atherton	$19.70	$17.10	$18.30	$14.80	$19.80
3	Berkeley	$14.40	$18.00	$16.40	$16.70	$19.30
4	Carmel-by-the-Sea	$18.80	$13.50	$18.70	$13.90	$15.70
5	Cupertino	$12.00	$16.20	$17.50	$17.80	$13.80
6	Fresno	$19.20	$15.60	$19.60	$15.90	$14.40
7	Laguna Beach	$18.90	$14.60	$16.70	$12.10	$13.90
8	Mailbu	$18.70	$17.80	$14.00	$18.50	$13.70
9	Pasadena	$17.00	$19.40	$17.10	$17.30	$17.30
10	San Francisco	$14.40	$14.00	$13.90	$15.40	$18.30

Figure 5-39 Pivot table data

To transform the year columns of data in Figure 5-39, they all have to have the same column name in the Destination Column on the Unpivot Transformation Editor. This is how all of the values will become rows. Once complete, each store will have five rows of data (one for each year of data), once the table is unpivoted. If a cell in one of the year columns is empty (Null), it would not be written out to the new table. Depending on the goals of the package, this may or may not be a problem.

If you need the rows to be written to the new table, even if there is no data for a particular year, type a zero in the corresponding cell in the spreadsheet (or whatever file type the data is in), before you create the package. This is the best solution, because if the data for a year is missing, you probably would not notice on some chart types, which would skew the data displayed on the chart.

The other option is to add a Conditional Split transformation to the package and send the rows that can be created (the good data) to one file, by checking to see if the value column is not null. If the value column is null (the bad data), send the row to a different file.

If you have a spreadsheet that looks like the one shown above in Figure 5-39, you will appreciate how the Unpivot Column option can help you import this non tabular data into a SQL Server database. This transformation is used to change the layout into one that a database supports. By support, I mean that the data will be changed to a layout that can be used to create a table or chart visualization. This data layout is often referred to as a PIVOTED LAYOUT. It does not lend itself to be used to create reports because the data is already pivoted (not in TABULAR FORMAT).

Exercise 5.9: Use The Unpivot Transformation

This exercise will show you how to transform the data shown above in Figure 5-39.

1. Rename a new package to E5.9 Unpivot data.

2. Add an Excel source ⇒ On the Excel Source Editor, click the New button ⇒ Select the ssis_data.xlsx file ⇒ Make sure that the First row option is checked. Remember the connection name, because you will rename it.

3. Select the Pivot Data table ⇒ Click OK.

4. On the Connection Managers tab, rename the connection to Ch5 Unpivot data.

Configure The Unpivot Transformation

On the Unpivot Editor shown in Figure 5-40, the only columns that you should check and rename are the ones that you want to unpivot.

In this exercise, this means that all of the year columns should be checked and given the same name in the Destination Column. This is how the column name is created in the destination table.

The **PASS THROUGH** option is used to select columns that will be written out for each row of data that is created. As you check the fields that will be unpivoted, the check mark (for the field) in this column is automatically removed.

Using the **PIVOT KEY VALUE COLUMN NAME** field is optional. It is used to create another column that will be added to the destination table. If used, the column will indicate where the data came from. Give this field a descriptive name, if used.

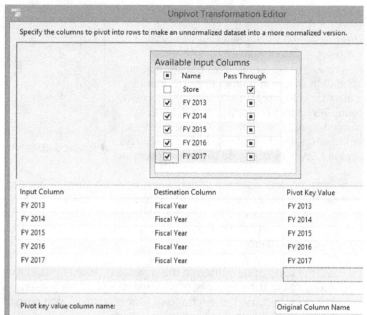

Figure 5-40 Unpivot Transformation Editor

1. Add the Unpivot transformation ⇒ Connect it to the data source.

2. On the Unpivot Transformation Editor, check the five year columns.

3. In the Destination Column for each row, type `Fiscal Year`.

4. In the Pivot key value column name field, type `Original Column Name`. You should have the options shown above in Figure 5-40.

Using The Union All Transformation As A Place Holder

There may be times when you want to be able to add a data viewer after a transformation, but have not added the next transformation or destination to the package. When that is the case, you can use the **UNION ALL TRANSFORMATION** as a place holder for a destination, without it being configured. The package will run without this transformation being configured.

This is what you will do in this part of the exercise, so that you can see how it works. The Union All transformation is covered in detail in the next chapter.

1. Add the Union All transformation ⇒ Connect it to the Unpivot transformation.

2. Add a Data Viewer after the Unpivot transformation ⇒ You may want to rearrange the order that the columns are displayed in, as shown in Figure 5-41. To do this, click the << button, then one by one, click on a column name and add them in the order that you want to see them in, on the Data Viewer.

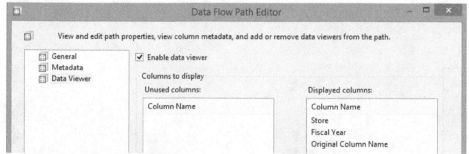

Figure 5-41 Data Flow Path Editor

3. Run the package. You should see the windows shown in Figure 5-42. On the left, you will see that nine rows came from the data source. After those rows went through the Unpivot transformation, 45 rows were created, which is what should happen. The 45 rows is what will be written to the destination file.

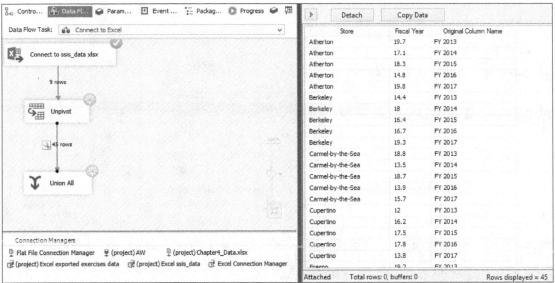

Figure 5-42 Unpivot processing and data output

At this point, on your own, you could add more transformations or write the data out to a file, because you know that the unpivot process worked as intended.

Exercise 5.10: Create A Package That Uses Multiple Data Sources

In this exercise, you will learn how to create a data flow that uses three data sources.

Create The First Data Flow

1. Rename a new package to `E5.10 Use 3 data sources.`

2. Add the Data Flow Task.

3. On the Data Flow tab, add a Flat File Source ⇒ Rename the source to `Mar2015 csv.`

4. On the Flat File Source Editor, check the Retain null values . . . option ⇒ Create a new connection named `Mar2015`, then select the Mar2015.csv file.

5. Display the Columns page ⇒ Click OK.

Create A Derived Column

In this part of the exercise, you will create a new column that will calculate the sales tax. By default, values in a csv file have the String data type. Fields with this data type cannot be used in an expression. Data types can be changed on the Advanced Editor.

1. On the Advanced Editor for the source, click on the Input and Output Properties tab ⇒ Flat File Source Output ⇒ Output Columns folder.

2. Click on the Amount column ⇒ Change the Data Type property to **NUMERIC [DT_NUMERIC]**, as illustrated in Figure 5-43.

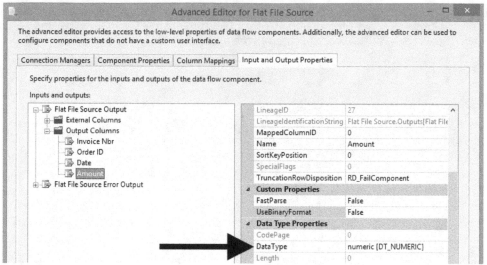

Figure 5-43 Data type changed

3. Add a Derived Column ⇒ Rename it to `Calculate sales tax` ⇒ Connect it to the source file.

4. On the editor, type `Tax` in the Derived Column Name field.

5. Create the following expression `Amount * .05`. You should have the options shown in Figure 5-44.

Derived Column Name	Derived Column	Expression	Data Type
Tax	\<add as new column>	Amount * .05	numeric [DT_NUMERIC]

Figure 5-44 Options for a new column

Create The Second Data Flow

1. Add a Flat File Source ⇒ Rename it to `June 2015 csv`.

2. Complete steps 4 and 5 in the Create The First Data Flow section, earlier in this exercise. In step 4, name the connection `June2015` and use the June2015.csv file.

3. Complete steps 1 and 2 in the Create A Derived Column section.

4. Right-click on the Calculate Sales tax task ⇒ Copy ⇒ Right-click on the canvas and select Paste.

5. Rename the task to `Calc sales tax june` ⇒ Connect it to the June 2015 source.

Sort The Data

In this part of the exercise, you will sort the data in the source file.

1. Add the Sort component ⇒ Rename it to `Sort descending` ⇒ Connect it to the Calc sales tax june component.

2. On the Sort Transformation Editor, check the Amount column ⇒ Change the Sort Type to descending.

   You should have the options shown in Figure 5-45.

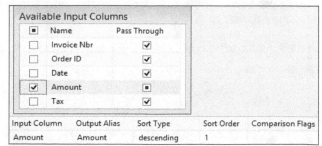

Figure 5-45 Sort options

Create The Third Data Flow

In this part of the exercise, you will create a source that will be mapped directly to the Union All transformation in an exercise in the next chapter.

1. Add a Flat File Source ⇒ Rename it to Sept 2015 csv.

2. Create a new connection named Sept2015, then select the Sept2015.csv file.

3. Display the Columns page ⇒ Click OK twice.

   The Data Flow tab should look similar to the one shown in Figure 5-46.

   In the next chapter, you will use the Union All transformation to combine the data in the two csv files, into a new table.

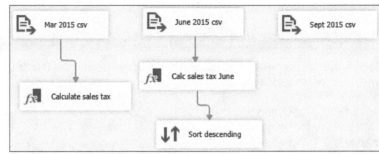

Figure 5-46 Data Flow layout

Audit Transformation

This transformation provides an easy way to add audit information to a destination file. It can be used instead of the Derived Column transformation, if it has the audit information that you want to use. This task adds fields to the destination file. It does not interfere with a any of the other fields in the package.

Figure 5-47 shows the editor. The options in the **AUDIT TYPE** drop-down list are the audit fields that can be added to the destination file.

The values that are added to the **OUTPUT COLUMN NAME** field, are the Audit Type names, but you can change them as needed. The Audit Type options are explained below.

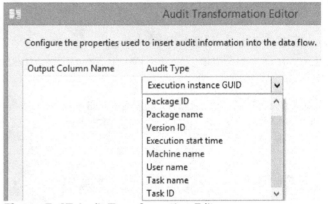

Figure 5-47 Audit Transformation Editor

EXECUTION INSTANCE GUID adds the guid number execution instance of the package.

PACKAGE ID adds the unique Package ID number.

PACKAGE NAME adds the name of the package.

VERSION ID adds the version guid number of the package.

EXECUTION START TIME adds the time that the package started running.

MACHINE NAME adds the name of the computer that the package was run from.

USER NAME adds the name of the user (from the computer information) that ran the package.

TASK NAME adds the task name (on the Data flow tab) of the Audit Task.

TASK ID adds the Audit Task unique ID number.

Exercise 5.11: Use The Audit Transformation

In this exercise, you will add the Audit transformation to an existing package and select some Audit Type options to write to the destination file.

Select The Audit Type Fields

1. Save a copy of the E5.4 package as `E5.11 Audit transformation.`

2. Delete the Ch5 Aggregate destination component.

3. Add the Audit transformation ⇒ Rename it to `Add audit fields` ⇒ Connect it to the Sort transformation.

4. On the Audit Editor, select the following Audit type fields from the drop-down list: Package name, Execution start time, User name and Task name.

5. In the Output Column Name column, change the Execution start time name to `Package run time` ⇒ Change the Task name to `Audit task name.`

   You should have the options shown in Figure 5-48.

Output Column Name	Audit Type
Package name	Package name
Package run time	Execution start time
User name	User name
Audit task name	Task name

Figure 5-48 Audit fields selected

Create The Destination File

In this part of the exercise, the destination file will be created and will include the fields from the Sort transformation and the audit fields.

1. Add a Flat File Destination component ⇒ Rename it to `Ch5 Write sort and audit fields` ⇒ Connect it to the Add audit fields transformation.

2. On the Flat File Destination Editor, click the New button.

3. On the Flat File Connection Manager Editor, type `Ch5 Audit task connection` as the connection name.

4. In the File name field, type `C:\SSIS Book\Ch5 Audit transformation.txt.`

5. Check the Column names option.

6. On the destination editor, at the bottom of the Mappings page, you should see the fields from the sort and audit transformation. Nine fields in total.

7. Run the package. 40 rows should be written to the destination file. Figure 5-49 shows the first few rows in the destination file.

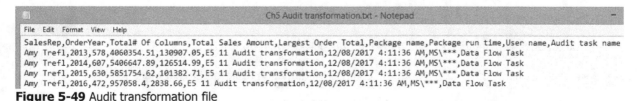

```
                                    Ch5 Audit transformation.txt - Notepad                                    –
File   Edit   Format   View   Help
SalesRep,OrderYear,Total# Of Columns,Total Sales Amount,Largest Order Total,Package name,Package run time,User name,Audit task name
Amy Trefl,2013,578,4060354.51,130907.05,E5 11 Audit transformation,12/08/2017 4:11:36 AM,MS\***,Data Flow Task
Amy Trefl,2014,607,5406647.89,126514.99,E5 11 Audit transformation,12/08/2017 4:11:36 AM,MS\***,Data Flow Task
Amy Trefl,2015,630,5851754.62,101382.71,E5 11 Audit transformation,12/08/2017 4:11:36 AM,MS\***,Data Flow Task
Amy Trefl,2016,472,957058.4,2838.66,E5 11 Audit transformation,12/08/2017 4:11:36 AM,MS\***,Data Flow Task
```

Figure 5-49 Audit transformation file

JOINING DATA

Overview

After reading this chapter and completing the exercises you will know how to use the following transformations.

- ☑ Union All
- ☑ Lookup
- ☑ Merge
- ☑ Merge Join
- ☑ Multicast

CHAPTER 6

Overview

So far, all of the exercises in this book have only used one table as the data source. Most databases are relational, meaning that a complete view of the data requires using two or more tables, to see all of the related data. For example, order information is usually stored in a minimum of three tables: Orders, Order Details and Products. Often, there are more tables that have order related data in a database, like customer information.

When setting up a new data warehouse, data from multiple existing tables and files may be needed to create one new table. You may also have the need to update data in one table, based on a value in a field in a different table. When either scenario is the case, the ability to join source tables is needed. SSIS has transformations that are used to join data in tables, including Lookup and Merge Join. This type of transformation is used to view/look up data in another table.

Union All Transformation

This transformation is used to combine data from two or more files into one output data set. And, as you learned in the previous chapter, the Union All transformation can also be used as a place holder, instead of using a destination file or another transformation, when testing a package.

While similar in functionality to the Merge transformation, that requires that the data be sorted before the data can be merged, the Union All transformation does not have this requirement. The data from each source or transformation that is connected to the Union All component is added/written to the destination source, one table after the other and the data is not sorted, while it is being written out. The Union All transformation works like the **UNION OPERATOR** in T-SQL.

Once the sources are linked to this transformation, the columns are automatically mapped if the column names are the same. You should confirm this before combining the data sources into one file or before the data is sent to another transformation. By default, the Union All transformation will automatically fix minor metadata inconsistencies like the length of string fields, for the same field. For example, if the length of one address field is 30 and an address field in another table has a length of 25, the length of 25 will be changed to 30.

Sometimes, when you make changes in a previous transformation, the Union All transformation will display the red error circle. I tend to delete the Union All transformation when I see the circle, then add the transformation back. Often, doing this causes the error to go away.

If you know that all of the column names in all of the sources that are connected to this transformation are the same, there is no need to open the editor, because the columns will automatically be mapped. If you are not sure, open the editor to confirm.

Exercise 6.1: Combine Data From Multiple Data Sources

In Exercise 5.10, you learned how to create flows for multiple data sources on the same Data Flow tab. If you recall, the package was not completed in that exercise. This exercise completes that package by writing the data from the data flows to the same output file, using the **UNION ALL TRANSFORMATION**.

1. Rename a copy of the E5.10 package to `E6.1 Union All transformation`.

2. Add the Union All component.

3. Connect the Calculate sales tax transformation, Sort descending transformation and the Sept 2015 source to the Union All component ⇒ Open the Union All Editor.

 The order that you connect components to the Union All transformation is the order that they are referenced in on the Union All Transformation Editor.

On the Union All Transformation Editor shown in Figure 6-1, the first column is a list of the fields that were created from the combination of the fields from all of the input sources. Notice that two fields in the last column have <ignore> instead of a field.

The Amount field was not mapped because it is not in the Sept 2015 source file. The Tax field is ignored because it was not calculated in the Sept 2015 source. If either field was in the Sept 2015 file, but had a different name, you could replace the <ignore> value by opening the drop-down list and selecting the field.

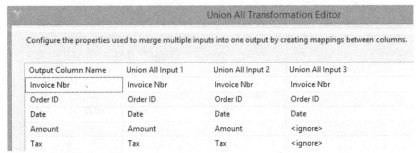

Output Column Name	Union All Input 1	Union All Input 2	Union All Input 3
Invoice Nbr	Invoice Nbr	Invoice Nbr	Invoice Nbr
Order ID	Order ID	Order ID	Order ID
Date	Date	Date	Date
Amount	Amount	Amount	<ignore>
Tax	Tax	Tax	<ignore>

Figure 6-1 Union All mappings

Create The Destination

In this part of the exercise, you will create a text file for the data from the three data flows to be written to.

1. Add the Flat File Destination ⇒ Rename it to `Ch6 Union All output` ⇒ Connect it to the Union All transformation.

2. Create a new delimited connection ⇒ Type `Ch6 Union Export` as the Connection manager name.

3. Type `C:\SSIS Book\Ch6 Union All exercise.txt`, as the file name.

4. Check the Column names option ⇒ Click OK.

5. Run the package.

    As shown in Figure 6-2, 107 rows from the first two data flows and 99 rows are from the third source were written to the destination file.

    It is not a requirement to send all of the data flows to the same destination table.

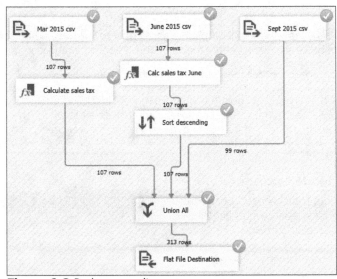

Figure 6-2 Package result

Joining Tables

More than likely, many of the packages that you will create, will need to use data in more than one table. There are two options, as explained below.

① Using one of the following transformations in SSIS: Lookup, Merge or Merge Join. More than one of these transformations can be used in the same package. If you find a package is running slow, remember that you can see how long the lookup process takes by looking at the last line (for the name that you gave the lookup or merge transformation task) on the **EXECUTION RESULTS TAB.**

② Join the tables outside of SSIS (in SSMS using the Query Designer). Quite frankly, this is the easiest option and because it is done outside of SSIS, it will not slow the packages down. The next chapter shows you how to join tables this way.

Lookup Transformation

As it's name indicates, this transformation is used to lookup data. If you are familiar with join types from using other software packages, the Lookup transformation is the equivalent of the **INNER JOIN**. The difference in SSIS is that the Lookup transformation is processed in the SSIS data flow, which is outside of the database engine. Tables can be joined from different database types. Another difference is that when done at the database level (in a query created in SSMS or in the Query Builder in SSIS), more than two tables can be joined at the same time. For example in an Inner Join, all of the following tables can be joined together: Order Header, Order Detail, Products, Customers and Sales Reps.

 The Lookup transformation can only create joins using two tables or data sets at a time. If you need to join data from more than two tables, you need to use multiple Lookup transformations. For example, if an order table needs data from the customer table and from the sales rep tables, you would have to create the following joins: Join #1) Orders table and Customer table, Join #2) Orders table and Sales Rep table. This is done by using the output from Join #1, as the input for Join #2.

Figure 6-3 shows some of the columns in the Order Detail and Product tables. As shown in the figure, these tables are linked on the Product ID field. That link is how columns from both tables can be used together to look up data.

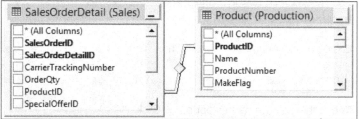

Figure 6-3 Order Detail and Product tables joined

 It is possible that the Lookup transformation will not find any matching records. When this is the case, multiple outputs are available for this transformation, including one for matched rows and one for rows that do not match.

 When using the Lookup transformation, it is a good idea that the largest table (usually the primary or fact table) is read into the component and the smallest table (the one that has the data that the primary table will lookup), is the table that is cached. The reason for doing this is because the table that is cached, blocks the flow when it is loaded into memory.

Cache Mode Options

The Lookup transformation has three cache modes, as shown in Figure 6-4. They are explained below.

They are used to let you select or trade off between resource usage and performance.

In some cache modes, the Lookup transformation initially stops the packages execution while the data is loaded into cache.

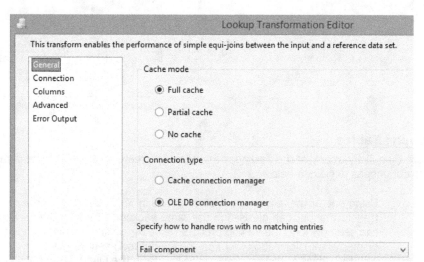

Figure 6-4 Lookup transformation cache mode

☑ In the **FULL-CACHE MODE**, one table is loaded into memory entirely. Rows in the other table are read in, in batches and the join operation is performed. Lookups against the table that is in memory is very fast. As shown in the figure, this is the default cache mode.

☑ In the **NO-CACHE MODE**, there is no caching upfront. This option is often used when you have decided that the lookup table is too large to cache all at once. Rows in the primary table are compared, one at a time to rows in the relational lookup table. This is probably the slowest of the three modes and the most likely to cause a performance issue when using a large data set. While probably the slowest mode, it is the best option if the lookup table has a lot of rows or if the data in the lookup table is volatile (the data changes frequently).

☑ The **PARTIAL-CACHE MODE** functions between the other two modes. Only the most recently used data is cached. When the cache gets too large, the least used cache data is discarded to make space for new data. This mode will increase the package run time, if there are a lot of rows that do not find a match in the lookup table. If you find that this is the case, once the partial cache option is selected, the options on the Advanced page, shown below in Figure 6-5, are enabled.

 If the lookup table is too large to be loaded into memory at one time (full-cache mode), select one of the other two options discussed above. The **CACHE TRANSFORMATION** can also be used to reduce memory usage. It is covered later in this chapter.

Partial-Cache Mode Advanced Options

The 32 and 64 bit cache options, shown in Figure 6-5, can be changed for each platform that the package could run on.

Checking the **ENABLE CACHE FOR ROWS WITH NO MATCHING ENTRIES** option, is used to force the task to remember the values that were not found in the lookup table. Doing this will help the performance. As show, the default cache allocation is 20%. You should increase this secondary cache value.

The **CUSTOM QUERY SECTION** shows the query that was automatically created to look up the values.

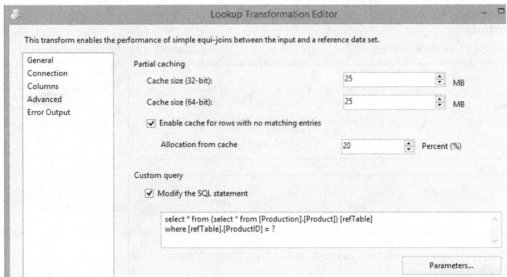

Figure 6-5 Advanced page lookup options

Exercise 6.2: Lookup Transformation

In this exercise you will use the Lookup transformation to get the product name from a different table.

1. Rename a new package to `E6.2 Lookup transformation`.

2. Create a source connection to the AW database ⇒ Rename the connection to `Order Detail table`.

3. On the editor, select the Sales.SalesOrderDetail table.

4. On the Columns page, clear the check mark for the following columns: Sales Order Detail ID, Carrier Tracking Number, Special Offer ID, row guid, and Modified Date.

Configure The Lookup Transformation

1. Add the Lookup transformation ⇒ Rename it to `Product Lookup` ⇒ Connect it to the source.

2. On the editor, on the Connection page, select the Production.Product table.

3. On the Columns page, link the tables on the Product ID field.

4. Check the Name column in the Lookup Columns table. This is the lookup field that will be added when the data set is written to the destination table. You can select as many lookup fields as needed.

5. In the Output Alias column, type `ProductName`, as shown in Figure 6-6 ⇒ Click OK.

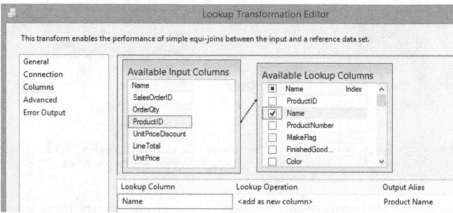

Figure 6-6 Lookup options selected

Configure The Destination

1. Create an Excel destination connection named `Create lookup table` ⇒ Connect it to the Lookup transformation.

2. On the dialog box, open the Output drop-down list and select Lookup Match Output, as shown in Figure 6-7.

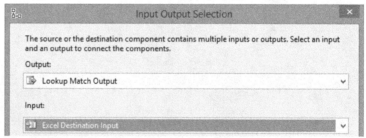

Figure 6-7 Lookup Input Output Selections

3. On the destination editor, use the Excel exported exercises data connection manager.

4. Select the Ch6 Lookup Product Name table.

5. On the Mappings page, all of the columns should be linked, including the Product Name column. Notice that the Product Name column (from the lookup table) has been added to the table ⇒ Click OK.

6. Run the package. Figure 6-8 shows some of the data that was written to the destination table in the Exported Exercise Data workbook.

	A	B	C	D	E	F	G
1	SalesOrderID	OrderQty	ProductID	UnitPriceDiscount	LineTotal	UnitPrice	Product Name
2	43659	1	776	0	2024.994000	2024.994	Mountain-100 Black, 42
3	43659	3	777	0	6074.982000	2024.994	Mountain-100 Black, 44
4	43659	1	778	0	2024.994000	2024.994	Mountain-100 Black, 48
5	43659	1	771	0	2039.994000	2039.994	Mountain-100 Silver, 38
6	43659	1	772	0	2039.994000	2039.994	Mountain-100 Silver, 42
7	43659	2	773	0	4079.988000	2039.994	Mountain-100 Silver, 44
8	43659	1	774	0	2039.994000	2039.994	Mountain-100 Silver, 48
9	43659	3	714	0	86.521200	28.8404	Long-Sleeve Logo Jersey, M
10	43659	1	716	0	28.840400	28.8404	Long-Sleeve Logo Jersey, XL

Figure 6-8 Lookup data added to a table

What Happens If A Matching Lookup Record Is Not Found?

Doing the steps below now, would append the same data to the destination table in Exercise 6.2 that you just added, unless you delete the current data from the table. If you are like me, curious, you will probably want to add two data viewers, one for the rows of data that found a match, that will be written to the output file and one for the rows of data that did not find a match in the lookup file. If so, do the following:

1. Add a data viewer right before the Create lookup table transformation.

2. Add a Union All transformation and connect it to the Lookup no match output, as shown in Figure 6-9.

    Figure 6-10 shows the data viewer for the Match Output. In this exercise, you will not see a data viewer popup for the No Match path. That is because all of the records found a match in the lookup table. If this data viewer appeared, you would probably create a destination file for the records that did not find a matching lookup record.

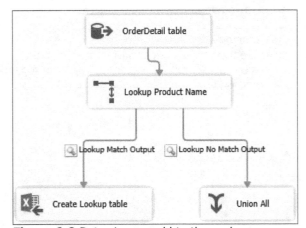

Lookup Match Output Data Viewer at Data Flow Task

SalesOrderID	ProductID	Product Name
43659	776	Mountain-100 Black, 42
43659	777	Mountain-100 Black, 44
43659	778	Mountain-100 Black, 48
43659	771	Mountain-100 Silver, 38

Figure 6-10 Data for Lookup match

Figure 6-9 Data viewers add to the package

Another Way To Cache Data

In the previous exercise, you learned how to use the Lookup transformation to get data from another table. The cache mode options were also covered. While these options work as intended, the cache data is only available for some OLE DB connections. What if you needed to look up data from an Excel file?

In the previous exercise, if the package had two or more data flows that needed to look up data from the same table, each data flow would need its own connection to the same lookup table. And the cached data would have to be reloaded each time each Lookup transformation was used.

If the table in each data flow had the same fields, they could be connected to a Union All transformation and then to a Lookup transformation. If that is not possible, the next section provides the alternative option.

Cache Transformation

When used with the Lookup transformation, the Cache transformation will load data to a cache file. In addition to being used in any Lookup transformation in the package, it can also be used to create a destination file. This reduces the database load and memory usage. Using the Cache transformation with the Lookup transformation means that all lookup transformations in the package can share the same cache and not reload it, each time that it is needed.

This transformation can also load the cache to a file so that it can be shared with other packages. This transformation is used to load a cache file to the data flow. This allows the Lookup transformation to perform lookups faster and use larger data sets for the lookup, without causing performance problems.

The Cache transformation has its own connection manager, named Cache Connection Manager. Like the other connection managers, the Cache Connection Manager is accessible from the Connection Managers folder.

The **CACHE CONNECTION MANAGER** is used in conjunction with the Cache transformation when the Cache transformation is used with the Lookup transformation. This connection manager can take data from just about any source and load it into cache for the Lookup transformation. The Lookup cache mode options only support OLE DB connections. This means that the lookup table could be in an Excel file or from a query, if the cache connection is used.

Exercise 6.3: Use The Cache And Lookup Transformations

In this exercise you will modify the E6.2 exercise by adding the Cache transformation to it. In addition to learning how to configure the Cache transformation, you will also get to see how a package that has multiple data flows looks.

While the lookup table used in this exercise does not have hundreds of thousands of rows, I wanted you to know about the cache information, so that on your own, when the need arises, you will be able to add the cache transformation to packages that use the Lookup transformation.

Modify The Control Flow Tab

1. Save a copy of the E6.2 package as E6.3 Cache transformation.

2. On the Control Flow tab, rename the Data Flow Task to Lookup Transformation.
   Each Data Flow Task has its own Data Flow tab, which is why I had you rename the Data Flow Task.

3. Add a Data Flow Task above the Lookup transformation task ⇒ Rename it to Cache Transformation ⇒ Connect it to the Lookup transformation task. Figure 6-11 shows the **DATA FLOW TASK DROP-DOWN LIST** on the Data Flow tab. You can select the data flow that you want to work on, by selecting it here or by right-clicking on the corresponding Data Flow Task on the Control Flow tab and selecting Edit.

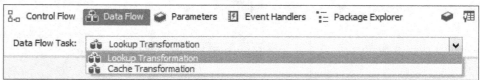

Figure 6-11 Data Flow Task drop-down list

Configure The Cache Transformation

1. On the Cache Transformation Data Flow Task (See Figure 6-11 above), add an OLE DB source. It is probably easier to use the Source Assistant and select the SQL Server AW connection.

2. On the editor, create the query shown in Figure 6-12. This query creates the values for the lookup table.

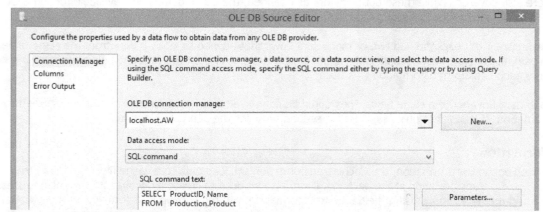

Figure 6-12 Query to retrieve the product names

3. Add the Cache transformation ⇒ Connect it to the OLE DB source.

4. Open the Cache Transformation Editor ⇒ Click the New button.

5. On the Columns tab, change the Index Position to 1 for the Product ID field, as shown in Figure 6-13 ⇒ Click OK. The Mappings page should look like the one shown in Figure 6-14.

The options on this tab are used to indicate which column(s) should be used as an index field and which column should be used as a reference field.

The **INDEX POSITION FIELD** is used to indicate that the field will be used to link (join) on.

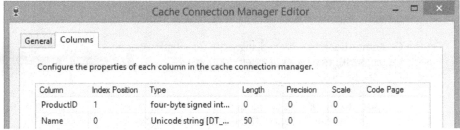

Figure 6-13 Cache Connection Manager Editor options

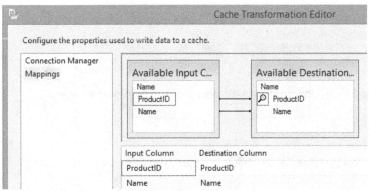

Figure 6-14 Mappings page options

6. On the Lookup Transformation data flow task, open the Product Lookup transformation editor ⇒ On the General page, select the Cache connection manager option, shown earlier in Figure 6-4.

7. On the Columns page, link the table on the Product ID column.

8. Check the Name column ⇒ Change the Output Alias to ProductName.

9. On the Excel Destination editor, select the Ch6 Cache Lookup Product Name sheet.

10. Run the package. When you view the table, you will see the same data that was shown earlier in Figure 6-8.

Creating Multiple Lookups

When using relational data, there will be times when there is a need to look up data from more than one table. This is not a problem. Just use as many Lookup transformations, as you need.

Exercise 6.4: Use Three Lookup Tables

In this exercise, you will learn how to create a package that looks up the customer name, sales rep and territory.

 While this exercise uses lookup tables that are in the same database, when you need to use lookup tables in different data sources, use the Cache Connection Manager discussed earlier in this chapter.

1. Rename a new package to E6.4 Use three lookup tables.

2. Create a connection to the AW database ⇒ Rename the connection to Order Header table.

3. On the editor, select the Sales.SalesOrderHeader table.

4. On the Columns page, only select the following fields: Sales Order ID, Order Date, Customer ID, Sales Person ID, Territory ID and Total Due. The last three ID fields selected, will be used to look up data in other tables.

5. Add three Lookup transformations ⇒ Rename them `Customer lookup`, `Sales Rep lookup` and `Territory lookup`.

Create The Customer Lookup

1. Connect the Customer lookup to the Order Header table.

2. On the Customer Lookup editor, display the Connection page ⇒ Select the **USE RESULTS OF AN SQL QUERY** option ⇒ Type the query below.

   There is a space between the single quotes. This query selects the Customer ID field and creates the Customer Name field, by combining the values in the First and Last Name fields ⇒ Click the Preview button. You should see the data shown in Figure 6-15.

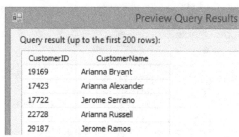
Figure 6-15 Customer name query results

```
SELECT CustomerID, FirstName + ' ' + LastName AS CustomerName
FROM    Sales.CustomerPII
```

3. On the Columns page, drag the Customer ID field in the Input table to the same field in the Lookup table ⇒ Check the Customer Name field.

Handling Records With No Match

It is possible that there is no matching record in the lookup table. When that is the case, the following options are available.

☑ Redirect the rows to an error output destination file, using the red arrow on the lookup transformation.

☑ Redirect the rows to a No Match Output, by selecting the **LOOKUP NO MATCH OUTPUT** option on the Input Output Selection dialog box. This option is used to write the rows to another file or connect the path to another transformation.

☑ Ignore that there is no match for some records and allow the records without a match to continue through the data flow.

The option that you select depends on how important the missing data is. For example, if the missing data is needed as a field that will be used in a calculation, or as a link to another table or needs to be looked up in another table, the row should be redirected. If the missing data will not be used in these types of scenarios, it may be okay to ignore the failure and allow the row to continue through the flow. An example of letting the row continue is when the destination file will be used to create a report. Hopefully, empty fields on a report will get someone's attention, so that the data can be corrected. <smile>

In this exercise, every order should at least have a customer. How can there be an order without someone (a customer) placing it? If a customer lookup did not find a match, there is a much bigger problem and the row should be redirected to another table.

1. On the General page, open the drop-down list and select **IGNORE FAILURE**.

> **Error Output Page Alternative**
> I find this easier to use the **SPECIFY HOW TO HANDLE ROWS . . . OPTION** on the General page, on the Lookup Transformation Editor [See Figure 6-4], then selecting the same option on the Error Output page, when I want the same option applied to all of the fields in the table.

Create The Sales Rep Lookup

1. Connect the Sales Rep transformation to the Customer lookup transformation ⇒ Open the Output drop-down list and select Lookup Match Output.

2. On the editors Connection page for the Sales Rep lookup, create the query below.

```
SELECT BusinessEntityID, FirstName + ' ' + LastName AS SalesRep
FROM   Person.Person
```

3. On the Columns page, drag the Sales Person ID field in the Input table to the Business Entity ID field in the lookup table ⇒ Check the Sales Rep field.

4. On the General page, open the drop-down list and select **IGNORE FAILURE**.

Create The Territory Lookup

1. Connect the Territory transformation to the Sales Rep transformation ⇒ Select the Lookup Match Output option.

2. On the editors Connection page for the Territory transformation, select the Sales.SalesTerritory table.

3. On the Columns page, drag the Territory ID input field to the Territory ID lookup field ⇒ Check the Name field ⇒ Change the Output Alias to `Territory`.

4. On the General page, open the drop-down list and select **IGNORE FAILURE**.

Finish The Package

1. Add the Union All transformation and connect it to the Territory lookup ⇒ Select the Lookup Match Output option.

2. Run the package.

    You should see that the number of rows is the same for each step, as shown in Figure 6-16.

    In this exercise that is what should happen, even if there were rows with missing data. That is because nothing was set up to handle rows that did not find a match for any of the three lookups.

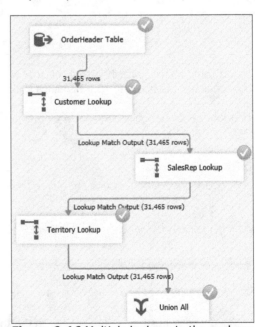

Figure 6-16 Multiple lookups in the package

Another Lookup Transformation Feature

Now that you have used the Lookup transformation, hopefully you have an idea of whether or not it is a transformation that you would use on your own. There is another feature that I think may be helpful.

In addition to using a data source in the same package to create a cache file, you can create a cache file using data from a different package. The table with the least amount of data is the one that should be loaded into the cache file. Once data is loaded into a cache file, it can be used by several data flows in several packages in the project. This includes being able to use the cache file in a Data Flow Task that is in a Foreach Loop Container.

Merge

As its name indicates, this transformation is used to merge data from two data sources into the same output file. What you may like about this transformation is that you can add additional components for error handling. While this transformation is similar to the Union All transformation covered earlier in this chapter, the Merge transformation has some requirements that you need to understand before deciding to use it, instead of using the Union All transformation. The requirements are explained below.

☑ If you need to use more than two paths, use the Union All transformation. By paths, I mean two or more arrows connecting to the Merge transformation. For example, if the flow has three Conditional Split transformations above the Merge transformation, only two of the Conditional Split transformations can connected to the same Merge transformation.

☑ The metadata must be the same for both tables. **METADATA** is data about other data. In this transformation, metadata refers to the data type. For example, the Order Amount field in one table cannot have the String data type and a numeric data type in the table being used in the Merge transformation.

☑ The data must be sorted exactly the same way on both paths leading into the Merge transformation, that you want to connect to it. This means that both tables must be sorted on fields that have the same data. Changing options on the Advanced Editor, as shown later in Figure 6-18, means that you do not have to actually sort the data, but can say that it is sorted. <smile> The ORDER BY clause in the Sort transformation can also be used to sort the data.

When you connect a path to the Merge transformation, you will see the dialog box shown in Figure 6-17.

Open the Input drop-down list and select **MERGE INPUT 1**, for the first path that you are connecting to the merge. The Merge Input 2 option is for the second path that you are connecting to this transformation.

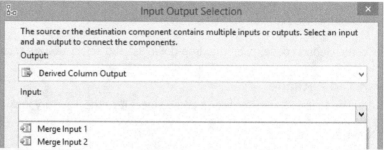

Figure 6-17 Input Output Selection dialog box (Merge transformation)

When the second component is attached to the Merge transformation, the Merge Input 2 path is automatically applied to it and you will not see the Input Output Selection dialog box.

The transformation is automatically configured by mapping the columns from the paths. You can select to not use a column of data, by selecting <ignore>.

Exercise 6.5: Merge Data

In this exercise, you will learn how to use the Merge transformation to write data from two text files into a new text file.

1. Rename a new package to `E6.5 Merge data`.

2. Add two Flat File Source components ⇒ Rename one to `MergeFile1` ⇒ Rename the other to `MergeFile2`.

3. Open the editor for Merge File 1 ⇒ Create a new connection named `Merge1` ⇒ Select the MergeFile1.txt file.

4. Open the Advanced editor for MergeFile1 ⇒ On the Input and Output Properties tab, click on the Flat File Source Output section ⇒ Change the **IS SORTED** property to True.

5. Display the fields in the Output Columns folder ⇒ Click on the Order ID field ⇒

   Change the **SORT KEY POSITION** property to 1, as illustrated in Figure 6-18.

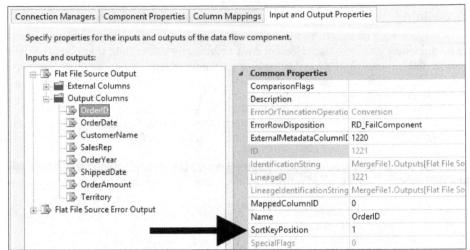

Figure 6-18 Sort Key Position property illustrated

 As long as the **IS SORTED** and **SORT KEY POSITION PROPERTIES** are set, the data in the table doesn't actually have to be sorted, but you did not hear that from me. <smile>

6. Repeat steps 3, 4 and 5 for the Merge2 source. Change the 1 to 2, in steps 3 and 4.

Set Up The Merge And Destination File

1. Add the Merge transformation.

2. Connect the MergeFile1 source to the Merge transformation ⇒ In the Input drop-down list, select the Merge Input 1 option.

3. Connect the MergeFile2 source to the Merge transformation ⇒ Open the Merge Editor.

   You should have the options shown in Figure 6-19.

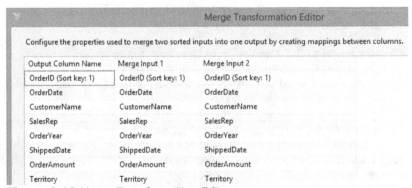

Figure 6-19 Merge Transformation Editor

4. Add the Flat File Destination ⇒ On the editor, create a new connection ⇒ Name the connection Ch6 Merge ⇒ Type C:\SSIS Book\Ch6 Merge exercise.txt, as the file name.

5. Run the package. 25 rows should have been written to the destination file. The top of the destination file should look like the one shown in Figure 6-20.

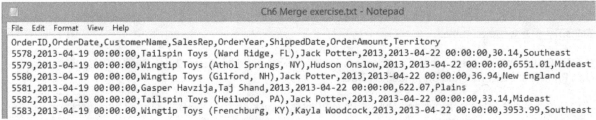

Figure 6-20 Merge file created from two input files

Merge Join

This transformation can perform the equivalent of an **INNER JOIN** or an **OUTER JOIN**, when two data flows are merged. It is useful when you have two different data sources, that have data that needs to be merged. For example, you need to merge data in an inventory system with the data collected from an app that the field sales reps use.

The Merge Join transformation will remind you of the Lookup transformation. This transformation is best suited when you need to merge/join tables that are in different data sources or you are not familiar enough with T-SQL to create a query. A benefit that the Merge Join transformation has over the Lookup transformation is that it does not create large cache files. It can also use reference data from the data flow path in addition to a data source transformation.

While there are some similarities between the Lookup transformation and the Merge Join transformation, there are some differences. The Merge Join transformation does not pre load data, cache a data set or do per record queries.

Like the Merge transformation, the Merge Join transformation uses a dialog box, as shown in Figure 6-21, to link the input data sources.

The difference is the Input field options. You have to select the join type that you need to use.

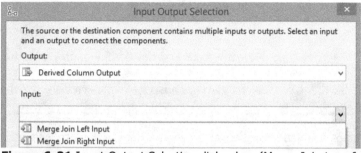

Figure 6-21 Input Output Selection dialog box (Merge Join transformation)

 It is important to note that if both tables are in the same database, it is quicker to create the join at the OLE DB source level (by creating a query), instead of using a transformation.

How To Set The Sort Properties

There are steps that must be completed to ensure that sorting is enabled properly. This is how the component will know that the data is presorted, as explained below.

① In addition to the data having to be sorted, the **IS SORTED PROPERTY** on both data sources Advanced Editor (Input and Output Properties tab), must be set to True.
② Once the Is Sorted property is set, the sort order of the columns needs to be set. The sorting for both data sources has to use the same column.

Why The Order By Clause Is Not Recognized
Even though the query uses an **ORDER BY CLAUSE** to sort the data, SSIS (the OLE DB source component) does not know this. That is because the **METADATA** that SQL Server returns after running the query only includes column names, data types and a few other items. The sort order is not included in the metadata. Because the Sort transformation is used, SSIS has to process the sort, so it knows that the data is sorted.

Exercise 6.6: Use The Merge Join Transformation

In this exercise, you will learn how to join the data in two tables in the same database. One table will be used to lookup the product name and product line for each row in the primary table.

1. Rename a new package to E6.6 Merge tables from a database.

2. Create a source connection to the AW database ⇒ Name it Order Detail ⇒ On the source editor, select the Sales.SalesOrderDetail table.

3. On the Columns page, remove the check mark for the following fields: Sales Order Detail ID, Special Offer ID, Unit Price Discount, rowguid and Modified Date.

4. On the Advanced Editors, Input and Output Properties tab, click on the OLE DB Source Output section ⇒ Change the Is Sorted property to True.

5. In the Output Columns folder, change the Product ID's Sort Key Position property to 1. Yes, I know what you may be thinking. That the Sort Key property should be set for the Sales Order ID field. This is what I thought also. Then I realized after getting an error when running the package, that the Merge Join transformation does not work that way.

6. Create a source connection to the AW database ⇒ Name it `Product table` ⇒ On the source editor, select the Production.Product table.

7. On the Columns page, clear the check mark for all of the fields, except Product ID, Name and Product Line.

 When you only need to select a few fields in a table, it is easier to remove the check mark at the top of the table (which clears the check mark for all of the fields), then check the ones that you need.

8. Change the Output Column for the Name field to `Product Name`, as shown in Figure 6-22.

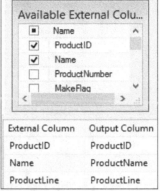

Figure 6-22 Product table options

9. Repeat steps 4 and 5 above for this table.

Configure The Merge Join Transformation

 The only columns that can be used to join the tables on the Merge Join Transformation Editor, are ones that the tables are sorted on.

1. Add the Merge Join transformation.

2. Connect the Order Detail source to the Merge Join transformation ⇒ In the Input drop-down list, select the Merge Join Left Input option.

3. Connect the Product table to the Merge Join transformation.

4. On the Merge Join Transformation Editor, the Product ID field should be checked, in the **JOIN KEY COLUMN**, in both tables ⇒ Change the Join type to **LEFT OUTER JOIN**.

The next step is used to select the fields in the order that you want them added to the destination table.

5. In the Order Detail table, check the following fields: Sales Order ID and Product ID ⇒ Change the Product ID Output Alias to `ProductNbr`.

6. Check the Product Name field.

7. In the Order Detail table, check the following fields: Order Qty, Unit Price and Line Total.

8. Check the Product Line field. You should have the options shown in Figure 6-23.

    The **JOIN TYPE FIELD** is used to select how to link the tables. The default join type is **INNER JOIN**.

    The other options in the drop-down list are **LEFT OUTER JOIN**, which you used in this exercise and **FULL OUTER JOIN**. This join type is also known as a **CROSS JOIN** or **CARTESIAN JOIN**. This join selects rows from both tables, whether or not there are matching rows in the other table.

Figure 6-23 Merge Join transformation options

The **SWAP INPUTS BUTTON** is used when the tables are not in the right order. Clicking this button will switch the left input table to the right input table and vise versa.

Sort The Data Before Adding It To The Destination

Because the records are currently sorted on the Product ID field, they will not be written to the destination table sorted in the order that they should be, which is by the Sales Order ID field. Therefore, the data needs to be sorted before it is written to the destination table.

1. Add the Sort transformation ⇒ Connect it to the Merge Join transformation.

2. On the Sort Editor, check the Sales Order ID field.

3. Create an Excel destination ⇒ Name it `Ch6 Merge Join` ⇒ Connect it to the Sort transformation.

4. On the editor, select the Excel exported exercises data connection ⇒ Select the Ch6 Merge Join table ⇒ Click on the Mappings page. All of the fields should be mapped.

5. Run the package.

    You should see that the Order Detail table had 121,317 rows at the beginning of the package and that is the same number of rows that were written to the destination table, as shown in Figure 6-24.

    In this exercise, that is correct because the data was not filtered. If fewer rows were written to the destination table, there is a problem, based on the specs for this exercise.

    While this package runs, it does not retrieve the lookup data from the Product table, as it should. I tried creating the package several different ways, using a variety of options. The more I tried, the worse it got. I know what the data in the destination table should look like because I created a query in the Query Builder. [See Chapter 7, Exercise 6.6 Recreated In Query Builder]

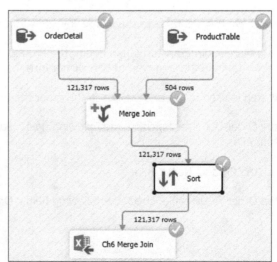

Figure 6-24 Package with a Merge Join transformation

Exercise 6.7: Merge Data From Two Sources

In this exercise, you will learn how to use the Merge Join transformation to join data from a table in the AW database and a sheet in an Excel workbook. The table in the database will be the primary table. The sheet in the Excel workbook will be the lookup table to get the sales reps names.

1. Rename a new package to `E6.7 Merge from 2 file types`.

2. Create a source connection to the AW database ⇒ Name the connection `Order Info table` ⇒ On the editor, select the Order Info table.

3. On the Columns page, only select the following fields: Order ID, Order Date, Customer Name, Sales Rep ID and Order Amount.

4. On the Advanced Editor, change the Is Sorted property to True, like you did in the previous exercise ⇒ In the Output Columns folder, change the Sales Rep ID's Sort Key Position property to `1`.

5. Create a source connection to the Excel ssis_data file ⇒ Name the connection `Sales rep table`.

6. On the editor, select the Sales Reps sheet ⇒ On the Columns page, clear the check mark for all of the fields, except the first two.

7. Repeat step 4 for the Excel source. Use the Rep ID field.

Configure The Merge Join Transformation

1. Add the Merge Join transformation.

2. Connect the Order Info table to the Merge Join transformation ⇒ In the Input drop-down list, select the Merge Join Left Input option.

3. Connect the Sales Rep table to the Merge Join transformation.

4. On the Merge Join Transformation Editor, change the Join type to **LEFT OUTER JOIN**.

5. On the Order Info table, check the following fields: Order ID, Order Date and Customer Name.

6. Check the Full Name field in the Sales Rep table ⇒ Change the Output Alias to `SalesRep`.

7. On the Order Info table, check the Order Amount field.

    You should have the options shown in Figure 6-25.

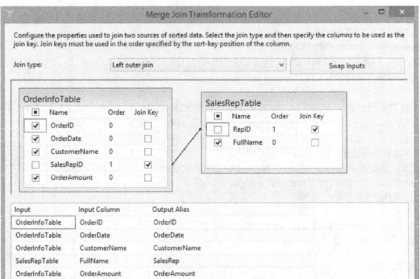

Figure 6-25 Merge Join Transformation Editor options

8. Add the Union All transformation and connect it to the Merge Join transformation ⇒ Run the package.

   You should see the output shown in Figure 6-26.

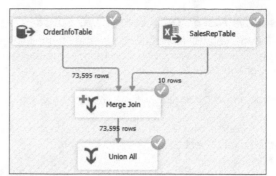

Figure 6-26 Data merged from 2 different sources

Multicast

This transformation is used to send data to two or more destinations. It does not alter the data. For example, the data is currently being written to a database and a user needs the same data in an Excel file. The additional file created can be the same destination file type as the one currently being used in the package. Once the Multicast transformation is connected, it can then be connected to other destinations or transformations.

This transformation is similar to the Conditional Split transformation in the fact that both can send data to multiple outputs. The difference is that the Multicast transformation sends all of the data to each of the destinations or other transformations that it is attached to.

Exercise 6.8: Send Data To Multiple Files

In this exercise, you will modify a package that currently sends the data to an Excel file, to also send the data to a text file.

1. Save a copy of the E6.2 package as E6.8 Multicast transformation.

2. Delete the arrow after the Product Lookup transformation.

3. Add the Multicast transformation below the Product Lookup transformation ⇒ Rename it to Send data to 2 files.

4. Connect the Multicast transformation to the Product Lookup transformation ⇒ Open the Output drop-down list and select Lookup Match Output.

5. Connect the Create Lookup table to the Send data to 2 files transformation ⇒ On the editor, select the Ch6 Multicast sheet.

6. Add a Flat File Destination ⇒ Rename it to Ch6 Multicast output file ⇒ Connect it to the Multicast transformation.

7. On the Flat File editor, create a new connection named Ch6 Multicast that connects to a new text file named Ch6 Multicast table.txt in the SSIS Book folder.

8. Check the Column names option ⇒
   The package layout should have the connections and transformations shown in Figure 6-27 ⇒
   Run the package.

   You should see that the same number of rows are written to both tables.

   While this exercise connected the Multicast transformation to destination files, it could also be connected to another transformation.

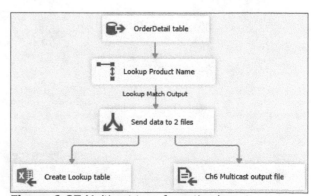

Figure 6-27 Multicast transformation layout

Logging The Data In A Package

After you have created packages in this book, you had the option of running the package and viewing information about the execution of the package, including warnings, errors and general information. When a package goes into production, it will probably be put on a schedule to automate running it. It would be helpful if there is a log file, so that you could see the status of the package.

The **LOGGING OPTION** is on the SSIS menu. This option is used to record package information at run time. This includes values in variables and parameters.

 Packages that are run from a catalog, automatically have events logged. [See Chapter 8, Configuring The Catalog]

Configure SSIS Logs Dialog Box

Figure 6-28 shows the dialog box that is used to create the log file for a package. The log file can store package run times and error information.

Providers And Logs Tab

The options in the **PROVIDER TYPE** drop-down list are used to select the type of log file that the logged data will be saved in. As needed, more than one log provider can be used in the same package. The options are explained below.

SQL SERVER The data will be written to a table in SQL Server.

WINDOWS EVENT LOG The data will be written to the Windows Event log. This file type can be read remotely.

TEXT FILES Writes the data to a csv file.

SQL SERVER PROFILER Writes the data to a file that can be captured in the SQL Server Profiler trace file.

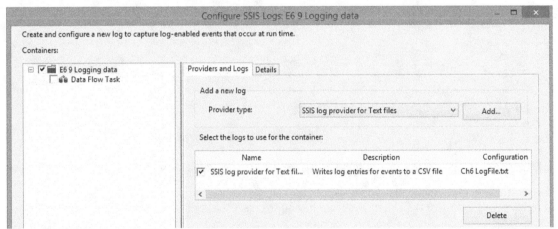

Figure 6-28 Configure SSIS Logs dialog box

 Tasks that are checked, but not enabled in the Containers list, means that the task will use the log settings of the parent container.

Details Tab

Figure 6-29 shows the Details tab options. These are the events that you can select to be logged. When or if the events that you select occurs, while the package is running, an entry will be written to the log file. The events displayed, depend on what is selected in the **CONTAINERS SECTION**, on the left side of the dialog box. By checking the first option (the package) in this section, the events selected will be applied to the other tasks in this section. Checking any of the other tasks, will write more events to the list.

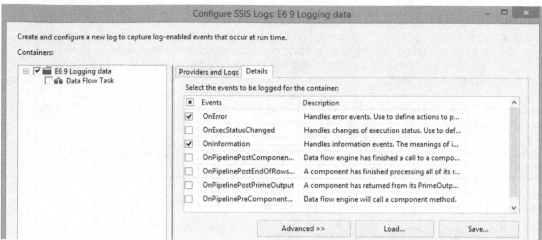

Figure 6-29 Details tab options

 Clicking the check box to the left of the Events heading shown above in Figure 6-29, will check all of the events.

Clicking the **ADVANCED BUTTON** displays the options shown in Figure 6-30. This screen is used to customize the events that will be logged. If you do not want to log an option that is checked, clear the check mark. For example, if you do not want the computer name logged for the On information event, clear the check mark illustrated in the Computer column.

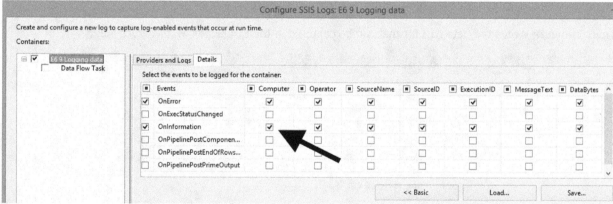

Figure 6-30 Advanced Details tab

The **SAVE BUTTON** is used to save the options that you select, to an XML file. Doing this will let you use the XML configuration file in another package. This will keep you from having to select the same options manually, for other packages.

The **LOAD BUTTON** is used to open an XML logging configuration file to use with the current package that is open.

Exercise 6.9: Add Logging Functionality To A Package

In this exercise you will learn how to add logging functionality to a package.

1. Save a copy of the E6.1 package as `E6.9 Logging data`.

2. Right-click on the Control Flow canvas ⇒ Logging.

3. Clear the check mark for the Data Flow Task in the **CONTAINERS LIST** ⇒ Check the E6.9 Logging data option.

Set Up The Log File

1. Open the Provider type drop-down list and select the SSIS log provider for text files option.

2. Click the Add button.

3. Check the log option that was just created.

4. In the **CONFIGURATION COLUMN**, open the drop-down list and select <New connection>.

5. On the File Connection Manager Editor, change the Usage type to **CREATE FILE**.

6. In the File field, type `C:\SSIS Book\Ch6 LogFile.txt`. You should have the options shown in Figure 6-31 ⇒ Click OK. You should have the logging options shown earlier in Figure 6-28.

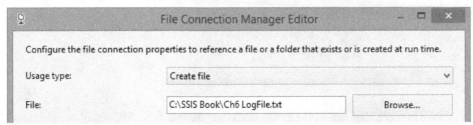

Figure 6-31 Options to create the log file

Select The Events To Be Logged

1. On the Details tab, check the following events: On Error, On Information, On Task Failed and On Warning.

2. Run the package ⇒ When the package is finished, open the Ch6 LogFile.txt file in Notepad.

From the options that were selected for this exercise, the last column is probably the one that you will be most interested in. That is because it lets you know each step that was executed, as shown in Figure 6-32.

```
Beginning of package execution.

016266,0x,Validation phase is beginning.

016262,0x,Prepare for Execute phase is beginning.

016263,0x,Pre-Execute phase is beginning.

876060,0x,The processing of file "C:\SSIS Book\Ch6 Union All Exercise.txt" has started.

876060,0x,The processing of file "C:\SSIS Book\Sept2015.csv" has started.
```

Figure 6-32 Log file

QUERY BUILDER CRASH COURSE

Overview

After reading this chapter and completing the exercises, you will have a better understanding of how to use Query Builder to create queries.

If you already know how to create queries using T-SQL or how to use Query Designer in SSMS or SSRS to create queries, you can skip this chapter, because Query Builder in SSIS, provides the same functionality as these tools. The exercises in this chapter are not used in the last chapter in this book.

CHAPTER 7

Overview

Truth be told, when I created the outline for this book, it was not even a consideration to cover Query Builder in any detail. By the time that I finished writing the first draft of Chapter 5, I decided to cover Query Builder enough for people that currently do not know T-SQL to be able to have a way to join tables, filter and sort data, and create basic expressions that may be needed for a package.

While there are transformations for joining and sorting, etc., they can be time consuming to set up and I thought knowing how to create this functionality in a single query, would make your life a little easier. As you have seen, a few exercises earlier in this book used Query Builder briefly. If you have used Query Designer in SSMS or SSRS, you are already familiar with Query Builder in SSIS.

This crash course in learning the basics of creating queries is not intended to and does not cover all of the functionality that Query Builder has, but it will go a long way towards helping you get familiar with creating queries, without knowing T-SQL. If you plan to learn SSRS, this chapter will be very helpful and put you ahead of the game.

The two most important things that I hope that you take away from this chapter are:

① If you do not know T-SQL, don't worry. This chapter covers the basics of creating queries without writing the code from scratch. While you will not be typing the queries from scratch, seeing the code generated, will hopefully make you a little more comfortable, when the time comes to learn T-SQL from scratch.

② Some of the functionality that the tasks and components on the Data Flow tab in SSIS have, can also be accomplished in a query. The benefit of a query is that the more "work" and "processing" that is done in a query, allows the package to run faster. And you will see that creating a query is usually easier then using a task or transformation. One query can create the same functionality that requires several tasks and transformations. For example, in one query, you can filter data, sort data, create new (derived) columns of data and join tables.

 If you have used the Query Designer in SSMS or SSRS, Query Builder has most of the same functionality. Why these tools do not have the same name, is beyond me. <smile>

The benefit that SSIS components and tasks have over Query Builder is that they support any database or file type that you can connect to. Query Builder only supports OLE DB and Excel data sources. If you want to use Query Builder with other file types, you can import the data into an OLE DB or Excel data source.

Query Builder

The illustrated sections of Query Builder in Figure 7-1, are explained below. The buttons on the toolbar are explained in Table 7-1.

The **DIAGRAM PANE** displays the tables used to create the data set and the joins (relationships) between the tables. (1)

The **CRITERIA PANE** (also known as the **GRID PANE**) displays the fields used in the query. This pane is also used to rename fields, sort the rows, create filters, groups and new columns (fields). (1)

The **SQL PANE** displays the T-SQL code, that is automatically generated from the diagram and criteria panes. As you add fields and make changes in the Criteria pane, you can see the code change in the SQL pane. You can also type code in this pane and modify the code that is automatically generated.

The **RESULT PANE** displays the rows that are retrieved when the query is run. This lets you check to ensure that the criteria created is retrieving the records that you expect. If some or all of the records displayed in this section are not what you need, make changes in the other sections, as needed.

(1) One feature in Query Builder that you will like, especially when first learning how to create queries, is that changes that you make in the top two sections of Query Builder, are automatically applied to the query (in the SQL pane section). For example, this means that if you check a field in the first section and later change your mind and uncheck the field, the field is also removed from the query.

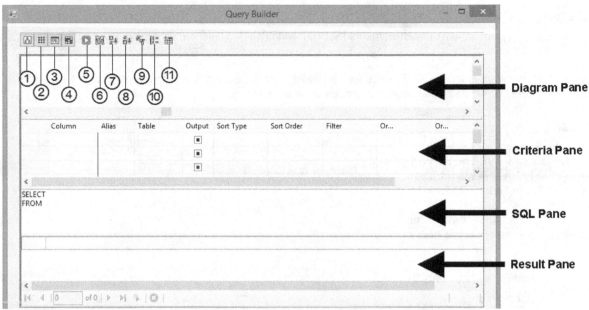

Figure 7-1 Query Builder

Button	Description
①	The **SHOW/HIDE DIAGRAM PANE BUTTON** displays/hides the Diagram pane.
②	The **SHOW/HIDE GRID PANE BUTTON** displays/hides the Grid (criteria) pane.
③	The **SHOW/HIDE SQL PANE BUTTON** displays/hides the SQL pane.
④	The **SHOW/HIDE RESULT PANE BUTTON** displays/hides the Result pane.
⑤	The **RUN BUTTON** runs/executes the query and displays the data that is retrieved, in the Result pane. (2)
⑥	The **VERIFY SQL BUTTON** checks the SQL syntax of the code, in the SQL pane. It does not display all of the errors at one time. The errors are displayed one by one, after you fix the current error.
⑦	**SORT ASCENDING** button. (3)
⑧	**SORT DESCENDING** button. (3)
⑨	The **REMOVE FILTER BUTTON** is only enabled after a filter has been created and the field used in the filter is selected, in the Diagram pane. The button is used to remove the filter. To me, it is easier to remove the filter criteria from the grid.
⑩	The **USE GROUP BY BUTTON** adds the GROUP BY column to the Grid pane. [See GROUP BY Clause] (2)
⑪	The **ADD TABLE BUTTON** displays the Add Table dialog box, shown in Figure 7-2. As its name implies, it is used to add tables and views to the diagram pane. (2)

Table 7-1 Toolbar buttons explained

(2) This option is also available on the shortcut menu in the Diagram pane.
(3) This button is only enabled when a field in a table, in the Diagram pane, is selected.

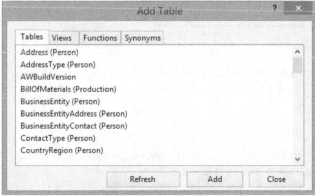

Figure 7-2 Add Table dialog box

SELECT Statement Clauses

As you have seen, a query has at least two statements (SELECT and FROM). There are other clauses, and they are explained throughout this chapter.

SELECT statements have what is known as **CLAUSES** (or parts). Each clause provides different functionality that relates to retrieving data. Some clauses are also referenced as **ARGUMENTS**.

FROM Clause

This clause is used to say what table(s) the fields used in the query are in. The SELECT statement shown in Figure 7-3 will retrieve all fields and rows in the Order Info table.

The bottom of the figure shows some of the records that were retrieved when the query was run.

Notice the SELECT and FROM statements in the middle of the Query Builder.

At the top of the Orders table (in the Diagram pane), you will see the ***(ALL COLUMNS)** option. Checking this option will cause all of the fields (columns) in the table to be retrieved when the query is run. This option does not display each field in the table, in the query.

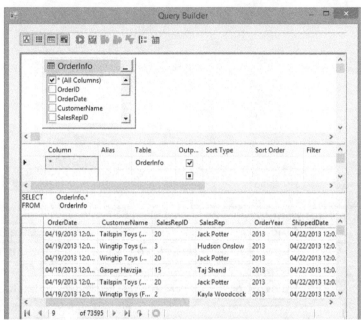

Figure 7-3 Basic query

Selecting Fields To Add To The Query

In Figure 7-3 above, the query retrieved all of the fields in the table. Most of the time, all of the fields in a table are not needed for a package. The solution is to only add fields that are needed, after the SELECT clause, as shown in Figure 7-4. To add fields, you can use any of the following: check them in the table at the top of the dialog box, open the Column drop-down list and select a field, or type the fields in on the SELECT line. Specifying fields to be retrieved is known as adding a **FIELD LIST** to the SELECT statement.

```
SELECT      OrderID, OrderDate, CustomerName, OrderAmount
FROM        OrderInfo
```

Figure 7-4 Fields added to the SELECT statement

> **Exercise Tips**
> ① After you rename the package, open the editor ⇒ Click the Build Query button.
> ② To add a table to the query, click the **ADD TABLE BUTTON**.

Exercise 7.1: Create A Basic SELECT Query

In this exercise you will learn how to create a query that selects a few fields in a table. You will also create a template to use as the starting point for the majority of the exercises in this chapter.

Create The Template

1. Rename a copy of the E5.3 package to `0 Ch7 Query Builder`. The first character in the package name is a zero. I gave it that name so that it will be at the top of the SSIS Packages folder, which will make it easier to get to. Just like the empty package file that you may have created earlier in Chapter 3.

The file will move up to the top of the SSIS Packages folder, once you make a copy of it, in the next section of this exercise. I will refer to this package as the "QB package".

. . . .

2. On the OLE DB Source Editor, delete the query (the text in the SQL command text box).

3. Open Query Builder and add the Order Info table ⇒ Click OK twice. You will see the red circle on the button on the Data Flow tab, but that's ok ⇒ Save the changes to the package.

Create The SELECT Query

1. Rename a copy of the QB package to `E7.1 Basic SELECT query`.

> **Selecting Fields**
> The order that you check the fields in, (in the tables) is the order that they will be added to the Criteria pane. It is customary to use the primary key field, as the first field in the query, if the field needs to be displayed in the query results or if it will be used to create criteria. Doing so, is not a requirement.

2. Check the following fields on the Order Info table: Order ID, Order Date, Customer Name, Order Amount and Sales Rep.

    The grid and query should look like the ones shown in Figure 7-5.

    The query shown, will also be displayed on the source editor in the SQL command text box.

Column	Alias	Table	Outp...	Sort Type
OrderID		OrderInfo	✔	
OrderDate		OrderInfo	✔	
CustomerName		OrderInfo	✔	
OrderAmount		OrderInfo	✔	
SalesRep		OrderInfo	✔	

```
SELECT    OrderID, OrderDate, CustomerName, OrderAmount, SalesRep
FROM      OrderInfo
```

Figure 7-5 Basic SELECT query

Create An Alias

An alias in Query Builder, is created to give a field a more user friendly name, that better describes the data stored in the field. This is the same as the Alias column that some transformations have. Doing this is not a requirement. It is usually done for one of the following reasons:

① The field contains a formula (aka expression), which means that it needs its own name.
② The data in the field will be used by an end user. Some field names may be cryptic to non IT people. For example, the data, from the query, will be exported to a spreadsheet that will be used by the Marketing department, or the query will be used by someone using SSRS to create reports. In either scenario, the person using the data, may not be familiar with the field names used in a table.

1. In the Alias column for the Order ID field, type `Order Nbr` ⇒ Press Enter.

> Notice in Figure 7-6, that brackets were automatically added around the name in the Alias column. That is because the name has a space in it.

Look at the query. Notice that **AS [ORDER NBR]** was automatically added after the Order ID field.

When reading the query, this lets you know that when the result of the query is used in a transformation or is written to a destination file, that "Order Nbr" will be used as the field name/column header, instead of Order ID.

Column	Alias	Table	Outp...	Sort Type	Sort
OrderID	[Order Nbr]	OrderInfo	✔		
OrderDate		OrderInfo	✔		
CustomerName		OrderInfo	✔		
OrderAmount		OrderInfo	✔		
SalesRep		OrderInfo	✔		

```
SELECT    OrderID AS [Order Nbr], OrderDate, CustomerName, OrderAmount, SalesRep
FROM      OrderInfo
```

Figure 7-6 Alias name created for a column

2. Click the Run button.

At the bottom of the Query Builder window, you should see the rows shown in Figure 7-7. These are the fields from the Order Info table that would be available to the transformations in the package, when using this query as the source. The columns in this section can be resized as needed, just as you do in Excel.

	Order Nbr	OrderDate	CustomerName	OrderAmount	SalesRep
▶	5578	04/19/2013 12:00:00 AM	Tailspin Toys (Ward Ridge, FL)	30.14	Jack Potter
	5579	04/19/2013 12:00:00 AM	Wingtip Toys (Athol Springs, NY)	6551.01	Hudson Onslow
	5580	04/19/2013 12:00:00 AM	Wingtip Toys (Gilford, NH)	36.94	Jack Potter
			•		
			•		
	5586	04/19/2013 12:00:00 AM	Tailspin Toys (Fieldbrook, CA)	30.14	Taj Shand
	5587	04/19/2013 12:00:00 AM	Wingtip Toys (Rose Tree, PA)	33.14	Taj Shand

|◀ ◀ | 1 | of 73595 | ▶ ▶| | 🔖 | ○ |

Figure 7-7 Query result

The difference is that the resizing is not saved when the query is saved.

3. Click OK twice ⇒ Save the package. At this point, you would add the transformations and destination, as needed.

DISTINCT Clause

Use the DISTINCT clause when you only want to retrieve one row of data for each unique value in the field(s) after the SELECT clause. Most of the time you will use the DISTINCT clause with one field.

I use this clause when I need to create a query that will be used as a list of values for a parameter. For example, if I needed a list of order dates from the Orders table, I would use the query shown in Figure 7-8.

```
SELECT DISTINCT OrderDate
FROM    OrderInfo
```

Figure 7-8 SELECT statement with DISTINCT clause

The Order Info table has several records that have the same order date. For values displayed in a parameter, each date only needs to be displayed once, in the parameter drop-down list. In this scenario, I am referring to a parameter field for a report created in SSRS.

WHERE Clause

This clause is used to create the filter criteria that the data has to meet to be retrieved. Filters can be created for fields that will not be used in a transformation or written to a destination table. In the previous exercise, the query retrieved all of the records in the table. The next exercise will show you how to create a filter.

Exercise 7.2: Create A Date Filter

In this exercise, you will create a query that filters the Order Date field to only retrieve rows if the field has a date in the specified range. Often, there is a need to select records that are in a date range, like 9/1/15 to 9/19/15 or for a specific year. The **BETWEEN OPERATOR** is used in the Filter column, when you want to select values that are in a range.

1. Rename a copy of the QB package to `E7.2 Date range filter`.

2. Add the following fields: Order ID, Customer Name, Order Date.

3. In the Filter column for the Order Date field, type `Between 9/1/15 and 9/19/15` ⇒ Press Enter. You should have the filter criteria and query shown in Figure 7-9. Notice that the WHERE clause converted the date field for you.

	Column	Alias	Table	Outp...	Sort Type	Sort Order	Filter
	OrderID		OrderInfo	✔			
	CustomerName		OrderInfo	✔			
	OrderDate		OrderInfo	✔			BETWEEN '09/01/2015' AND '09/19/2015'

```
SELECT    OrderID, CustomerName, OrderDate
FROM      OrderInfo
WHERE     (OrderDate BETWEEN CONVERT(DATETIME, '2015-09-01 00:00:00', 102) AND CONVERT(DATETIME, '2015-09-19 00:00:00', 102))
```

Figure 7-9 Filter criteria and query

4. Run the query.

    You should see the rows shown in Figure 7-10. If you scroll down the list of rows, you will see that all of the rows have an Order Date in the date range that you created.

OrderID	CustomerName	OrderDate
56545	Tailspin Toys (Avenal, CA)	09/07/2015 1...
56546	Tailspin Toys (Cherry Grove B...	09/07/2015 1...
56547	Amarasimha Vinjamuri	09/07/2015 1...

Figure 7-10 Result of the filter criteria

Exercise 7.3: Create Multiple Filters

The previous exercise showed you how to create range filter criteria for a date field. If you needed to select specific sales reps, a range filter would not work. You would need filter criteria for each sales rep that you want to include. To get these values for this exercise, I looked in the Order Info table and randomly selected these ID values. No magic involved. <smile>

1. Rename a copy of the QB package to E7.3 Multiple filters.

2. Add the following fields: Order Date, Customer Name, Sales Rep ID and Sales Rep.

3. In the Filter column for the Sales Rep field, type Jack Potter. You should have the filter criteria and query shown in Figure 7-11.

Column	Alias	Table	Outp...	Sort Type	Sort Order	Filter
CustomerName		OrderInfo	✔			
SalesRepID		OrderInfo	✔			
SalesRep		OrderInfo	✔			= N'Jack Potter'

```
SELECT    OrderDate, CustomerName, SalesRepID, SalesRep
FROM      OrderInfo
WHERE     (SalesRep = N'Jack Potter')
```

Figure 7-11 Filter criteria for one sales rep by name

4. In the OR column for the Sales Rep ID field, type 3 or 7 ⇒ Press Enter. This will select the sales rep for ID number or 3 or 7.

Figure 7-12 shows the query.

The **WHERE CLAUSE** will select rows when the Sales Rep field equals Jack Potter or if the Sales Rep ID field equals 3 or 7. This means that as long as one of these three filter conditions are met, the row will be retrieved.

```
SELECT    OrderDate, CustomerName, SalesRepID, SalesRep
FROM      OrderInfo
WHERE     (SalesRep = N'Jack Potter') OR
          (SalesRepID = 3 OR
           SalesRepID = 7)
```

Figure 7-12 Multiple filter criteria

5. Run the query. You will only see rows that meet one of the values on the WHERE clause, shown above in Figure 7-12.

6. Clear the check mark in the **OUTPUT COLUMN** for the Sales Rep ID field.

    The query will no longer display this field on the SELECT statement, as shown in Figure 7-13. Compare this figure to Figure 7-12.

```
SELECT    OrderDate, CustomerName, SalesRep
FROM      OrderInfo
WHERE     (SalesRep = N'Jack Potter') OR
          (SalesRepID = 3 OR
           SalesRepID = 7)
```

Figure 7-13 Modified filter query

7. Run the query. While the Sales Rep ID field is not displayed in the Result pane at the bottom of the dialog box, the filter criteria for the field is still used.

Changing The Order Of Fields In The Grid
If you have the need to reorder the fields in the grid, click on the light gray square, to the left of the field that you want to move. Then hold the mouse button down and drag the mouse pointer up or down, to the location where you want the field moved to.

Exercise 7.4: Extract And Convert Parts Of A Date Field

If you need to sort data by year or need to use the month name, as part of a group, you need a way to get that information from a date field. Functions are used to extract this data from a date field.

The new columns of data that you will create in this exercise is the same as using the **DERIVED COLUMN TRANSFORMATION** that was covered in Chapter 4.

Extract The Year From A Date Field

You have seen the **YEAR FUNCTION** used in Chapter 5, Exercise 5.3. Now, you will learn how to use this function.

1. Rename a copy of the QB package to E7.4 Date field query.

2. Add the Order Date field.

3. Click in the row below the Order Date field ⇒
    Open the drop-down list shown in Figure 7-14 and select the
    Order Date field.

    Yes, the same field can be added to the criteria pane more
    than once.

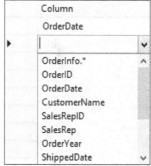

Figure 7-14 Column drop-down list

4. Click before the field name and type YEAR(⇒ Click at the end of the field and type a).

5. In the Alias column, type OrderYear2. The reason that I added the 2 after the field name is because the table already has a field named Order Year.

6. Run the query.

    You should have the criteria and query shown
    in Figure 7-15.

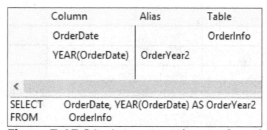

Figure 7-15 Criteria to extract the year from the date field

Extract The Month Number From A Date Field

In this part of the exercise, you will learn how to extract the month number. This value is often used when there is a need to group by year, then by month. Grouping or sorting on the month name, will not put the month names in calendar order, which is what is requested or needed in most situations. Sorting on the month name would display the months in alphabetical order, which probably is not what you want.

The **MONTH FUNCTION** is used to extract the month number from a date field.

1. In the row below the YEAR formula, type MONTH(OrderDate).

2. In the Alias column, type MonthNumber. The query should look like the one shown in Figure 7-16. If you want, you can run the query.

```
SELECT    OrderDate, YEAR(OrderDate) AS OrderYear2, MONTH(OrderDate) AS MonthNumber
FROM      OrderInfo
```

Figure 7-16 Formula to extract the month number

Extract The Month Name From A Date Field

This part of the exercise will show you how to get the month name. The **MONTH NAME FUNCTION** is used to extract the month name. Displaying the month name is often used in financial reports. It is also used a lot in a crosstab/pivot table report, as the column headings.

In Chapter 5, Figure 5-29, the Year column headings could be replaced with month names. This would allow the data for a specific year to be displayed by month name. To get the month names in calendar order, the data would have to be sorted by the month number that you learned how to create in the previous part of this exercise.

If you have the need to use the Month Name function, you may as well create the Month Number formula at the same time, as they are often used together.

1. On the next row in the grid, in the first column type MONTHNAME(OrderDate).

2. In the Alias column, type MonthFullName. Your query should look like the one shown in Figure 7-17.

SELECT	OrderDate, YEAR(OrderDate) AS OrderYear2, MONTH(OrderDate) AS MonthNumber,
	{ fn MONTHNAME(OrderDate) } AS MonthFullName
FROM	OrderInfo

Figure 7-17 Query that creates year, month number and month name columns

3. Run the query.

You should see the columns shown in Figure 7-18. I scrolled down the list to select the data to shown in the figure, so that you could see different values in the three new columns of data, that were created in this exercise.

OrderDate	OrderYear2	MonthNumber	MonthFullName
04/26/2013 ...	2013	4	April
04/26/2013 ...	2013	4	April
04/26/2013 ...	2013	4	April
04/26/2013 ...	2013	4	April
09/03/2014 ...	2014	9	September
09/03/2014 ...	2014	9	September
09/03/2014 ...	2014	9	September

Figure 7-18 Result of the date formulas

Calculate The Order Processing Time

In Chapter 4, Exercise 4.7, you learned how to create a derived column to calculate the order processing time. In this part of the exercise, you will create the same formula.

1. On a new row in the grid, type DATEDIFF(dd, OrderDate, ShippedDate).

2. Type OrderProcessingTime in the Alias column, as shown in Figure 7-19.

Column	Alias	Table
OrderDate		OrderInfo
YEAR(OrderDate)	OrderYear2	
MONTH(OrderDate)	MonthNumber	
{ fn MONTHNAME(OrderDate) }	MonthFullName	
DATEDIFF(dd, OrderDate, ShippedDate)	OrderProcessingTime	

Figure 7-19 Columns for the query

The reason that the Table column is empty for most of the fields is because the fields are calculated fields.

3. Run the query. The number in the Order Processing Time column displays the number of days between the Order and Shipped dates.

I don't know about you, but the first two steps above are much easier to create then using the Derived Column transformation, and you can run the query to see the results immediately, instead of having to enable the Data Viewer in SSIS. <smile>

Sorting The Data In A Query

By default, the data retrieved in the query is not sorted. To sort the data, select the first column that you want to sort on, then select if you want the data in the column to be sorted in ascending or descending order. You can sort on more than one column. Columns that are sorted on do not have to be displayed in the query results. In a way, sorting data is like grouping data, because all records that have the same value in the field(s) used in the sort, are displayed together.

Sorting data in a query, accomplishes the same functionality that the **SORT TRANSFORMATION** does. The benefit of sorting data in a query is that it requires less processing power, which is a good thing. <smile>

ORDER BY Clause

This clause is used to sort the data that is retrieved in the query. Once you select a field to sort on, you will see an A to Z icon with an arrow next to the field in the table. This icon indicates how the field is sorted, as illustrated later at the top of Figure 7-20. If a sort order is not selected, the field will be sorted in ascending order. When the descending sort order is selected, DESC will automatically be added to the ORDER BY clause. If you type in the SQL code to create the sort, you have to type DESC in, to specify that the field should be sorted in descending order.

Exercise 7.5: Sort The Data

In this exercise you will modify the WHERE clause to sort on the following three fields: Customer Name, Order ID and Order Date.

1. Rename of copy of the QB package to `E7.5 Sorting data`.

2. Add the following fields: Order ID, Order Date, Order Amount and Customer Name.

3. In the **SORT ORDER** column for the Customer Name field, type $1 \Rightarrow$

    In the Sort Order column for the Order ID field, type $2 \Rightarrow$

    In the Sort Order column for the Order Date field, type 3.

    You should have the options illustrated in Figure 7-20. When you run the query, you should see the rows shown in Figure 7-21.

    By looking at the data shown in Figure 7-21, it is difficult to tell if or how the data is sorted.

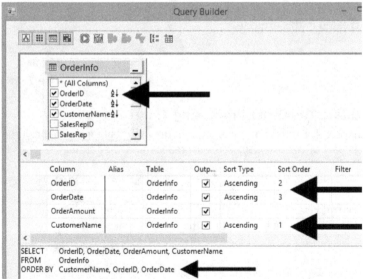

Figure 7-20 ORDER BY criteria to sort on three fields

You could place the fields in the order that the data is sorted by, to make it easier to see the sort order.

A group could be created for the Customer Name field. This would display all of a customers orders together.

OrderID	OrderDate	OrderAmount	CustomerName
1	01/01/2013 ...	23153.23	Aakriti Byrraju
45	01/01/2013 ...	472.31	Aakriti Byrraju
495	01/09/2013 ...	1381.07	Aakriti Byrraju
1318	01/25/2013 ...	35.66	Aakriti Byrraju
1387	01/28/2013 ...	87.27	Aakriti Byrraju

Figure 7-21 Result of ORDER BY criteria in Figure 7-20

GROUP BY Clause

This clause takes sorting one step further by creating a summary (a total) for rows that have a common value in the field(s) being grouped on. The two tasks that are needed to create a GROUP BY clause, are explained below.

① You have to decide which field(s) will be used to create a group. The unique values in these fields create the group. For example, the Orders table has a sales rep and order date field. All orders that have the same sales rep and order date could be used to create a group. Each group creates a row in the data set.

② You have to decide what other fields will be used to create a summary row. These fields would not be placed on the GROUP BY clause. Usually, these fields do not have values that make sense to group on, or if they could be grouped on, it would not add value to the report. Some of these fields may need to have some type of summary value created, like a count or total (sum). Fields that fall into this category can use functions to create the summary value. These summary values are displayed when the value in at least one of the Group By fields change. In the scenario discussed above, the summary values would be displayed on the report when the sales rep name or order date changes.

 Keep in mind that when a GROUP BY clause is used, each field must go into one of the categories discussed above. Fields that do not use an aggregate function are included on the GROUP BY clause after the fields that are aggregated on.

Sorting vs Grouping Data

The biggest difference between sorting and grouping records is that sorting displays all of the detail records and grouping, displays a summary of the sorted detail records. Think pivot table or crosstab layout. Another difference is that grouping records allows calculations to be added to the query. These calculations are created by using what is known as an **AGGREGATE FUNCTION**.

Exercise 7.6: Use The Group By Option

In this exercise, you will use the Group By option to group the orders by sales rep and year. It is a good idea to add the fields that will be grouped on to the grid, in the order that you want the rows of data grouped. In this exercise, the rows should be grouped by sales rep, then by the order year.

1. Rename a copy of the QB package to E7.6 Group By clause.

2. Add the Sales Rep field to the grid.

3. Create a formula using the Order Date field, to extract the year. (Refer back to Exercise 7.4, if necessary.) ⇒ Type YearEnding in the Alias column.

4. Add the Order ID field to the grid ⇒ In the Alias column, type # of sales for the year.

5. Click the **USE GROUP BY BUTTON** on the toolbar.

6. Open the Group By drop-down list for the Order ID field ⇒ Scroll down and select **COUNT DISTINCT**. The options in the drop-down list are not in alphabetical order.

7. Sort the Year Ending column in ascending order. Your grid and query should look like the ones shown in Figure 7-22.

Column	Alias	Table	Outp...	Sort Type	Sort Order	Group By
SalesRep		OrderInfo	&#10003;			Group By
YEAR(OrderDate)	YearEnding		&#10003;	Ascending	1	Group By
OrderID	[# of sales for the year]	OrderInfo	&#10003;			Count Distinct

```
SELECT     SalesRep, YEAR(OrderDate) AS YearEnding, COUNT(DISTINCT OrderID) AS [# of sales for the year]
FROM       OrderInfo
GROUP BY   SalesRep, YEAR(OrderDate)
ORDER BY   YearEnding
```

Figure 7-22 Group By criteria

8. Run the query. Figure 7-23 shows the first few rows of data retrieved by the query.

    Each row of data shown in the figure, is a summary (a distinct count) of the total number of sales (orders) for each sales rep, for each year that they have data in the table.

    This exercise is the equivalent of using the **PIVOT TRANSFORMATION**, but has more functionality.

SalesRep	YearEnding	# of sales for the year
Amy Trefl	2013	1942
Anthony Grosse	2013	1936
Archer Lamble	2013	1986
Hudson Hollin...	2013	1908
Hudson Onslow	2013	1945
Jack Potter	2013	1969
Kayla Woodcock	2013	2014

Figure 7-23 Result of the Group By criteria

For example, if the Order Amount criteria shown at the bottom of Figure 7-24 was added, the total amount of each sales rep sales would be displayed, as shown in Figure 7-25.

Column	Alias	Table	Outp...	Sort Type	Sort Order	Group By
SalesRep		OrderInfo	✔			Group By
YEAR(OrderDate)	YearEnding		✔	Ascending	1	Group By
OrderID	[# of sales for the year]	OrderInfo	✔			Count Distinct
OrderAmount	[Total Sales Amount]	OrderInfo	✔			Sum

Figure 7-24 Order Amount criteria added to the query

SalesRep	YearEnding	# of sales for the year	Total Sales Amount
Anthony Grosse	2013	1936	1139290.92
Jack Potter	2013	1969	4550210.14
Kayla Woodcock	2013	2014	18917300.02
Sophia Hinton	2013	1966	5545219.97

Figure 7-25 Result of Order Amount criteria being added to the query

HAVING Clause

As needed, this clause is used with the GROUP BY clause. The HAVING clause is used to select which grouped rows will be retrieved. Using it, will remind you of the WHERE clause discussed earlier, because it filters the group rows, that are created by the GROUP BY clause.

Exercise 7.7: Using The HAVING Clause

In this exercise, you will add the HAVING clause to the GROUP BY query that you created in the previous exercise. The HAVING clause will be used to select sales reps whose yearly number of orders is greater than or equal to 2,000.

1. Rename a copy of the E7.6 package to `E7.7 HAVING clause query`.

2. In the Filter column for the Order ID field, type `>=2000`. The grid and query should look like the ones shown in Figure 7-26.

Column	Alias	Table	Outp...	Sort Type	Sort Order	Group By	Filter
SalesRep		OrderInfo	✔			Group By	
YEAR(OrderDate)	YearEnding		✔	Ascending	1	Group By	
OrderID	[# of sales for the year]	OrderInfo	✔			Count Distinct	>= 2000

```
SELECT     SalesRep, YEAR(OrderDate) AS YearEnding, COUNT(DISTINCT OrderID) AS [# of sales for the year]
FROM       OrderInfo
GROUP BY SalesRep, YEAR(OrderDate)
HAVING     (COUNT(DISTINCT OrderID) >= 2000)
ORDER BY YearEnding
```

Figure 7-26 Modified query with a HAVING clause

3. Run the query.

    Figure 7-27 shows the first few rows of data.

    All of the rows have a value equal to or greater than 2,000, in the last column.

SalesRep	YearEnding	# of sales for the year
Kayla Woodcock	2013	2014
Amy Trefl	2014	2083
Anthony Grosse	2014	2130
Archer Lamble	2014	2139

Figure 7-27 Result of the Order ID filter criteria

JOIN Clause

This clause is used to link tables. Tables used with this clause have to be linked to a table in the FROM clause in the SELECT statement.

The first part of the JOIN clause lists the tables that are being joined. The next part of the JOIN clause (after the word "ON") contains the field from each table that will be used to link the tables.

As covered in the previous chapter, many of the packages that you create, will need data from more than one table. As shown in Figure 7-28, the Customer ID field is displayed. The data set would be more useful if it contained the customer name instead.

SELECT OrderID, CustomerID, OrderDate
From Sales.Orders

Figure 7-28 Query using the Customer ID field

Figure 7-29 shows the SELECT statement that retrieves the Customer Name field in the Customers table, from a second table.

```
SELECT   Sales.Orders.OrderID, Sales.Orders.CustomerID, Sales.Orders.OrderDate, Customers.CustomerName
FROM     Sales.Orders INNER JOIN
         Sales.Customers ON Sales.Orders.CustomerID = Customers.CustomerID
```

Figure 7-29 SELECT statement with a JOIN clause

Using More Than One Table In A Query
When more than one table is used to create a query, each field must be referenced by its table name. Not doing this will create an error. The good news is that when using Query Builder, the table name for each field used in the query, is automatically added to the code, as shown above in Figure 7-29.

If you type in the code, shown above in Figure 7-29, you have to type in the table name. In the query shown earlier in Figure 7-26, table names were not needed because the query only used one table.

Exercise 7.8: Join Tables

So far in this chapter, all of the queries that you have learned to create, only used one table. In this exercise, you will learn how to create a query that uses data in two tables. Joining tables provides the same functionality as the **LOOKUP, MERGE** and **MERGE JOIN TRANSFORMATIONS** that were covered in the previous chapter. The difference is that joining the tables in a query is much easier. The caveat is that the tables that need to be joined, have to be in the same SQL Server database or Excel workbook. As needed, data from other sources can be imported into the database, as you learned, when using the Import and Export wizard.

The Order Detail table contains all of the items for each order. By design, the table stores the Product ID field. Most of the time, the product name is displayed, instead of the Product ID. The Product Name field is stored in a different table and will be "looked up", so to speak.

1. Rename a copy of the QB package to `E7.8 Join 2 tables.`

2. Delete the Order Info table. (Click on the table ⇒ Press the Delete key.)

3. Add the Sales Order Detail (Sales) table ⇒ Add the Product (Production) table.

As you can see, a link was automatically created between the tables, on the Product ID field. As shown in the query in Figure 7-30, an **INNER JOIN** was automatically created from the Order Detail table to the Product table. The Product table is the lookup table. All of the rows in the Order Detail table need to be retrieved, whether or not there is a matching record in the Product table.

```
SELECT
FROM     Sales.SalesOrderDetail INNER JOIN
         Production.Product ON Sales.SalesOrderDetail.ProductID = Production.Product.ProductID
```

Figure 7-30 Inner Join link between tables

If you are not sure that the default join that is created, is what you need, right-click on the link between the tables. You will see the shortcut menu shown in Figure 7-31.

The Select All options are used to pick the type of join that you need. In this exercise, all of the rows in the Order Detail table need to be retrieved, so you would select the first option.

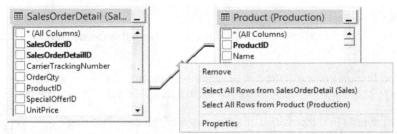

Figure 7-31 Join shortcut menu

4. Select the first Select All option, shown above in Figure 7-31. Notice that the join type changed in the query, to the Left Outer Join, as shown in Figure 7-32.

```
SELECT
FROM      Sales.SalesOrderDetail LEFT OUTER JOIN
          Production.Product ON Sales.SalesOrderDetail.ProductID = Production.Product.ProductID
```

Figure 7-32 Modified join type

5. In the Order Detail table, check the Sales Order ID and Product ID fields.

6. In the Product table, check the Name field.

7. In the Order Detail table, check the following fields: Order Qty and Unit Price. The query should look like the one shown in Figure 7-33.

```
SELECT    Sales.SalesOrderDetail.SalesOrderID, Sales.SalesOrderDetail.ProductID, Production.Product.Name,
          Sales.SalesOrderDetail.OrderQty, Sales.SalesOrderDetail.UnitPrice
FROM      Sales.SalesOrderDetail LEFT OUTER JOIN
          Production.Product ON Sales.SalesOrderDetail.ProductID = Production.Product.ProductID
```

Figure 7-33 Query using data from two tables

In the previous chapter, you learned that SSIS did not know that the data was sorted, when a query sorted the data. The solution was to use the Advanced Editor to change the Is Sorted property and the Sort Key Position property.

Unless you make the same changes on the Advanced Editor, you will have the same problem when using a T-SQL query as the data source, even if the query has an **ORDER BY** clause. The reason is because the OLE DB source component works in what is called a **PASS-THROUGH PROCESS**, which means that the source component does not know that the ORDER BY clause exists. While column names and data type metadata is passed through, the sort order is not passed through.

8. Run the query.

Figure 7-34 shows the first few rows that were retrieved. Now, you can see the name of the products.

All of the rows shown in the figure have the same Sales Order ID because the items (products) were purchased on the same order. If you scroll down the list, you will see different Sales Order ID numbers.

SalesOrderID	ProductID	Name	OrderQty	UnitPrice
43659	776	Mountain-100 Black, 42	1	2024.994
43659	777	Mountain-100 Black, 44	3	2024.994
43659	778	Mountain-100 Black, 48	1	2024.994
43659	771	Mountain-100 Silver, 38	1	2039.994
43659	772	Mountain-100 Silver, 42	1	2039.994
43659	773	Mountain-100 Silver, 44	2	2039.994
43659	774	Mountain-100 Silver, 48	1	2039.994
43659	714	Long-Sleeve Logo Jersey, M	3	28.8404
43659	716	Long-Sleeve Logo Jersey, XL	1	28.8404

Figure 7-34 Result of a query with data from two tables

Create A Line Item Total

This field stores what is often referred to as the Extended Price. It is calculated by multiplying the quantity (how many of the item was ordered) times the price of the item. The Order Detail table has the Line Total column, which holds the value that I am referring to. This part of the exercise will show you how to create the formula to calculate the Line Item Total.

1. On an empty row in the grid, type `OrderQty * UnitPrice`.

2. In the Alias column, type `LineItemTotal`, as shown in Figure 7-35.

Column	Alias	Table
SalesOrderID		SalesOrder...
ProductID		SalesOrder...
Name		Product (P...
OrderQty		SalesOrder...
UnitPrice		SalesOrder...
Sales.SalesOrderDetail.OrderQty * Sales.SalesOrderDetail.UnitPrice	LineItemTotal	

Figure 7-35 Line item total formula

3. Run the query.

    You should see the last column shown in Figure 7-36.

SalesOrderID	ProductID	Name	OrderQty	UnitPrice	LineItemTotal
43659	776	Mountain-100 Black, 42	1	2024.994	2024.994
43659	777	Mountain-100 Black, 44	3	2024.994	6074.982
43659	778	Mountain-100 Black, 48	1	2024.994	2024.994
43659	771	Mountain-100 Silver, 38	1	2039.994	2039.994
43659	772	Mountain-100 Silver, 42	1	2039.994	2039.994
43659	773	Mountain-100 Silver, 44	2	2039.994	4079.988
43659	774	Mountain-100 Silver, 48	1	2039.994	2039.994
43659	714	Long-Sleeve Logo Jersey, M	3	28.8404	86.5212
43659	716	Long-Sleeve Logo Jersey, XL	1	28.8404	28.8404

Figure 7-36 New column of data created

Exercise 7.9: Linking To More Than One Table

The JOIN TRANSFORMATIONS that were covered in Chapter 6, have one limitation that queries do not have. That is only being able to only link to one other table at a time. In a query, you can link to as many related tables, as necessary. When a third table is added to the query, it can be linked to either of the tables that are already in the query.

In this exercise, you will modify the package that you created in Exercise 7.8, by adding two more tables and selecting fields from them. The Order Header table will be the primary table in the package. It contains the main information about each order. It has the Customer ID field, but not the customer name. The customer information is stored in the Customer table.

Add And Link The Tables

1. Rename a copy of the E7.8 package to `E7.9 Query with multiple tables`.

2. Delete all of the fields in the grid.

3. Add the Sales Order Header (Sales) table. This is the main order table. The Order Detail table will be linked to this table.

4. Right-click on the link between the Order Header and Order Detail tables ⇒ Select the All rows from Sales Order Header (Sales) option.

5. Add the CustomerPII (Sales) table ⇒ Drag the Customer ID field in the Order Header table to the Customer ID field in the Customer table ⇒ Right-click on the link between these tables and select the Sales Order Header option. The FROM CLAUSE in the query should look like the one shown in Figure 7-37.

```
SELECT
FROM      Sales.CustomerPII RIGHT OUTER JOIN
          Sales.SalesOrderHeader ON Sales.CustomerPII.CustomerID = Sales.SalesOrderHeader.CustomerID LEFT OUTER JOIN
          Sales.SalesOrderDetail ON Sales.SalesOrderHeader.SalesOrderID = Sales.SalesOrderDetail.SalesOrderID LEFT OUTER JOIN
          Production.Product ON Sales.SalesOrderDetail.ProductID = Production.Product.ProductID
```

Figure 7-37 Query with four linked tables

Select The Fields To Create The Query

1. In the Order Header table, check the Sales Order ID and Order Date fields.

2. In the Customer table, check the First Name and Last Name fields.

3. In the Order Detail table, check the Order Qty and Product ID fields.

4. In the Product table, check the Name field.

5. Run the query. You do not have to wait for all of the rows to be processed.

   You can click the Red stop button, at the bottom of the dialog box. You should see the rows shown in Figure 7-38.

SalesOrderID	OrderDate	FirstName	LastName	OrderQty	ProductID	Name
51657	06/27/2013 ...	Arianna	Bryant	1	799	Road-550-W Yellow, 42
51657	06/27/2013 ...	Arianna	Bryant	1	716	Long-Sleeve Logo Jersey, XL
70717	04/15/2014 ...	Arianna	Alexander	1	782	Mountain-200 Black, 38
70717	04/15/2014 ...	Arianna	Alexander	1	873	Patch Kit/8 Patches
49716	02/15/2013 ...	Jerome	Serrano	1	795	Road-250 Black, 52
54264	08/12/2013 ...	Jerome	Serrano	1	976	Road-350-W Yellow, 48
53264	07/27/2013 ...	Arianna	Russell	1	878	Fender Set - Mountain

Figure 7-38 Data from four tables

You will see rows that have the same Sales Order ID number, Order Date and First and Last Name fields. That indicates that more than one item was on the order. If you look at rows like that, you will see that the Product ID field has a different number for each row. If nothing else, this is the functionality that queries have over transformations.

Exercise 7.10: Recreate Exercise 6.4 Without Using The Lookup Transformation

In Exercise 6.4, you created a package that used the Lookup transformation to get data from three tables, to combine with the primary table. This exercise will show you how to create the same functionality of all of the components and transformations shown in Chapter 6, Figure 6-16, by creating **ONE** query. Yes, just one query. <smile>

Select And Link The Tables

1. Rename a new QB package to E7.10 Replace Lookup transformations.

2. Delete the Order Info table.

3. Add the following tables: Sales Order Header, Sales Territory, CustomerPII and Person.Person.

4. Delete the link between the Territory and Customer tables.

5. Right-click on the link between the Order Header and Territory tables ⇒ Select the Order Header option.

6. In the Order Header table, link the Customer ID field to the same field in the Customer table ⇒ Change the link to Select all from the Order Header table.

7. In the Order Header table, link the Sales Person ID field to the Business Entity ID field in the Person table ⇒ Change the link to Select all from the Order Header table. You should have the FROM statement, shown in Figure 7-39.

```
SELECT
FROM    Sales.SalesOrderHeader LEFT OUTER JOIN
        Person.Person ON Sales.SalesOrderHeader.SalesPersonID = Person.Person.BusinessEntityID LEFT OUTER JOIN
        Sales.CustomerPII ON Sales.SalesOrderHeader.CustomerID = Sales.CustomerPII.CustomerID LEFT OUTER JOIN
        Sales.SalesTerritory ON Sales.SalesOrderHeader.TerritoryID = Sales.SalesTerritory.TerritoryID
```

Figure 7-39 FROM statement

Select The Fields To Create The Query

1. Add the following fields from the Order Header table: Sales Order ID, Order Date and Total Due.

   Notice that the ID fields in the Order Header table that were used to link to other tables, were not added to the query. That is because they are not needed in the query.

2. Check the First Name field in the Customer table ⇒ In the first column in the grid, click after the First Name field and type + ' ' + LastName ⇒ Click in the Alias column and type CustomerName.

   Notice that Query Builder added the letter N to the expression.

 The reason that I had you check the First Name field is so that Query Builder would know which table the First Name field is in. As you can see, the same field names are in the Person table. Doing this keeps you from having to type in the table name in the expression. If you look at the query, you will see that the table name was automatically added. Less typing for us! <smile>

3. Check the First Name field in the Person table ⇒ Create the same expression that you created in step 2 ⇒ Type SalesRep in the Alias column.

4. Check the Name field in the Territory table ⇒ In the Alias column, type Territory.

The grid should look like the one shown in Figure 7-40.

Column	Alias	Table	Output
SalesOrderID		SalesOrderHeader (Sales)	✔
OrderDate		SalesOrderHeader (Sales)	✔
TotalDue		SalesOrderHeader (Sales)	✔
Sales.CustomerPII.FirstName + N' ' + Sales.CustomerPII.LastName	CustomerName		✔
Person.Person.FirstName + N' ' + Person.Person.LastName	SalesRep		✔
Name	Territory	SalesTerritory (Sales)	✔

Figure 7-40 Fields selected to be retrieved

5. Run the query. Figure 7-41 shows some of the rows retrieved.

Notice that 31,465 rows were retrieved, which is the same number of rows that was retrieved in Exercise 6.4.

SalesOrderID	OrderDate	TotalDue	CustomerName	SalesRep	Territory
53485	07/31/2013 12:00:00 AM	65910.6732	Pilar Ackerman	Syed Abbas	Australia
53492	07/31/2013 12:00:00 AM	20135.1188	Jenny Lysaker	Syed Abbas	Australia
53502	07/31/2013 12:00:00 AM	35912.8785	Jeff Hay	Syed Abbas	Australia

Figure 7-41 Data retrieved from four tables

Views

Views are usually created by a Database Administrator, or someone that has administrator rights to the database. Views are used to get data from a variety of tables and combine the data into a "view". This makes it easier to access the fields that you need, from different tables.

A view is a **DATASET** (the result) of a query and usually retrieves a subset of the data in a data source. Views are stored in the database and are like tables, but they do not have the physical characteristics of a table. For example, records cannot be added to or deleted from a view. New fields cannot be added to a view unless the query that creates the view is modified to include more fields. The field length or data type cannot be changed in a view, like it can in a table.

Views are created when the same record set, calculations or query needs to be used in several reports or in SSIS, for several packages. The IT department will create views, so that people do not have direct access to the live data and to prevent people from having access to some fields in a table. Using a view means that you would not have to select the same options over and over again, in the Query Designer, each time that you create a data set.

Instead of selecting all of the tables, fields and options in the Query Designer like you have done this chapter, select the view in the database, instead of the individual tables. Figure 7-42 shows views in the sample database.

Usually, views have data from more than one table. For example, in the previous exercise, you joined three tables and selected the fields from each table that you needed. Essentially, that is a view.

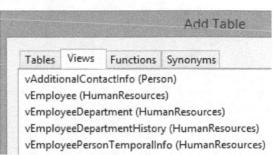

Figure 7-42 Views in the AW database

Being able to create queries, allows you to create a view, if you do not have administrator rights to the database to create a view. Instead of creating the query in Query Builder, create the query in the Query Designer in SSMS and save the query as an **.SQL FILE**, like the one that you used in Chapter 4, Exercise 4.1. That way, it can be used as many times as needed to create packages.

Exercise 6.6 Recreated In Query Builder

The goal of Exercise 6.6 was to merge data from two tables and create a new table from the merged data. As I said in Chapter 6, I don't know why I could not get it to work as I expected. If I did something wrong, I do not know what it is. It is possible that the Merge Join transformation is not designed to function the way that I think it should. Be that as it may, Figure 7-43 shows the query and some of the data that it generated. As you can see, the product name is filled in for every item. In Exercise 6.6, that was not the case. It only filled in each product name once in the new table. I hope that this query helps, if you have the need to create the same or similar functionality.

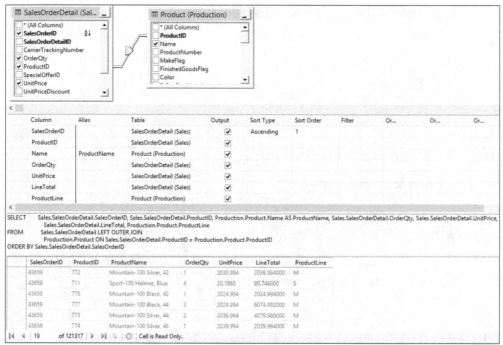

Figure 7-43 Query to create the destination table in Exercise 6.6

This concludes the Query Builder crash course. I hope that you feel a little more at ease, if you need to create a basic query on your own.

USING VARIABLES, PARAMETERS AND CONTAINERS

 Overview

After reading this chapter and completing the exercises you will:

- ☑ Understand the role that expressions play in creating a package and be able to create basic expressions
- ☑ Learn about the Expression Builder
- ☑ Create static and dynamic variables
- ☑ Be able to create and use parameters to pass values
- ☑ Be able to set up containers
- ☑ Know how to create breakpoints
- ☑ Understand the basics of creating a catalog

CHAPTER 8

Overview

If you have completed all of the exercises in the previous chapters, you are well on your way to being able to create packages that have a lot of functionality. This chapter will introduce you to variables, parameters, containers and expressions. Having an understanding of these tools will help you add even more functionality to packages and take your package design skills to the next level.

On your own, you will probably find out quickly that many of the packages that you initially create, will need to be changed to be dynamic, so that they can support using different values each time that they are run. In addition to making your life easier in the long run, the number of packages that need to be created and maintained, will be reduced. What you will learn in this chapter is that expressions are a major component of making packages dynamic. When a package is run, an expression is evaluated and based on the result of the expression, different actions are taken. Before you start frowning, many of the expressions that you will use on a regular basis are pretty easy to create, as long as you can keep an open mind.

Expressions

As covered above, this chapter will teach you new skills. While the majority of the exercises so far, have allowed you to keep from writing code, some of the functionality covered in this chapter requires creating expressions.

Expressions are created using functions, operators, variables, literals and parameters. Expressions are a key component to creating what is known as a **DYNAMIC PACKAGE**. Expressions are created to set a property in a component or task. When the package is run, the expression is evaluated and used in the property that it was created for. Expressions can be created to do any of the following. Functionality like this, is what makes a package dynamic.

☑ Include the current date as part of the filename.
☑ Retrieve email addresses from a file to populate the To field on an email.
☑ Load several files from a folder that have the same file extension.
☑ Run a series of steps based on a condition.

In Chapter 4, I discussed data types and how it is important to get them right. This is especially true when creating expressions. And if you already know T-SQL, you will find that some data types have different names.

In Chapter 5, you learned how to use the Derived Column transformation. You created an expression to calculate the sales tax. [See Chapter 5, Figure 5-44] As briefly covered in Chapter 5, the expression language used on a data flow component is a combination of C#, T-SQL and Visual Basic. Expressions created on the Expression Builder use the same syntax.

 When creating a **BOOLEAN EXPRESSION** like the one shown below, it is not a requirement to capitalize True and False. They are not case sensitive. @[User::BooleanField] == False

Task Editor Expressions Page

Most tasks on the Control Flow tab have the page shown in Figure 8-1. This page displays the properties that can be set dynamically.

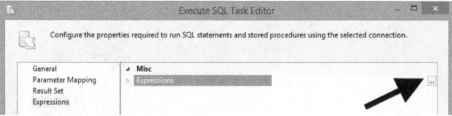

Figure 8-1 Expressions page

The **EXPRESSIONS FIELD** is used to dynamically set a property at run time, using an expression. This field can use an expression, a variable or a constant value.

Opening Expression Builder

This dialog box is available on an editor that has an Expressions page, as shown above in Figure 8-1, by following the steps below.

   ① From the Expressions page, click on the Expressions option to display the button illustrated above in Figure 8-1.
   ② Click the ellipsis button to open the Property Expression Editor, shown in Figure 8-2.
   ③ Open the Property drop-down list and select the property that you want to create the expression for.
   ④ Once a property is selected, click the ellipsis button. You will see the Expression Builder, shown in Figure 8-3.

This dialog box is used to select the property that the expression will be created for.

The expression can be typed in or click the ellipsis button to use the Expression Builder, to create the expression.

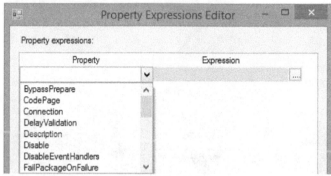

Figure 8-2 Property Expressions Editor

Expression Builder

SSIS packages have several locations that expressions can be created from.

One location, on the Derived Column transformation, was discussed earlier.

Figure 8-3 shows the Expression Builder. This dialog box provides access to system and user variables.

Both versions of the Expression Builder are almost identical. The biggest difference is that the Expression Builder shown in the figure, allows you to test the expression. The Expression Builder on a transformation editor does not have this functionality. [See Chapter 5, Figure 5-18]

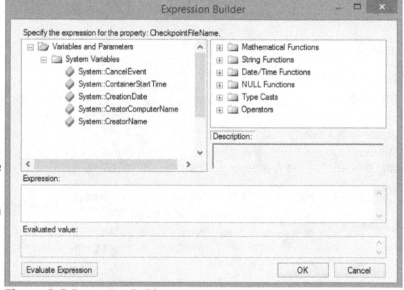

Figure 8-3 Expression Builder

The other difference is that the Expression Builder in Figure 8-3 does not have the Columns folder that transformation editors have.

Click the **EVALUATE EXPRESSION BUTTON** to see the value created by the expression.

Other Places To Create Expressions From

   ☑ Clicking on a connection on the Connection Managers tab, displays the Properties window, shown in Figure 8-4. Clicking on the Expressions property and then clicking the ellipsis button, displays the dialog box shown earlier in Figure 8-2.
   ☑ Chapter 3 introduced you to precedence constraints. In Chapter 6 Exercise 6.3, you learned how to create a basic constraint. The **PRECEDENCE CONSTRAINT EDITOR** can be used to create an expression for an evaluation, by selecting an expression evaluation option, then clicking the ellipsis button at the end of the Expression field.

☑ The **EXPRESSION TASK** is used to create expressions that set the value for variables that are used in the control flow. Selecting the Edit option on the shortcut menu for this task, opens the Expression dialog box shown above in Figure 8-3. The only difference creating an expression using this task, is that the expression is not tied to a particular property like it is when the Expression Builder is opened from a transformation. [See Expression Task]

☑ When the **VARIABLES WINDOW** (shown later in Figure 8-7) is displayed and a variable is selected, click the ellipsis button at the end of the Expression property, or in the Properties window, shown in Figure 8-5.

☑ The **EXECUTE SQL TASK** that was created in Exercise 3.6, by the Import and Export Wizard, has the SQL statement property. It can be used to create a query, on the dialog box shown in Figure 8-6 or on the Query Builder. The query is often used to set a variable or file connection. The query will be run by this task.

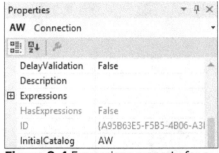

Figure 8-4 Expressions property for a connection

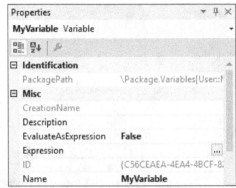

Figure 8-5 Expression property for a variable in the Properties window

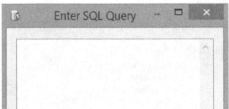

Figure 8-6 Enter SQL Query dialog box

Expression Task

As its name suggests, this control flow task is used to create expressions. This task can be used instead of the **SCRIPT TASK**. Some uses of the Expression task are:

☑ Auditing the number of files that run through a loop.

☑ Set a variable to an expression at run time.

☑ Adding it to a Foreach Loop Container, which can be used to loop through the files in a folder, that need to be loaded into a database. The expression would create a counter and be incremented by 1, each time another file is read.

Understanding Variables

A variable stores a value. This value is passed to or accessed by other objects like parameters or used in code. There are two types of variables: **SYSTEM** and **USER DEFINED**.

SYSTEM VARIABLES are pre-defined variables that are built into SSIS. They are read only. You cannot create or modify them. The left side of Figure 8-3 shown earlier, displays some of the system variables that are available.

The focus in this chapter is user defined variables, because they are the type that you can create. Both can be used in a package to help in the control flow, hold data and many other tasks. Variables are a way for objects in a package to talk to each other. They can be used in the following ways:

☑ In an expression for precedence constraints.

☑ To combine several values together.

☑ Set a components property.

☑ To pass a set of values between objects (an array).

☑ In the Script Task component.

☑ In logic expressions.

☑ To store an expression that can be used in several places in a package. This is sometimes referred to as an **EXPRESSION BASED VARIABLE.**

☑ Send values to parameters that will be used in T-SQL queries and stored procedures.

The variables created in SSIS are the same as variables that are used in programming languages. Variables are set internally in a package. Variables store one of the following types of values:

☑ Static value, meaning the value does not change. This is also known as a hard coded value.

☑ Dynamic value, is set based on a condition. The value can be set once or modified as many times as necessary, while the package is running.

When a package is in design mode, variables can be created, renamed, deleted and have the data type changed. At runtime, a variable is locked and only the value of the variable can be changed. The default scope of a variable is the entire package. Variables that are scoped at the component level (a task, container, event handler) means that only the component or any of its sub components will have access to a variable. Keep the following in mind when creating variables.

☑ **VARIABLE NAMES ARE CASE SENSITIVE.** vCounter and vcounter are two different variable names.

☑ **DON'T USE VARIABLE NAMES THAT ARE SIMILAR** to others in the package or the project. This can make it confusing to remember what the variables are used for. Variables cannot be set to **NULL** in SSIS. Each variable data type has its own default value when data is not present. For example, a string variable uses an empty string.

User Defined Variable Properties

The options on the Variables window shown in Figure 8-7, are not the only properties that variables have. When you click on a variable name in the window, additional properties are displayed in the Properties window, as shown in Figure 8-8.

When the **EVALUATE AS EXPRESSION PROPERTY** is set to True, the variable becomes dynamic so to speak, because the value will be defined by the formula created on the **EXPRESSION PROPERTY**. The value of a variable is either a literal value or can be defined dynamically. Variables are used as an alternative to using expressions because they can be set by using the **SCRIPT TASK**. Variables can store expressions that can be used throughout the package.

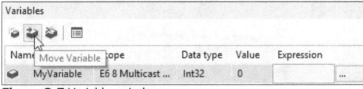

Figure 8-7 Variables window

You can type the expression directly on the Variable window, or click the ellipsis button at the end of the Expression field.

Once an expression is created, the **EVALUATE AS EXPRESSION** property on the Properties window is automatically set to True, as shown in Figure 8-8. This means that the expression can be used to set the value.

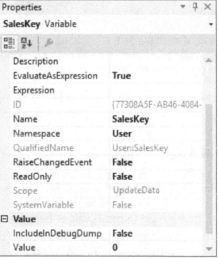

Figure 8-8 Properties for a variable

Value And Expression Fields On The Variables Window
You only need to use one of these fields to create a variable. Use the Value field when you want to use the same fixed value throughout the package. Use the Expression field when the value will change, based on a condition.

Displaying System Variables

By default, the Variables window only displays user defined variables. If you want to display system variables in the window, follow the steps below.

1. Click the GRID OPTIONS BUTTON (the last one) one the Variables window.

2. On the dialog box shown in Figure 8-9, check the SHOW SYSTEM VARIABLES OPTION.

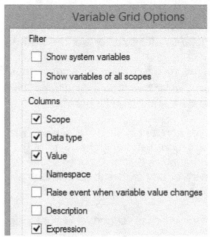

Figure 8-9 Variable Grid Options dialog box

Creating User Defined Variables

Below are locations that variables can be created from.

- ☑ SSIS menu ⇒ Variables, displays the window shown earlier in Figure 8-7.
- ☑ As covered in Chapter 4, source and destination editors can use variables to select data to retrieve or select the data to export. This is accomplished by using one of the following data access mode options: TABLE NAME OR VIEW NAME VARIABLE or SQL COMMAND FROM VARIABLE.
- ☑ Right-click on the Control Flow tab canvas ⇒ Variables.

What Is Scope?

Scope refers to where the variable can be used. Scope can be set for a component. This means that the variable can only be used with that component. The scope can also be set at the package level, meaning that the variable can be used anywhere in the package.

If you create a variable at the package level, as shown earlier in Figure 8-7, you can change the scope by clicking the MOVE VARIABLE button on the Variables window.

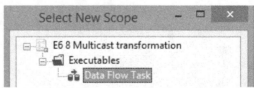

You will see the dialog box shown in Figure 8-10. Click on the item (level) that you want the variable moved to, then click OK.

Figure 8-10 Select New Scope dialog box

Variables And Parameters

It is hard to discuss variables without including parameters in the discussion. That is because they have many of the same options or features in common, as listed below.

- ☑ Both are used to move values between package components.
- ☑ They are also used to make a package dynamic.
- ☑ They use the same data types. [See Chapter 4, Table 4-1]
- ☑ Both are placeholders and use the same fields to be created. The fields used to create variables and parameters are Name, Data Type, Scope and Value.

Parameters are scoped at the package or project level. Variables created in SSIS can be scoped to the package level or to a specific component in the package.

Variables And Parameters Have The Same Data Types
While variables and parameters have the same data types, they are slightly different from the data types that you have used for other features in SSIS. Most of the time for variables and parameters, you will probably use one of the following data types: DateTime, Int32 (for numeric values) and String.

Using A Variable In A Query

Often, a variable is used to pass a value in a T-SQL query, either in the Execute SQL Task or on the source editor, when using a query to retrieve the data for the package. When that is the case, you would create a query like the one shown later in Figure 8-16.

The ? on the WHERE clause is the placeholder for the variable name. Then you create a parameter that will use the variable. Each time the package is run, you have the ability to change the variables value. This is what makes a package dynamic. In this scenario, the variable is actually being used to filter (select) the data that will be written to the destination.

Variable Name Tip
I put a lower case v in front of variable names, so that I do not mistake a variable for a field in a table. Doing this is optional.

Understanding Parameters

If you used SSIS 2008 or earlier, parameters are the replacement for the configuration files and tables that you may have used.

Parameters are a relatively new feature to SSIS. They are similar to variables because they store values and can be used in an expression to set a variable or package parameter. Parameters are set externally. By externally, I mean that they are not created in a task, transformation or component. This means that they can be used in expressions and be used in different parts of the package. Parameters can also be used to override almost any SSIS property.

Initially, parameters can be created in a package, on the Parameters tab or from the Solution Explorer. Parameters can be set as a default for a package or project. They can also be set as an execution value. As you have seen in previous chapters, there are a lot of properties that can be set in transformations and tasks. After you have created a project or package parameter, it can be used to set a variable package property or used in any expression.

SSIS supports the following types of parameters:

- ☑ **PROJECT PARAMETERS** are like project connections, meaning that they are created at the project level and can be used in any package in the project.
- ☑ **PACKAGE PARAMETERS** are created at the package level and can only be used in the package that it is created in. Create this type of parameter when you know that the value that the parameter stores, is specific to a package.

You will only see the Parameters tab for packages that are created in a project that is in the **PROJECT DEPLOYMENT MODEL**.

Parameters cannot be changed by an expression like variables can.

Parameters Tab

Figure 8-11 shows the Parameters tab and the options used to create input parameters.

The parameters created on this tab are package level and are different from variables because they can be passed from a job. Parameters also have the two properties explained below that variables do not have.

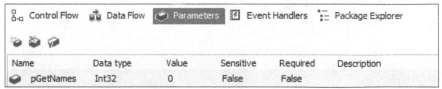

Name	Data type	Value	Sensitive	Required	Description
pGetNames	Int32	0	False	False	

Figure 8-11 Parameters tab

The **SENSITIVE PROPERTY** is used to encrypt the value in the catalog database. Setting this property to True, makes the parameter secure. When enabled (set to true), the value is displayed as ***, like a password or as NULL. [See Understanding The Catalog]

Setting the **REQUIRED PROPERTY** to True, forces the parameters value to be set at run time.

Project Parameters

To create a project parameter, right-click on the **PROJECT.PARAMS** file in the Solution Explorer ⇒ Select Open, as shown in Figure 8-12.

This displays the file in the workspace, as shown in Figure 8-13. The options are the same as the ones shown above in Figure 8-11. The difference is that the parameters will be saved in the Project.Params file.

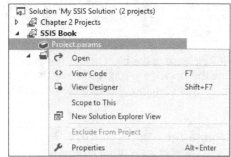

Figure 8-12 Project.params file shortcut menu

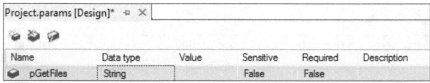

Figure 8-13 Project.params file

Parameterize Dialog Box

The dialog box shown in Figure 8-14 is used to link an existing parameter, to the task or create a new parameter to link to the task on the Control Flow tab.

To open the dialog box, right-click on the task that you want to apply the parameter to or create a parameter for ⇒ **PARAMETERIZE**. The options are explained below.

The **PROPERTY** option is used to select the task that you want the parameter applied to.

The **DO NOT USE PARAMETER** option is used to remove the parameter from the selected task.

The **USE EXISTING PARAMETER** option is used to select an existing parameter to apply to the task.

The **CREATE A NEW PARAMETER** option is used to create a new parameter to apply to the task.

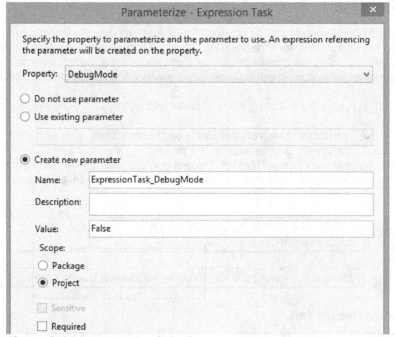

Figure 8-14 Parameterize dialog box

The **VALUE** option is used to type in the default value for the parameter.

The **SCOPE** option is used to select one of the following:
- ☑ Select **PACKAGE** when you want to be able to modify the package without having to edit and redeploy the package.
- ☑ Select **PROJECT** when you want to provide external data to one or more packages in the project.

SENSITIVE and **REQUIRED OPTIONS** [See Parameters Tab, earlier in this chapter]

. . . .

What Makes A Package Dynamic?

A package is considered dynamic when it can be reconfigured, often based on a condition, at run time. Examples of dynamic functionality include selecting email addresses based on territory, selecting orders based on the sales amount and creating export file names.

Expressions can be created for variables to use to make a package dynamic. Expressions can be created for a task or property. Parameters can be created and used with an SQL query to make a package dynamic. The expressions can use functions, operators and literals. Expressions can be created in variables, which can be passed to a parameter to make a package dynamic. When the package is run, the expression is evaluated. The next exercise will show you how to make a package dynamic, by using a parameter.

Variables vs Parameters

Overall, variables and parameters provide the same type of functionality, each are better suited for different tasks, as explained below.

☑ Use a variable when you only need to create or save a value in a specific parameter.

☑ Use a parameter when you want to set the property value outside of the package, regardless of whether or not the property is required.

☑ Use a parameter when using the project deployment model (covered later in this chapter). Parameters are the better choice when it comes to replacing package configurations to create a dynamic solution.

While variables and parameters can both be used to make a package dynamic, the differences between the two are listed below.

☑ Variables can use a hard coded value or an expression to calculate the value.

☑ There is no option in a parameter to create an expression. The value in a parameter can be changed at run time. Parameters can be used in an expression.

> **Parameter Name Tips**
> ① Just like I use a lower case v to denote a variable field, I use a lower case p to denote a parameter field, to distinguish it from a field in a table. Doing this is optional.
> ② When used to map a variable to a parameter, the name, for example, $Package::pGetData, indicates that the parameter is a package parameter. Parameter names are case sensitive and must start with a $ (dollar sign) and be followed by either the word "Package" or "Project", depending on the type of parameter that you are referencing. You would reference a parameter this way on the OLE DB Source Editor, with a query that uses a parameter to retrieve data, as shown later in Figure 8-16. The ? on the **WHERE CLAUSE**, in the figure, is the place holder for the parameter value. On the Source Editor, click the **PARAMETERS BUTTON** to display the dialog box shown later in Figure 8-17. You would type the parameter name in the Variables column. This is most often used with a stored procedure.

Exercise 8.1: Create A Project Level Parameter

In this exercise you will learn how to create a project level parameter that selects the Sales Rep ID. The value will be used to select the records that will be written to a text file.

Create The Project Level Parameter

In this part of the exercise, you will learn how to create a parameter that can be used by any package in the project. The value will be passed to the package when it is run. Doing this will make the package dynamic. When you create packages on your own, that need to select data based on a value, creating a parameter is a good option. An example is Exercise 4.1, where the order year was hard coded into the query.

1. In the Solution Explorer window, open the Project.params file.

2. Click the Add Parameter button.

3. In the Name field, type `pSalesRep`.

4.   In the Value field, type a 7 ⇒ In the Description field, type `Sales Rep ID number` as shown in Figure 8-15.

This parameter will store the value of the sales rep whose data will be sent to the destination file.

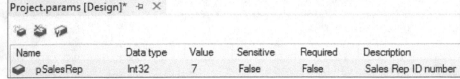

Name	Data type	Value	Sensitive	Required	Description
pSalesRep	Int32	7	False	False	Sales Rep ID number

Figure 8-15 Project parameter

5.   Save the changes to the parameter file, then close the file.

Create A Query That Uses A Parameter

In this part of the exercise, you will create a query to select the table and some of the fields in the table. You will also set the source to use the parameter value on the WHERE clause in the query.

1.   Rename a new package to `E8.1 Package with a parameter`.

2.   Create a source connection to the AW database.

3.   On the OLE DB Source Editor, select the SQL command data access option ⇒ Type the query below, as shown in Figure 8-16.

```
SELECT OrderID, OrderDate, CustomerName, SalesRepID, SalesRep, OrderAmount,
Territory
FROM OrderInfo
WHERE SalesRepID = ?
```

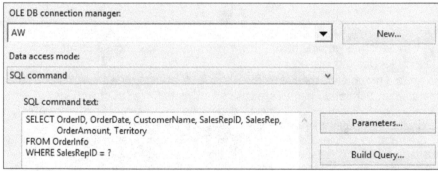

Figure 8-16 Query that uses a parameter

4.   Click the Parameters button ⇒
In the Variables drop-down list, scroll to the bottom and select the $Project::pSalesRep parameter, as shown in Figure 8-17.

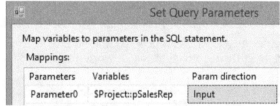

Figure 8-17 Set Query Parameters dialog box

5.   Click OK to close both dialog boxes.

Create The Destination File Connection

1.   Add a Flat File Destination ⇒ Connect it to the source ⇒
Name the destination `Write to Ch8 SalesRep file`.

2.   On the destination editor, create a new delimited connection manager that uses the `C:\SSIS Book\Ch8 SalesRep.txt` file ⇒ Name the connection `Ch8 SalesRep parameter`. You should have the options shown in Figure 8-18.

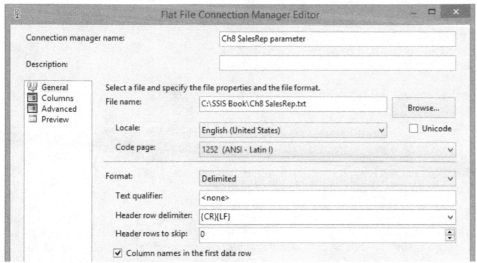

Figure 8-18 Flat File destination options

3. Check the Column names option.

4. Run the package. You should see that 7,276 rows were written to the destination file.

5. Open the Ch8 SalesRep.txt file in Notepad. You should see that the Sales Rep ID for all of the rows is 7, as illustrated in Figure 8-19. That is the default value that you set up for the parameter.

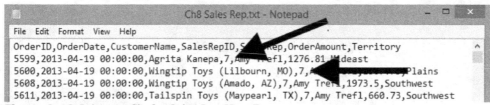

Figure 8-19 Sales rep file for Sales Rep ID = 7

On your own, you do not have to add the Sales Rep ID field to the output. I did it in this exercise so that you could see that the parameter is working as intended.

Change The Parameter Value

In this part of the exercise, you will change the parameters value and run the package again.

1. Open the Project.params file.

2. Change the Value field to 2 ⇒ Save the changes ⇒ Close the file.

3. Run the package again. 7,474 rows will be written to the file. When you view the text file, you will see that all of the rows have the Sales Rep ID 2.

If this package was deployed to the catalog, you could create what is known as an **ENVIRONMENT**. This would let you configure the parameter (by enabling the User environment variable), so that when the package is run (in production mode), you could select the value that would be passed to the parameter in the query.

When deployed, using the parameter will work like parameters do in SSRS or Crystal Reports™. By that I mean that each time the package is run, you will be prompted to enter a value for the parameter that will be passed to the package.

Breakpoints

In addition to using data viewers on the Data Flow tab,
setting breakpoints can also be helpful when testing a package.
This option is available for tasks on the Control Flow tab.

Figure 8-20 shows a container that has at least one breakpoint,
which is denoted by the (red) circle.

Figure 8-20 Container with a breakpoint

This feature will remind you of the Data Viewer tool that you have learned how to use. One difference between a breakpoint and a data viewer is that a breakpoint is applied to a task, not between tasks. This means that you have the ability to see more detailed information, while the package is running.

Breakpoints are helpful when you need to figure out why a package is not working as intended. This includes packages that run, but do not generate any errors. Breakpoints let you stop a package while it is running, to see the status or values in variables or the data. Breakpoints display data on the **LOCALS** and **WATCH WINDOWS**, in the Debug mode workspace.

Creating A Breakpoint On A Task

When you have the need to create a breakpoint, follow the steps below.

1. Right-click on a task ⇒
   EDIT BREAKPOINTS.

   You will see the dialog box
   shown in Figure 8-21.

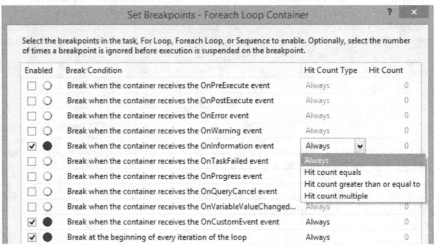

Figure 8-21 Set Breakpoints dialog box

2. In the **ENABLED COLUMN**, check the break conditions that you want to use.

The break conditions stop the package from running at different points during the task. The conditions and when the package stops the task are explained below.

ON PRE EXECUTE Right before the task runs. (1) (2)
ON POST EXECUTE Right after the task is finished running. (1) (2)
ON ERROR When the task generates an error. (1)
ON WARNING When the task generates a warning. (1)
ON TASK FAILED When the task fails. (1)
ON PROGRESS When the progress of the task is updated.
ON QUERY CANCEL When the task can cancel the execution.
ON VARIABLE VALUE CHANGED When the variables value changes. This condition requires that the **RAISE CHANGED EVENT PROPERTY**, on the Properties window, for the variable be set to True [See Figure 8-8]. This property can also be displayed on the Variables window, by checking the Raise event option, shown earlier in Figure 8-9.
ON CUSTOM EVENT When a custom task defined event happens.
ITERATION OF THE LOOP Right before each loop cycle starts. This break condition is only available for the For Loop or Foreach Loop Container tasks. Keep in mind that this break condition is executed, each time a loop occurs. This means that if the loop is executed 500 times, the break condition can be executed 500 times if the Hit Count Type and Hit Count options are not changed from the default values. (1)

(1) This is a common breakpoint to use.
(2) This break condition is used to view the value in a variable, before and after a task.

The **HIT COUNT TYPE** and **HIT COUNT OPTIONS** are used to set the maximum number of times that a breakpoint occurs before the breakpoint stops the package. The **HIT COUNT TYPE** property has the following options:

☑ **ALWAYS** The breakpoint stops the package every time the breakpoint hits.

☑ **HIT COUNT EQUALS** The breakpoint stops the package when the breakpoint reaches the number of times specified in the Hit Count property, as shown above, at the bottom of Figure 8-21.

☑ **HIT COUNT GREATER THAN OR EQUAL TO** The breakpoint stops the package when the breakpoint reaches the number of times specified in the Hit Count property and every time after that.

☑ **HIT COUNT MULTIPLE** The breakpoint stops the package when the breakpoint reaches the number of times specified in the Hit Count property, then in multiples of the Hit Count value. If the Hit Count property is 2, the package stops every other time the breakpoint hits.

Containers

As you have learned, the Control Flow tab is used to organize the workflow of the package. There may be times when the workflow requires more than one set of tasks or actions, or even a set of repeating actions. When any of these scenarios is the case, the solution is to add a container to the Control Flow tab for each set of tasks that need to be kept together. One way to understand the functionality of containers is to think of them as small self-contained packages.

Containers are used to logically group tasks together or to add structure to the package. They are also used to set up tasks that need to be repeated. Variables and event handlers can be created for the scope of the container, instead of for the entire package. Containers can also be nested, meaning one container can have another container in it.

Once a container has been added and the tasks have been added to a container and configured, the next step is to connect the containers using precedence constraints. Figure 8-22 shown below, is an example of a control flow with containers. Containers are most helpful when two or more tasks need to be kept together or repeated (looped). While it will not hurt anything to have a container that only has one task that does not need to be repeated, there really is no benefit setting up a container for that purpose. The container types are listed below. They are explained later in this chapter.

☑ **FOR LOOP CONTAINER** (3)
☑ **FOREACH LOOP CONTAINER** (3)
☑ **SEQUENCE CONTAINER**

(3) This container works the same as the function with the same name, which is used in many programming languages.

Figure 8-22 shows two containers with tasks. Containers are also a way to combine tasks into groups.

When this type of layout is used, the workflow can be controlled by the success or failure of the container. By that I mean that all tasks in the container must complete successfully for the container to be successful. That in turn will allow the task after the container to be executed.

Figure 8-22 Control flow with two containers

If more than one container is used on the Control Flow tab, all of the items in the first container must be completed, before tasks in the other containers can run. This requirement only applies to containers that have linked tasks with precedence constraints.

Because the control flow and data flow are separate, when looping is added to the control flow, the tasks on the Data Flow tab should not have to be changed.

 Earlier, three types of containers were discussed. Quiet as it's kept, there is a fourth container. There is no option on the toolbox for it. The truth is that we have been using it all along, but did not know it. No, I was not holding out on you, that is not my style. I did not know either, until I started doing some research for this chapter. This is what I found out. The name of this mystery container is **TASK HOST CONTAINER**. It is the default container in SSIS and is used behind the scenes. It is automatically assigned to each task. All packages have this container, even though you cannot see it.

 Container Tips

① The task names in each container must be unique.

② Containers can be nested, meaning that a container can be added to an existing container, just like a task.

③ A task in a container cannot be linked (connected) to anything outside of the container. Doing so, will generate an error. A container can be linked to a task or container outside of itself.

④ All of the tasks in a container can be run at the same time by right-clicking on the container and selecting Execute Container, the same way a package is run.

For Loop Container

This container is used to create a work flow that will cause the tasks in it to be repeated, until the condition that you create is evaluated to be false. This container is used to create the equivalent of a programming loop, meaning that the task(s) in the container will continue to be evaluated until the expression evaluates to false. Once evaluated to false, the external task that is connected to the container can be processed. Figure 8-23 shows the editor for the For Loop container. The properties are explained below.

The **INIT EXPRESSION** property is used to create the expression that will initialize the variables value that will be used in the loop. This property sets the initial value for the variable.

The **EVAL EXPRESSION** property is used to create the Boolean expression that has to evaluate to false. This expression evaluates the value in the variable. The expression will stop the loop from processing or continuing.

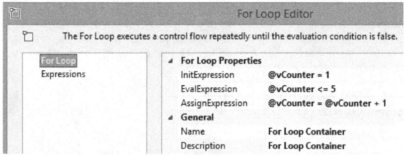

Figure 8-23 For Loop container properties

The **ASSIGN EXPRESSION** property is used to create an expression that changes the value in the Eval Expression property.

Exercise 8.2: Create A For Loop Container

This chapter has covered a variety of control flow features. This exercise will show you how to use a variable as a counter field by creating an expression for the container. In this exercise, you will learn how to create the following:

☑ A variable that will be used as a counter.
☑ A For Loop Container.
☑ A breakpoint.

Create A Counter Variable

In this part of the exercise, you will create a counter field that will count from 1 to 5. The variable will be used in an expression in the container to check the value, thus creating a loop.

1. Rename a new package to E8.2 Create A For Loop Container.

2. If the Variables window is not displayed, right-click on the control flow canvas ⇒ Variables.

3. In the Variables window, click the **ADD VARIABLE** button.

4. In the Name field, type vCounter ⇒
    In the Value field, type a 1. Your variable should have
    the options shown in Figure 8-24.

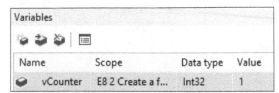

Figure 8-24 vCounter variable options

Configure The Container

In this part of the exercise, you will customize a container by creating an expression for the counter to loop through. You will use the For Loop Properties discussed earlier.

1. Add a For Loop Container to the canvas.

2. On the editor, type the expressions below. When finished, you should have the values shown earlier in Figure 8-23.

    Init Expression @vCounter = 1
    Eval Expression @vCounter <=5
    Assign Expression @vCounter = @vCounter + 1

Add A Breakpoint

In this part of the exercise, you will create a breakpoint that occurs at the start of every loop.

1. Right-click on the container ⇒ Edit Breakpoints.

2. Check the last condition, Break at the beginning of every iteration of the loop.

3. Run the package.

> **Breakpoint Options**
> When a breakpoint stops the package. Click the Continue (green) button on the toolbar to go to the next breakpoint if one exists or through the rest of the package. Clicking the blue button stops the package at the breakpoint.

> **Using The Watch Window**
> You can use the Watch window to see the values in the variables, when a breakpoint has stopped the package. The steps below show you how to open a Watch window.
> 1. Click the Debug button on the menu ⇒ Windows ⇒ Watch, as shown at the top of Figure 8-25.
> 2. Type in the variables name that you want to see the values of, in the Name column, as shown in Figure 8-26.

Figure 8-25 shows options that you can use when running a package.

Figure 8-25 Debug menu

4. At the bottom of the canvas, you should see a tab named **WATCH** or **WATCH1**. Display the tab. (Windows ⇒ Watch ⇒ Watch 1)

5. In the Name field, type vCounter ⇒ Press Enter.

    The Watch window should look like the one shown in Figure 8-26, when you click on the arrow to the left of the counter field. Doing this displays the variables properties.

    The current value in the variable is 1. The red circle on the container should have a yellow arrow in it.

    If you want to change one of the values, while in Debug mode, right-click on the row and select **EDIT VALUE** ⇒ Type in the new value that you want to use.

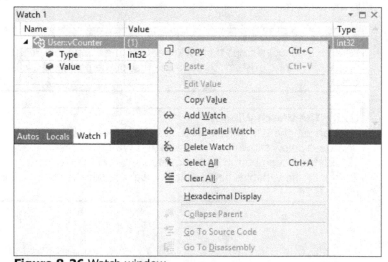

Figure 8-26 Watch window

6. On the toolbar at the top of the workspace, click the **CONTINUE** button, shown in Figure 8-27, to continue running the package. In the Watch window, you should see that the variable has changed to 2. At this point, you know that the counter is working properly.

Figure 8-27 Continue and Stop debugging buttons

7. You can keep clicking the Continue button or click the Stop debugging button.

The **LOCALS WINDOW** shown in Figure 8-28, displays the values of all user and system variables. The variables on this window can be added to the Watch window by right-clicking on the variable and selecting **ADD WATCH**.

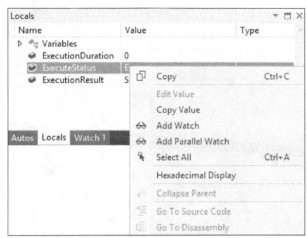

Figure 8-28 Locals window

The **CALL STACK WINDOW**, shown in Figure 8-29, is a debugging window that is used to help resolve a problem with the package.

The window displays a list of tasks that have run up to the breakpoint. Initially, this window is in the same group of windows, as the Output window, but it can be moved to another group of windows.

Figure 8-29 Call Stack window

Foreach Loop Container

This container is used to create a workflow that repeats the task(s) in the container. A popular use for this container is looping through files in a folder or looping through records in a table, until there are no more files or records to be processed. It can also be used to send email to each email address in a record set.

Use this container when you need to loop through several tasks or components (also known as a **COLLECTION**). This container is used to create a recurring loop for a data set or enumeration (a list). During the looping process, the container assigns the value from the item to a variable. The variable can be used by connections or tasks inside or outside of the container.

Foreach Enumerators

The type of item that the container will process (loop through) depends on the enumerator that is selected on the Collections page, on the Foreach Loop Editor. The options are explained below. The first three are the most popular.

☑ **FOREACH FILE ENUMERATOR** performs an action for each file in the selected folder. Checking the **TRAVERSE SUBFOLDERS** option will perform the same action for the selected folders, sub folders. Usually, a specific file type extension is selected, but that is not a requirement. Figure 8-30 shows the options to use this enumerator. This is probably the most used enumerator.

☑ **FOREACH ITEM ENUMERATOR** will loop through a list of items (columns) by clicking the **COLUMNS BUTTON** shown in Figure 8-31.

☑ **FOREACH ADO ENUMERATOR** will loop through a list of tables or rows in a table from an ADO record set, by selecting the necessary options and apply the task(s) in the container to each table or rows in the table. (4)

☑ **FOREACH ADO.NET SCHEME ROWSET ENUMERATOR** will loop through an ADO.NET data source. For example, this enumerator can be used to get a list of tables in the AW database used in this book. (4)

☑ **FOREACH FROM VARIABLE ENUMERATOR** is used to loop through an SSIS variable or an array.

☑ **FOR EACH NODELIST ENUMERATOR** uses the options shown in Figure 8-32 to loop through a node list in an XML document.

☑ **FOREACH SMO ENUMERATOR** loops through a list of SQL Server Management Objects (SMO). This option can be used to get a list of views in an SQL database. (4)

☑ **FOREACH HDFS FILE ENUMERATOR** uses the options shown in Figure 8-33 to loop through the files in a Hadoop Distributed File System (HDFS).

(4) I could not get this enumerator to display the enumerator options. The last time that I used this enumerator was in SQL Server version 2012 and it displayed the fields. I posted questions in the forum and sent emails to tech support, but did not receive any replies.

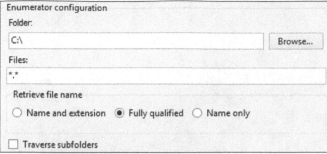

Figure 8-30 Foreach file enumerator options

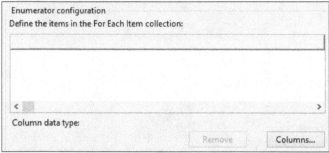

Figure 8-31 Foreach item enumerator options

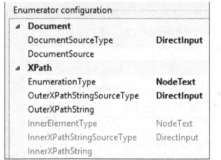

Figure 8-32 Foreach Nodelist enumerator options

Figure 8-33 Foreach HDFS File enumerator options

Exercise 8.3: Copy Files From One Folder To Another

There may be times when you need to use files that have a specific file type, that are in a folder that has files with a variety of file types. For example, all of the sales reps may save their orders weekly, in the same folder on a server. In the package that you are creating, the sales reps weekly order files need to be in a specific folder, that is different then the one that the files are initially saved to. The only thing that the file names have in common is that they are .csv files.

In this exercise, you will learn how to use the **FOREACH FILE ENUMERATOR** to copy files in one folder to another folder.

Moving Files From One Folder To Another
The steps in this exercise are the same if you need to move files from one folder to another. Instead of selecting the "copy" options in the steps, select the Move option.

1. In Windows Explorer, create a folder named `Ch8 Foreach File` in the SSIS Book folder. This is the folder that the csv files will be copied to.

2. Save a new package as `E8.3 Copy files to folder`.

3. In the Variables window, create a variable named `vGetcsvfiles` ⇒ Change the Data type to String ⇒ Type `vFile` in the Value field, as shown in Figure 8-34.

In this exercise, you can use any name that you want in the Value column because this variable will only be used to hold the name of the file that is currently being processed in the loop.

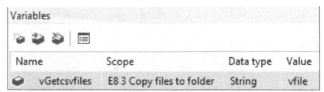

Figure 8-34 vGetcsvfiles variable options

Configure The Foreach Loop Container

1. Add the Foreach Loop Container to the canvas ⇒ On the editor, display the Collection page ⇒ Select the Foreach File Enumerator option.

2. Click the Browse button ⇒ Select the SSIS Book folder. This is the folder that has the files that will be copied.

The **FILES** field is used to select all of the files in the folder or specific files. ***.*** is the default value for the Files field and will select all of the files in the folder that was selected in step 2.

3. Change the value in the Files field to ***.csv**, as shown in Figure 8-35.

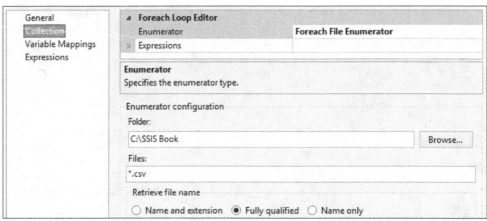

Figure 8-35 Foreach File Enumerator options

Retrieve File Name Section

The options in this section, shown at the bottom of Figure 8-35, are explained below.

Select the **NAME AND EXTENSION** option when you are using a specific file in the folder, like usethisfile.csv.

The **FULLY QUALIFIED** option uses the folder and file name. In this exercise, the *.csv is the full file name because when the package is run, the * will select each file that has the .csv extension.

The **NAME ONLY** option is used to select files based on the name that you type in the Files field. This means that if the folder has test.txt, test.jpg and test.csv, they will all be selected if you type "test" in the Files field.

4. On the Variable Mappings page, open the Variable drop-down list and select the variable that you created earlier. Accept the default Index value of zero. You should have the options shown in Figure 8-36 ⇒ Click OK.

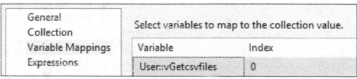

Figure 8-36 Variable Mappings page options

Configure The File System Task

This task will be used to copy the csv files from one folder to another.

1. Drag a File System Task into the container ⇒ On the editor, select the Copy file operation, if it is not already selected.

2. In the **DESTINATION CONNECTION** drop-down list, select **<NEW CONNECTION . . .>**. This property is used to select the destination location. In this exercise, that would be the folder that you created at the beginning of this exercise.

3. On the File Connection Manager Editor, open the Usage type drop-down list and select Existing folder. As you see, there is an option to create a folder. You could select that option to create the folder that you created in Windows Explorer at the beginning of this exercise.

4. Click the Browse button ⇒ Select the Ch8 Foreach File folder, as shown in Figure 8-37 ⇒ Click OK.

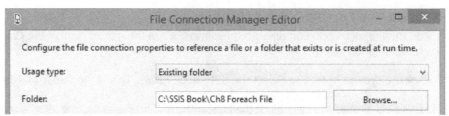

Configure the file connection properties to reference a file or a folder that exists or is created at run time.

Usage type: Existing folder

Folder: C:\SSIS Book\Ch8 Foreach File   Browse...

Figure 8-37 Connection options for an existing folder

5. Change the **IS SOURCE PATH VARIABLE PROPERTY** to True ⇒
    Change the Source Variable property to User::Getcsvfiles.

    You should have the options shown in Figure 8-38 ⇒ Click OK.

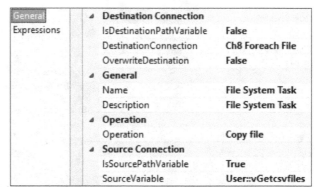

Figure 8-38 File System Task options

 The **OVERWRITE DESTINATION PROPERTY**, shown above in Figure 8-38, is used to select whether or not files in the destination should be over written. On your own, you need to decide what is right for the package that you are creating.

6. Run the package ⇒ When finished, look in the Ch8 Foreach File folder. You should see csv files. The number of files that you see, depends on whether or not you have completed all previous exercises that created a csv file.

Exercise 8.4: Import Data From Multiple Files

 The Import and Export Wizard can import several tables at one time, but it cannot import the data from several files into the same table in an SQL database or any database for that matter.

In this exercise you will learn how to configure the Foreach Loop Container and **FOREACH FILE ENUMERATOR**. The configuration will include importing the data in each file (of the same file type), in a folder, to a new table in the AW database. The data will be imported from csv files. On your own, you can use the steps in this exercise as a blueprint to import data from other file types.

Create The Source And Destination Connections

1. In Windows Explorer, create a folder named Ch8 LoadcsvFiles in the SSIS Book folder.

2. In the SSIS Book folder, copy the following files to the folder that you just created. AppendToFactSales.txt, June2015.csv, Mar2015.csv and Sept2016.csv. The .txt file is being copied to the folder to demonstrate that only the files that you select, will be loaded to the new table in the AW database.

3. Rename a new package to E8.4 Load data from multiple files.

4. Add a Data Flow Task ⇒ Rename it to Load multiple files.

5. Create a Flat File Source connection named `Load files` ⇒ On the editor, click New ⇒ In the Connection manager name field, type `Ch8 Loadcsvfiles`.

6. Click the Browse button ⇒ Navigate to the Ch8 LoadcsvFiles folder ⇒ Click on the June2015.csv file.

7. Check the Column names in the first row option ⇒ Display the Columns page ⇒ Click OK.

Create A Table In The AW Database

In this part of the exercise, you will create a table. It will be the table that the data in the csv files will be imported into.

1. Create a destination connection to the AW database ⇒ Connect it to the Load Files source connection.

2. On the OLE DB Destination editor, click the New button across from the Name of the table or the view field.

3. Change the table name to `csvfiles` ⇒ Change the Date field name to `InvoiceDate`, as shown in Figure 8-39 ⇒ Click OK.

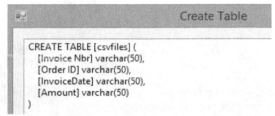

```
CREATE TABLE [csvfiles] (
    [Invoice Nbr] varchar(50),
    [Order ID] varchar(50),
    [InvoiceDate] varchar(50),
    [Amount] varchar(50)
)
```

Figure 8-39 Changes for the new csvfiles table

 On your own, on the Create Table dialog box, you should change any fields that should have a different data type. For example, the data type for the Invoice Nbr field should be changed to INT and the data type for the Invoice Date field should be changed to Date.

4. Check the Keep Nulls option.

5. On the Mappings page, map the Date field to the Invoice Date field ⇒ Click OK.

If you ran the package now, only data from one file in the folder, would be added to the new table that you just created. To force all of the files in the folder to be read, the Load multiple files (Data Flow Task) has to be moved into a container.

Configure The Foreach Loop Container

1. On the Control Flow tab, add a Foreach Loop Container ⇒ Move the Load multiple files task into the container.

2. On the containers editor, display the Collection page. The Foreach File Enumerator option should be selected.

3. Click the Browse button ⇒ Select the Ch8 LoadcsvFiles folder ⇒ Change the Files field to `*.csv`, as shown in Figure 8-40.

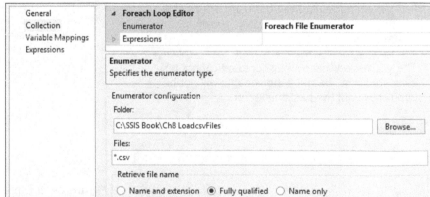

Figure 8-40 Collection page options

It is a good practice to use something on the Files field to only select the files that you want to use. That is because it is possible that other files could be added to the folder and you may not know it. If that happens, the package will fail, because the other files probably will not have the same columns.

4. On the Variable Mappings tab, open the Variable drop-down list and select <New Variable>.

5. In the Name field, type `vCurrentFile`, as shown in Figure 8-41 ⇒ Click OK.

   The Variable Mappings page should look like the one shown in Figure 8-42 ⇒ Click OK.

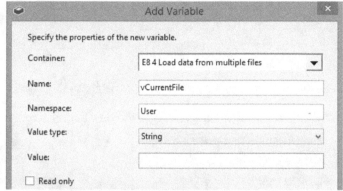

Figure 8-41 Add Variable dialog box

The vCurrentFile variable will store the name of the file that is currently being processed in the container.

Should something happen when the package is running, knowing what file was being used at the time the package got an error, may help you resolve the problem.

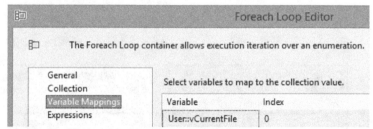

Figure 8-42 Variable Mappings page options

Add An Expression To The Connection

In this part of the exercise, you will create an expression on the source connection, to use the variable that was created in the previous part of this exercise.

1. On the Connection Managers tab, click on the **CH8 LOAD CSV FILES** connection. You should see the properties for the connection in the Properties window ⇒ In the Misc section, click the ellipsis button in the **EXPRESSIONS** field.

2. On the Property Expressions Editor dialog box, open the Property drop-down list and select **CONNECTION STRING** ⇒ Click the ellipsis button in the Expression field.

3. On the Expression Builder, expand the Variables and Parameters folder ⇒ Drag the User::vCurrentFile variable to the Expression field, as shown in Figure 8-43.

   The expression that you just created cannot be evaluated now, because the variable will not be populated until the package is run.

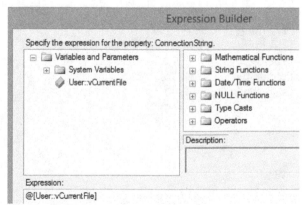

Figure 8-43 Expression Builder options

4. Click OK.

   You should have the expression shown
   in Figure 8-44 ⇒ Click OK.

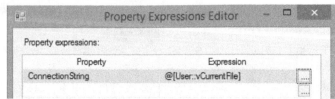

Figure 8-44 Property Expressions Editor

5. Run the package.

The package will read each csv file in the folder and write the records in each file to the csvfiles table in the AW database. If you look on the Progress tab, you will see that the June2015 file has 108 rows and 107 rows were written out. That is correct because the header row should not be written to the csvfiles table. The same is true for the other two tables.

Also notice that the .txt file in the Ch8 LoadcsvFiles folder was not used. That is correct because you specified to only use .csv files. On your own, you would probably move the csv files that were written to the destination table, to another folder or delete them in the package. Otherwise, the next time the package is run, the data in the three csv files would be written to the table in the database again. This means that the table in the database would have duplicate records, which is probably not what you want.

Sequence Container

This container is used to organize tasks and other containers into smaller sets of tasks to help structure the work flow of the package. This container is helpful when the package has a lot of tasks and components. That is because you can use this container to divide the tasks into smaller sections, if you will. The way that I visualize this container is that adding a few of them to a package is like creating sub folders and putting related tasks in each of the sub folders.

Sequence containers look like the other containers that were discussed, when added to the canvas. Figure 8-45 shows a sample sequence container that has four tasks. The tasks in the container must run before the task outside of the container (named Last Task), can run.

Unlike the For Loop and Foreach Loop containers, the Sequence container does not have an editor. Changes can be made on the Properties window. Below are some scenarios where using a Sequence container would be helpful.

Figure 8-45 Sequence container example

☑ Being able to set properties for several tasks at the same time, by placing them in a container, then setting the properties for them in the container.
☑ Setting up an event that is applied to all tasks in the container. For example, sending an email if any task in the container fails.
☑ Setting the scope of a variable to a container.
☑ If the package has multiple data flows, like a data flow for each of the following departments: Finance, HR and Marketing. Each of these departments have different data sets and will need different processing. Create a Sequence Container for each department, then put the control flow components for each department in its container.
☑ Grouping related tasks.

Groups

This feature looks like a container, but is not a container. It is however, another way to group components together. It mostly functions like a Sequence Container. The differences between a group and Sequence container are discussed below.

☑ Groups do not have precedence constraints, only the tasks in a group can have precedence constraints.

☑ Groups do not have as much functionality as a Sequence container.

☑ Groups can be created on the Data Flow tab.

☑ A task in a group can be connected to a task outside of the group.

☑ Properties cannot be passed into a group.

☑ Groups cannot be disabled, like they can in a Sequence container.

☑ Properties for the tasks in a group, cannot be set at the group level, like they can for containers. This means that the properties cannot be shared between the tasks in a group.

Creating A Group

The steps below show you how to create a group.

1. Select all of the tasks that you want to put into a group.

   An easy way to do that is to use the mouse to draw a box around all of the tasks that you want to put into a group, as shown in Figure 8-46.

   You will see the dashes on the border move ⇒ Release the mouse button.

   You will see a black border around each task that is selected.

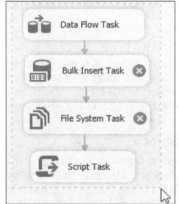

Figure 8-46 Tasks selected to be grouped

2. Right-click on one of the selected tasks ⇒ Select Group.

   You will see the group, shown in Figure 8-47.

   Additional tasks can be added to a group by dragging them into the group container.

Figure 8-47 Group created

Deploying Packages

The rest of this chapter provides an overview of the deployment options that are available in SSIS. On your own, you can select the option that works best for you. In depth coverage of deploying packages is beyond the scope of this book.

SSIS Catalog

The SSIS catalog contains information about the package components. If can only be used with the Project Deployment model. This tool improves the way that packages are deployed in the SQL Server environment, including the ability to run and manage packages, using Power Shell or T-SQL. This is in addition to using SSMS. With the catalog in SQL Server, you have access to views and reports. The catalog can be queried in SSMS.

A catalog is a database that packages are stored in. The name of the database is SSISDB. <clever name - smile> There can only be one catalog per database instance. When a package that is in a catalog is run, information about the packages execution and errors are stored in the database.

How To Create An SSIS Catalog

On your own, you can follow the steps below to create a catalog.

1. Open SSMS ⇒ Connect to your local instance of the database.

2. In the Object Explorer window, right-click on the **INTEGRATION SERVICES CATALOGS** folder and select Create Catalog, as shown in Figure 8-48.

    If the Create Catalog option is not enabled, it means that a catalog has already been created.

    Enabling the Common Language Runtime (CLR) integration option (the first option shown below in Figure 8-49) allows you to fully utilize the catalog.

    A password must be entered to encrypt the data. The password will protect the encryption key.

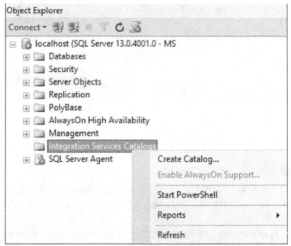

Figure 8-48 Integration Services Catalogs folder

3. On the dialog box shown in Figure 8-49, check the **ENABLE CLR INTEGRATION** option ⇒ Check the **ENABLE AUTOMATIC EXECUTION OF INTEGRATION SERVICES** option.

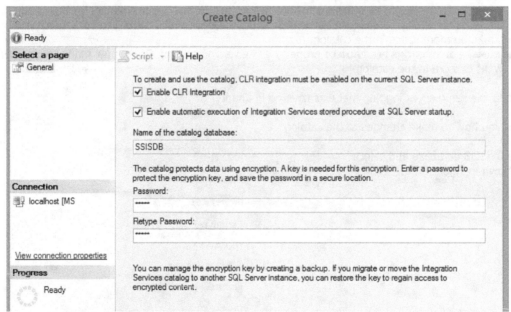

Figure 8-49 Create Catalog dialog box

4. Type in a password ⇒ Click OK. The catalog database will be created. Once created, you will see the database in the Integration Services Catalogs folder.

SQL Server Agent

If enabled, the Enable automatic execution option creates a job that will clean up the SSIS catalog tables.

To run this job, the SQL SERVER AGENT, shown earlier in Figure 8-48, must be enabled and started.

To start the agent, right-click on it, and select Start, as shown in Figure 8-50. When prompted if you are sure, click Yes.

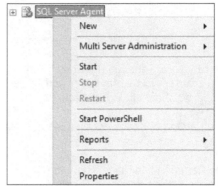

Figure 8-50 SQL Server Agent shortcut menu

Configuring The Catalog

After the catalog is created, you have the ability to change some of the catalogs properties, shown later in Figure 8-52. Some properties that you may want to change are explained below.

☑ The **CLEAN LOGS PERIODICALLY** property is used to select whether or not the log files are deleted from the catalog. Selecting True will cause the log files to be deleted every X number of days. X equals the value in the Retention Period property. (5)

☑ The **RETENTION PERIOD (DAYS)** property is used to select how many days you want to keep operational data (ie., warning or error messages) in the catalog. In most situations, the default of 365 days is too long.

☑ The **SERVER-WIDE DEFAULT LOGGING LEVEL** property is used to select the level of event logging detail that is captured and saved in the catalog. The options are None, Basic (the default), Performance, Verbose and Runtime Lineage. A higher level of detail (like Verbose or Runtime Lineage) will cause the packages to run slower and will take up more space in the catalog. (5)

☑ The **MAXIMUM NUMBER OF VERSIONS PER PROJECT** property is like version control. Select how many versions of a project you want to store in the catalog.

(5) This option refers to the same event logging that was covered in Chapter 6.

The steps below show you how to make changes to the catalog.

1. Right-click on the SSISDB database and select **PROPERTIES**, as shown in Figure 8-51.

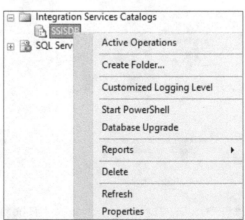

Figure 8-51 Catalog database

 The properties in the Operations Log and Project Versions sections that are not enabled, are automatically updated when packages in the catalog are run.

2. On the Catalog Properties dialog box, you may want to make the following changes, as shown in Figure 8-52.

   Retention Period (days) - 45

   Maximum number of versions per project - 5

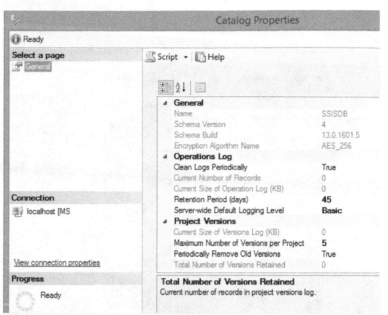

Figure 8-52 Catalog Properties dialog box

Creating Folders In The Catalog Database

Folders are used to store multiple projects. Think of a catalog project as the equivalent of a Solution in SSIS. Each catalog needs at least one folder. Usually, you may want a separate folder for each solution.

1. To create a folder, right-click on the SSISDB database and select **CREATE FOLDER**, as shown earlier in Figure 8-51.

2. In the Folder name field, type the name that you want to use for the folder name.

3. While optional, typing in a description is helpful to explain the types of packages that will be stored in the folder. Figure 8-53 shows the folder options. Once the folder is created, you will see it under the catalog folder, as shown in Figure 8-54.

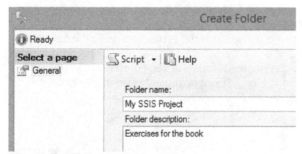

Figure 8-53 Create Folder dialog box

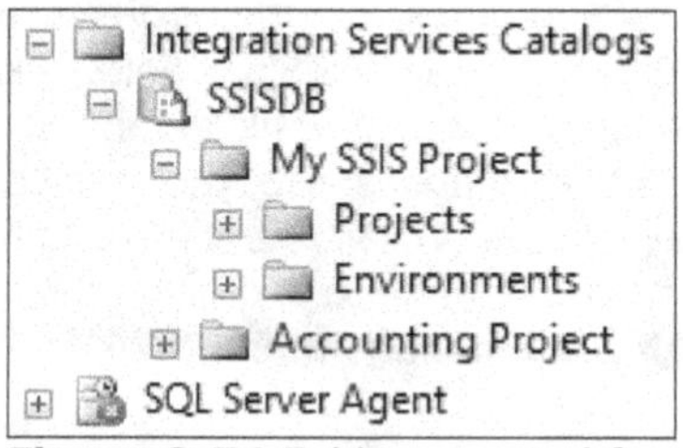

Figure 8-54 Folders created for the catalog

Deployment Models

There are two models for deploying packages, as explained below. Packages that have been set to be excluded from the project, are not displayed.

① **PROJECT DEPLOYMENT MODEL** deploys all of the packages in a project, at the same time. This model has more features than the package model, like the SSIS catalog. This model uses the Deployment wizard.

② **PACKAGE DEPLOYMENT MODEL** is the oldest of the two models. It can deploy one package or several packages at the same time. This model is mostly used for backward compatibility with older SSIS frameworks. There are two ways to deploy packages using this model, as explained below.

☑ Open the package in SSIS ⇒ File ⇒ Save Copy As.

☑ In SSMS, right-click on the **PROJECTS** folder ⇒ Select **IMPORT PACKAGES**, as shown in Figure 8-55. This option opens the wizard shown in Figure 8-56.

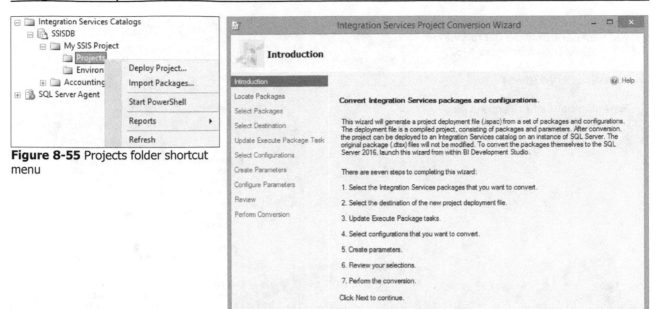

Figure 8-55 Projects folder shortcut menu

Figure 8-56 Integration Services Project Conversion Wizard

You can switch between the models, by doing one of the following in SSIS:

① Right-click on an SSIS project folder in the Solution Explorer and select Convert to Package (or Convert to Project) Deployment model. This option converts all packages in the project, regardless of the folder.
② Right-click on the SSIS Packages folder and select Convert Deployment model.

Deploying Packages To The Catalog

Earlier, creating and setting up the catalog was covered. This section covers getting packages in the catalog. The Deployment Wizard is the easiest tool to use to accomplish this task. There is more than one way to access the Deployment Wizard, as explained below.

① **USE SSMS** In SSMS, right-click on the Projects folder under the folder that you want to deploy the packages to, as shown earlier in Figure 8-55 ⇒ Select **DEPLOY PROJECT**.
② **USE THE .ISPAC FILE** (.ispac is the file extension) The name of the file is the project name in the Solution. This compressed file contains all of the project, package and parameter files. Double-clicking on this file options the Deployment Wizard. This file is in the bin\development folder of your project folder. For example, below is the path and filename to the file for the SSIS Book project used in this book. C:\SSIS Book\My SSIS Solution\SSIS Book\bin\development\SSIS Book.ispac.

Integration Services Deployment Wizard

This wizard is used to deploy packages in the Project Deployment model. It sends a SSIS project or package to the catalog on an SQL Server.

1. To open this wizard in SSIS, right-click on a package ⇒ **DEPLOY PACKAGE.**

   You will see the dialog box shown in Figure 8-57.

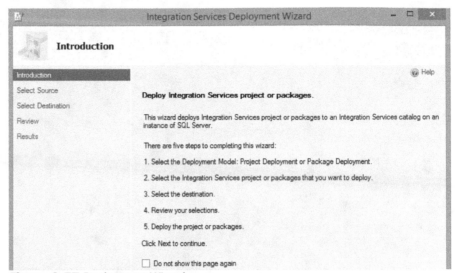

Figure 8-57 Deployment Wizard

2. Click Next. You will see a list of packages in the project, as shown in Figure 8-58, if the Package Deployment option is selected, as illustrated in the figure. Figure 8-59 shows the options for the Project Deployment model.

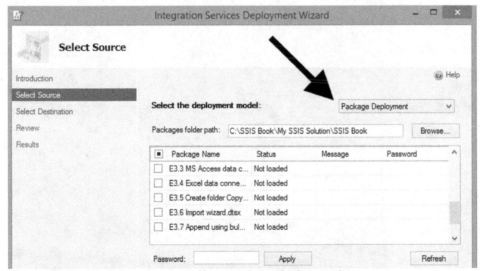

Figure 8-58 Select Source screen (for a package deployment)

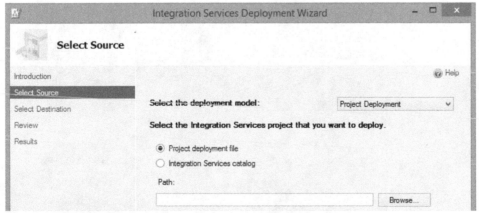

Figure 8-59 Select Source screen (for a project deployment)

INDEX

CPSIA information can be obtained
at www.ICGtesting.com
Printed in the USA
BVHW010915020520
579078BV00005B/462